WHEN EVILS WERE MOST FREE

"The poet Czeslaw Milosz has observed that those 'who are alive receive a mandate from those who are silent forever.' George Gabori . . . has accepted that mandate. His memoir . . . gives eloquent testimony to the memory of the millions of victims silenced forever by the twin lunacies of our century, communism and fascism.

". . . His is a powerful tale, all the more remarkable because Gabori was able to remain the man his father and grandfather taught him to be. The book is a tribute to those who helped him survive . . . Three were especially important: the priest at Dachau who encouraged him to remain steadfast in the faith of his father; the old Jewish industrialist, also at Dachau, who taught him that 'justice is a sort of passion for dealing decently with people'; and the respected Hungarian poet George Faludy who, every night for three years at Recsk, gave lectures, recited poetry, and reminded his fellow prisoners of the humanist tradition.

"Gabori recounts his story simply, sometimes with an ironic wit, but never with bitterness, pretension or self-consciousness."

—Maria Horvath,
Books in Canada

WHEN EVILS WERE MOST FREE

MOST FREE

George Gabori

Translated from the
author's Hungarian version
by Eric Johnson
with George Faludy

SEAL BOOKS
McClelland and Stewart-Bantam Limited
Toronto

*This low-priced Seal Book
has been completely reset in a type face
designed for easy reading, and was printed
from new plates. It contains the complete
text of the original hard-cover edition.*
NOT ONE WORD HAS BEEN OMITTED.

WHEN EVILS WERE MOST FREE
*A Seal Book / published by arrangement with
Deneau Publishers & Company Limited*

PRINTING HISTORY
*Deneau edition published May 1981
Serialized on CBC Radio Booktime program, April 26 through
May 14, 1982
Seal edition / June 1982*

*Seal Books are published by McClelland and Stewart-Bantam
Limited. Its trademark, consisting of the words "Seal Books"
and the portrayal of a seal, is the property of McClelland and
Stewart-Bantam Limited, 25 Hollinger Road, Toronto, Ontario
M4B 3G2. This trademark has been duly registered in the Trademarks Office of Canada. The trademark, consisting of the word
"Bantam" and the portrayal of a rooster, is the property of and
is used with the consent of Bantam Books, Inc. 666 Fifth Avenue, New York, New York 10103. This trademark has been duly
registered in the Trademarks Office of Canada and elsewhere.*

PRINTED IN CANADA

0 9 8 7 6 5 4 3 2 1

To my wife, Ibi, and my daughter, Susan

Contents

The author wishes to express his thanks
to the Multicultural Programme of the
Department of the Secretary of State of
the Government of Canada for support
toward the translation of this work.

Coming of Age in Putnok

WHEN I WAS NINE YEARS OLD my father, victorious after a long argument with my grandfather, took me out of our town's only *cheder* and enrolled me in its only public school. Overnight I was transported from the world of Hebrew letters and monotonously repeated texts to the still stranger world of Hungarian letters, patriotic slogans and walls covered with maps.

Grandfather rolled his eyes and predicted trouble, but it seemed he was wrong. I sat beside a boy my own age named Tivadar, a gentile—everybody was a gentile in that school except me. Tivadar and I got along famously until, after two or three weeks, he approached me in the schoolyard one day and asked me if it was true what the others were saying, that "we" had murdered Jesus.

Strange to tell—for this was 1933 and we were in Hungary—I had never heard about this historical episode, and I left Tivadar amicably enough, promising to ask my father about it. We met again the next morning and I told him what I had learned: that the Romans had killed Jesus, and that anyway Jesus had been a Jew, like me, so what did it matter to the Christians?

"That's not true," said Tivadar menacingly.

"My father does not lie," I replied.

By now a crowd had gathered around us and there was nothing for it but to fight it out. There were cheers and laughter as Tivadar hit me in the nose before I got my jacket off. It was not the first time I had tasted my own blood, but it was the first time a Christian had made it flow. Tivadar was flushed with pleasure and excitement at the applause and not at all expecting it when I lashed out with my fist and sent him sprawling backward on the cobbles. The crowd of boys groaned and shouted to Tivadar to get up and kill the Jew, but poor Tivadar did not move. Frightened, I grabbed my jacket and shoved my way through the crowd stunned into silence by this overturning of the laws of nature.

They were silent at home too when I told them what had happened. My father sent for me from his office in the afternoon, and I entered cap in hand. He always wore a braided Slovak jacket at work and looked more like a peasant than a Jewish wine merchant.

"Well, who started it?" asked my father, wearing an expression I had never seen on his face before. I was not at all frightened.

"He did. I told him what you said about Jesus and he challenged me."

My father clamped his teeth on his cigar and nodded, looking right through me.

"Jews don't fight," he finally said.

"Then why did you put me in a Christian school?" I asked in a loud, outraged whine.

"That's why I put you there, my son," he said at last, then swept me up and kissed me on the forehead. "You're learning fast; only next time don't hit him quite so hard."

Then he sent me out quickly and I stopped on the landing, startled to hear loud, whooping, solitary laughter coming out of my father's office.

During the first fifteen years of my life Admiral Horthy's Hungary was far from the worst place in Eastern Europe for a Jew. The reasonably tolerant Austro-Hungarian Empire and Count Karoly's liberal government were long gone; but gone too were the Communist dictatorship of 1919 and the so-called White Terror that followed Admiral Horthy's triumphal march to power. Having got rid of all the real and potential opponents he could get his hands on—and not a few innocent bystanders—the admiral had set up a mildly fascist regime in which, as Hungarians were fond of pointing out, he was the regent of a nonexistent monarch, an admiral without a navy in a country with no seacoast. It was all a far cry from Western democracy. On the other hand it was infinitely better than those twin Slavic nightmares, Poland and the Soviet Union. A quarter of the population existed in misery, but it had not yet occurred to anyone to ensure that that quarter consisted of Jews.

Of course a majority of the population were anti-Semitic—where were they not?—but we spoke Hungarian like everyone else, not Yiddish, and it had been a long, long time since there had been a pogrom. The general attitude toward us was best summed up by the novelist Mikszath, who reminded the nation that "an anti-Semite is someone who hates the Jews more than necessary."

My ancestors, the Grosz family, had arrived in Hungary sometime early in the nineteenth century, fleeing the Cossack knout and sword. Abandoning some *shtetl* surrounded by sunflowers periodically fertilized by Jewish blood, they led their wagons into Hungary leaving *Yiddishkeit* strewn along the trail behind them. Caftans and fur-trimmed hats gave way to jackets and caps; the plaintive songs of the Diaspora faded in the din of Gypsy violins and the crashing boots of the csardas. After two generations only two things separated us from the rest of the population: we reverenced a Book, and our neighbours loathed us.

My great-grandparents had settled in the town of Putnok, a dusty little baroque museum that seemed to have gone to sleep sometime during the reign of Franz Joseph I and was still waiting, slumbering tranquilly in the rolling hills of northern Hungary, for its prince to return. My great-grandfather had set up as a wine merchant and had worked himself into an early grave. But he had prospered, prospered to a degree unheard of in those parts unless one was an aristocrat like Count Putnoki, the local lord. The count excited a good deal of comment by scrupulously returning my grandfather's greetings in the street. A man who knew nothing about money except how to spend it, he respected my grandfather for being an initiate in the deeper mysteries of actually making it. So by 1924, the year I was born, the family Grosz was fairly rich, stubbornly Jewish and thoroughly Hungarianized—a combination calculated to infuriate everyone from Zionists to gentry, from Communists to Nazis.

Our evolution into this cultural hybrid had not been altogether smooth however. When as an infant I had toddled from room to room in our large house, I was in fact journeying through three different worlds: the narrow cosmos of the illiterate gentile servant girls in the kitchen, all gossip and whipped cream when my mother was not looking; my father's book-lined den, redolent of nicotine-impregnated leather, German philosophy, modern literature, enlightenment, assimilation and *Angst*; and finally the medieval gloom, mystery and peace of my grandfather's room. That murky, slightly musty cavern was the bastion of my security from my earliest days, long before I knew it for what it was: a museum of our origins. There were long shelves of tattered and crumbling Hebrew books, and the air was thick with candle wax and gentleness. Whenever he was not in the synagogue, my grandfather could be found in the centre of that room, sitting beside a huge stove dating from the days of Maria Theresa, rocking in prayer, plucking at his silver beard and always ready to raise me to the level of his lap and so closer to the Almighty. It was a room from the ghettos of Poland, a scene that might be found on a side street in Jerusalem.

The glue that held these sharp contrasts together beneath one roof was an almost tangible love. When my father took out of his wardrobe an aged moth-eaten uniform and told me that my great-grandfather had worn it as a private in Kossuth's army of liberation in 1848, or showed me his own brilliantly blue, gold-piped Royal Hungarian officer's uniform from World War I, my grandfather's deprecating wave of the hand and muttered Hebrew comment in no way altered the look of pride on his face.

In this confusing atmosphere, where after Hebrew prayers and gefilte fish my father was apt to give me a little lecture on the philosophy of Nietzsche, I grew up loving and admiring both men with almost equal intensity. But while my elder brother, Andrew, was drawn more to our grandfather, to

Hebrew grammar, Talmud and the synagogue, the gravitational pull of our father's world proved stronger in my case. Sitting at his knee on a leather ottoman beneath an oil lamp in which his cigar smoke shot up to the beams, I spent evening after evening hearing the plots of Victor Hugo, Anatole France and Dostoevsky long before I could read. But there were hours in my grandfather's room as well, learning about Moses, Masada, the Diaspora, about the One and Eternal God Who was everything for us, His chosen people. I was vaguely aware that there was a tug of war going on with me as the prize, but it was conducted with such charity that the only suffering it caused me as I grew was sometimes to keep me indoors listening to low, intense lectures when I preferred to be out playing with my friends.

And with my enemies! For by the age of thirteen I had enlisted Tivadar as my second-in-command and together we ruled over a sizable band of would-be delinquents, both Jewish and gentile. Known as the Yellow Peril after a pamphlet Tivadar had discovered at home, we created havoc among the geese in the market place and despair in the hearts of our rival gangs. Our favourite way of travel was over perilously sloping roof tops and our preferred activity pitched battles in the lumber yard, after hours, each army flying its flag above stacks of fresh-cut resinous pine, hurling mud bombs and mauling one another with wooden swords. As puberty overtook some of us, warfare gave way to feverish speculation behind those same lumber piles, the mystery of life growing more exciting even as it became less mysterious.

By this time the discovery that I had made the first, and only, time I beat up Tivadar had become something of a habit with me, and a scandal to the good Christians of Putnok. Although short for my age, gangling, hook-nosed and obviously Jewish, when confronted by a Jew-baiter anywhere close to my own size I was apt to leave him on the ground. I was the despair of Jewish and Christian mothers both, albeit for quite different reasons, and only my father had to look away to hide his grin as he took me mildly to task for bloodying yet another anti-Semitic nose. I was not much use to the world at the age of thirteen, but if we had had a Zionist of the Jabotinsky variety in Putnok I think it would have warmed his heart to see me in action.

As I approached my fourteenth birthday, Christmas Day

1938, the rumblings we had been hearing out of Germany finally reached little Putnok. More and more often my father, who had become thinner and thinner and obviously ill, turned the radio dial to Berlin and we all listened to the lunatic ravings of Herr Hitler. Then my father took to his bed and the house was filled with a steady stream of physicians and weeping women. My grandfather had died the previous year, leaving my father and myself alone with our spiritual doubts. Since then he had continued to do his best, with the help of Goethe, Lessing, Tolstoy and Voltaire, to turn me into a gentleman and a humanist. Now my father called me to his bedside and told me, in reference to what we had been hearing on the radio, that the barbarians were on the move again and we were going to be in trouble.

"And what shall I do, father?" I asked simply—for we both knew he was dying and somehow we both found it easy to talk about it.

"Remember what your grandfather told you," he replied, and closed his eyes to sleep.

This was so unexpected a piece of advice that I was still wondering weeks after my father's funeral what he had meant by it. It would be another twenty years before I realized, in the hardest possible way, that in fact his ideals and my grandfather's were really one and the same and that the political ideologies I was now investigating in reaction to the rising tide of fascism all around us—Marxism, anarchism, Trotskyism—all stemmed from something fatally different: a longing to change the world to suit one's own taste, not, as in the case of those two good men, a simple desire that each man should be treated with justice.

Hitler annexed Austria and was at our very borders now. The insane hatred toward Jews that Radio Berlin had trumpeted could now be heard from Radio Vienna. Taking advantage of this, Hungary's own Nazis sharply increased their activities and began pressuring Admiral Horthy's government to follow Hitler's lead.

With their usual lack of originality, the gentlemen in Budapest decided that a little persecution of the Jews might ease the situation. Two anti-Jewish laws designed to curtail Jewish social and economic activities were enacted in quick succession. First, we were allowed only eight years of schooling. The immediate result for me was that I awoke one morning to find that my formal education was at an end. The economic laws forced my family to close the doors of the wine business. My Uncle Gabriel came to announce the news, and to my surprise a great calmness descended over my mother as she sat across from him at the dining table beneath the chandelier my father had brought from Vienna. I had expected tears and lamentations, but without batting an eyelash she coolly began discussing how to sell out on the best possible terms—which, within several weeks, she had done. We had no business, but for the time being we were still quite well off. Hungarian anti-Semitism turned out to be as class-conscious as every other national institution. The laws were really aimed at small businessmen, those who lived from hand to mouth. For these the new laws meant instant poverty. Within two years of their enactment over forty percent of Hungarian Jews were left without any visible means of support.

It was clear that since I could no longer go to school, and since there was no family business for me to enter, I would have to learn a trade. My mother called a family council. The whole crowd of aunts, uncles and cousins poured in, and after hours of lively discussion over poppy-seed pastry and endless cups of coffee, I was summoned to hear my fate. I was going to Budapest to live with my father's sister, my Aunt Lina.

Several months went by, months in which World War II, after initial hesitations, burst into flame all around our Hungarian island. Meanwhile the ponderous machinery of family connections ground into action, eventually producing an opening for me in a small leather-working establishment in the capital. As the weeks went by the relatives trooped regularly through our dining room, eating ever greater masses of pastry and assuring one another that our communal disaster was only temporary. Anti-Semitism came and went in Hungary, they reasoned. "The dish is never as hot on the table as in the oven." And, after all, they pointed out comfortingly to one another, this was Hungary, not Germany or Russia.

Then one autumn day in 1940, shortly after the new prime minister, Count Teleki, signed an agreement making Hungary a party to the Tripartite Pact between Germany, Italy and Japan, almost all the relatives arrived to accompany my mother, my brother and myself to the little railway station of Putnok. Amidst a crowd of peasants and travellers, fat Aunt Rosa smothered me in kisses and Uncle Gabriel shook my hand and boomed encouragement, twirling his moustache and making remarks about the girls of the capital. I stood

among them weighed down by parcels of walnut preserves,
cookies and bagels, and my father's huge leather suitcases. In
the turmoil of noise, confusion, smoke and tears, I said good-
bye to my mother and then to all the others, who suddenly fell
silent. My brother, Andrew, was eyeing me with a strange
mixture of sorrow and envy, and we were both overcome with
embarrassment to find ourselves on the verge of tears.

I found a compartment in which no one looked at me with
that particular gaze Nazis reserve for Jews and waved at the
slowly receding, tearful little group on the platform. I was
sixteen years old and beginning a new life.

2

A Political Initiation

THE CITIZENS OF BUDAPEST, like those of nearly every capital between the Baltic and the Black Sea, have always thought of their city as a sort of eastern Paris. And, indeed, nestled in a broad bend of the Danube overlooked by a mountain, it has a site—if not the accompanying architecture—that Paris and Vienna might envy.

As Europe entered the second year of its agonizing suicide, Budapest was still desperately devoted to chic. Dandies and *boulevardiers* sported carnations, monocled roués conspicuously read the *Times* at curbside tables (though few of them knew a word of English) and fashionable and not-so-fashionable ladies learned their coquetry and their conversation from the lyrics of operettas and the drawing-room comedies of Molnar.

Above all, it was a city devoted to a rigid class structure, the inhabitants of the elegant quarters taking careful note of one another's clothing, brand of cigarette and latest witticisms. As for the majority, the working class, like the blacks in Johannesburg they were seldom seen in the centre except as menials. For the most part they kept to their own districts, the shabby outskirts or slums like Angyalfold (the Field of Angels), where they could be found six to a room.

Among the qualities which the glittering Austro-Hungarian monarchy had neglected to foster in its Hungarian subjects was a taste for serious thought of any kind, except that which leads to immediate gain. In the capital of a country that prized (and still prizes) intelligence—but which has never produced a philosopher—jokes, anecdotes and politics reigned supreme, especially jokes, those highly polished stories that so often enabled the Magyar to bear the otherwise insupportable but which in situations calling for wisdom were apt to trivialize thought to the point of imbecility. There were jokes about Hitler walking on water, jokes about Goering's sex life; but there were no jokes about the national mania for regaining the territories lost after World War I.

After the defeat of 1918 the Allies had parcelled out sizable chunks of Hungary to Czechoslovakia, Rumania and Yugoslavia, thus stranding some four million Hungarians outside their own country. Their plight was real enough, but Admiral Horthy's government found it a useful tool for distracting the population from their own catastrophic social problems. Propaganda for reconquering these territories aroused almost pathological mass enthusiasm, an obsession that was pushing the country into Hitler's embrace.

Not that I had any realization of all this or would have for some time to come. As the train from Putnok grated its way through the grim outskirts of Budapest that autumn night in 1940, I had nothing on my mind but the glittering sight that gradually unfolded as we reached the centre of the city. World War II was in full bloom, but Budapest was ablaze with more lights than any city between Lisbon and Tokyo. When I stepped onto the platform a sleeping car across the way began disgorging its passengers and I was swept up by a crowd that seemed to consist largely of painted ladies with poodles and gentlemen who looked like card sharps posing as counts—as no doubt some of them were. I was surrounded by more wholehearted vulgarity than I had ever seen at one time. My

Jewish heart was revolted; as for the rest of me, it was absolutely dazzled.

Aunt Lina turned out to be an enormously tall old lady of that rare species, the Jewish Amazon. Past her prime now, she was drawn and bent from the strain of bringing up two daughters and a son on a widow's slender income, from years of pinching pennies and trying to keep up appearances. She loomed above the crowd on the platform like a heron examining a shoal of fish. Then she swooped down accurately and plucked me from the swirling mass.

I knew from the beginning that my welcome in Aunt Lina's house was due largely to the fact that my father had been the only member of the family to help her out over the years. Also, the money she was receiving for my room and board was desperately needed. But for all that she was kind to me, being one of those perplexing women who show their grimmer side only when things are going well, which for the time being they were not.

Aunt Lina's flat had four rooms. As her son and two daughters were living at home, I was assigned a sofa, where the next morning I awoke with the imprint of upholstery all over me. I greeted my first Budapest dawn amidst huge cushions and surveyed the threadbare remains of Aunt Lina's former splendour, sipping coffee as the early morning light revealed sagging velvet-covered chairs and enough antimacassars to suggest that Aunt Lina must once have made a corner in the lace market.

Then I was sent out to find my workshop, and, bundled up against the cold wind blowing in from the eastern plains, I scurried along avenues cushioned with soggy leaves, trying to convince myself that it was after all an interesting experience to sink within twenty-four hours from the bourgeoisie, through the decayed middle class, to settle, any minute now, on the bottom—the working class.

The leather workshop, when I finally found it, turned out to be a long hall surrounded by windows like a veranda. Down the centre ran a wide bench at which craftsmen and apprentices sat on stools leaning over marble cutting boards. I was handed over to an old master craftsman, Janos, who set about training me from the first minute with benevolent gruffness.

All that first day I eyed my fellow workers with astonishment. There seemed to be no Jews among them, yet not one anti-Semitic remark was made, not even the casual sort that in Hungary passes for tolerance. It took awhile to overcome shyness on both sides, but by lunchtime on the second day I found myself completely accepted by all twenty and had learned—what my family did not know—that this was a union shop, its workers members of a Social Democratic trade union, the only mildly leftist sort of organization legal in the country.

The idea of trade unionism was, to say the least, a novelty to me. I do not think I had ever heard the word mentioned in my father's house. Old Janos and the others began explaining its principles to me during breaks, and at first my reservations were so strong—I was after all my father's son—that I even suspected their motives. But my objections crumbled when Janos put a gnarled hand on my shoulder and began damning Hitler and nazism to hell, cursing the Germans for their attack on Poland and the stupidity of the Hungarian government for toadying to them.

Gradually the others told me stories that had leaked out of Poland, news that had certainly not yet reached Putnok: of mass executions, Jews being forced to dig their own graves before being shot into them, people packed into vans and killed by carbon monoxide. Hearing gentiles express outrage at the fate of Jews was something entirely new in my experience, and within a few days I became convinced of three things: that my fellow workers were thoroughly decent men; that if the Nazis came to power in Hungary the Jews would not only be persecuted, but they would be killed; and that in the whole of our wretched country the only people who seemed even faintly interested in doing anything about it were the Social Democrats.

As I was growing up, the political life of Hungary had seemed restricted to Budapest, where it hovered like a *fata morgana*. For twenty years the governing Party of Unity had won all elections by the unoriginal expedient of holding open ballots everywhere except the larger cities. When criticized for this, Count Bethlen, prime minister throughout the 1920s, imperturbably maintained that "secret ballots are incompatible with the candid nature of the Hungarian people." So in towns like Putnok a prospective voter for the opposition had to go to one polling station, a government supporter to another. And at the former there was always a battery of notaries, judges and others who, with the help of public-spirited policemen and teachers, took the names of those voting the wrong way. Public servants lost their jobs, publicans their licences, well-to-do peasants found their taxes tripled, and tenant farmers were apt to be evicted from their dirt-floored hovels if they dared oppose the government.

Sometimes, however, the opposition polls simply did not open on election day, or if they did those who entered were beaten up. My father never went near the polls on the grounds that it was not worth the trouble to support the sham opposition that sat in parliament. But sometimes things did not even get to that point. One opposition candidate, an overoptimistic young liberal, had some years before shown up in Putnok to campaign with his wife. They were arrested at the station. After a lengthy interview the couple was sent back to Budapest, he for vagrancy, his wife for suspected prostitution. In rural Hungary there was simply no point in having a political opinion.

But in Budapest I was discovering a very different situation. Everyone here had strongly defined political views, even those who had nothing else. Out of sixteen daily newspapers that fanned the flames beneath this cauldron of opinion, I soon discovered that only two were worth reading: the *Magyar Nemzet*, or *Hungarian Nation*, and the *Nepszava*, or *Voice of the People*. The first was the mouthpiece of the non-socialist opposition, the second the official organ of the Social Democratic Party.

Although Hungary was nominally neutral at the end of 1940, it had sided with the Axis Powers to an extent that permitted it to reoccupy parts of northern Hungary, Ruthenia and Transylvania lost after World War I. The government, and Admiral Horthy himself, were indebted to Hitler for this favour, and it put them in a situation, odd even by Hungarian standards, of both fearing and hoping for a German victory. They censored the press heavily, so that while fourteen papers tended to take a pro-German line (or to complain that the government was not sufficiently pro-German), the *Magyar Nemzet* and the *Nepszava*, both dedicated to telling the truth, were often confiscated before they appeared or else arrived at the newsstands with whole columns left blank by the censors. Both papers were pro-British and foresaw that the alliance with Germany would lead Hungary into the usual national catastrophe.

It was the first time in my life that I had read what was

obviously true in a newspaper, and I was infuriated by the blanked-out columns. The *Magyar Nemzet* was better written, yet I soon realized that the sort of opposition it expressed was based on little more than a vague liberalism. The Social Democratic *Nepszava*, on the other hand, spoke for a political party that had fought for decades to change Hungary from a semifeudal state into a parliamentary democracy, for equality before the law and for the distribution of the enormous latifundia among the country's "three million beggars," as the landless peasants were quite accurately called. It denounced the war and damned discrimination, both religious and racial; in short it was antifascist, and my heart went out to it and to those who published it from the first time I got my hands on a copy.

Through Janos and my other fellow workers I gradually pieced together the history of the Social Democratic Party. It had played a role in Count Karoly's brief liberal government after World War I. Then when Bela Kun's Communist dictatorship took power, many of its leaders had fled to Vienna. In the autumn of 1919 Admiral Horthy rode into Budapest in the wake of a Rumanian army and was elected regent by a parliament whose members were understandably influenced by the fact that the admiral's troops were sitting on the balconies with their rifles trained on the assembly. Having just experienced Kun's Red Terror, the country now reeled under the White Terror that began Horthy's regime. Throughout all this only the Social Democrats had the courage to denounce the murders, robberies and frauds of Horthy's lieutenants, an endless list of crimes usually committed with politics as the pretext and hard cash as the motive.

The editor of the *Nepszava*, Bela Somogyi, had been a teacher in a primary school in the provinces. By no means a typical intellectual, he was a learned yet simple man whose only passion was for justice. Day after day he assailed the crimes and the criminals in the press, until finally Horthy (who in any case never had the acumen to distinguish between a Social Democrat and a Communist) ordered his officers to shut the man up. A group led by one Lieutenant Emil Kovarcz shoved Somogyi and a young man on his staff into a military vehicle one evening as they were walking home from the editorial offices. They were driven to the bank of the Danube, where the officers gouged out their eyes, bound them with barbed wire and threw them, still living, into the river.

The police established these facts—Hungary being, after all, a civilized country—and then filed them away at the suggestion of the regent. At the time I was learning all this I also learned that Emil Kovarcz was now a member of parliament.

Perhaps more than anything else, it was the story of the death of Somogyi and the nauseating facts of Kovarcz's career that made me decide, shortly after my seventeenth birthday, to throw my lot in with the Social Democrats. Every day as I walked to work I passed the party's headquarters, an unprepossessing little house of two stories on a side street. Unlike the headquarters of the other parties, this one had no cars parked in front and no policeman to tell a young onlooker to stop gaping and move along.

I discovered that the present leaders of the party were from every conceivable class and background. Anna Kethly came from an ancient Hungarian family and had been a teacher; Illes Monus was a Jewish intellectual; the head of the party, Karl Peyer, famous for his personal courage, had been born into the country's German minority, many of whose members were now agitating for the Nazis. And it seemed that in a city where politicians did little but intrigue against one another, the Social Democratic leaders lived in unaccountable harmony.

One morning on my way to work I saw a well-dressed man enter the little headquarters on Conty Street. As if it were the most natural thing in the world, he stopped to shake hands with the porter. I had never seen anyone shake a porter's hand before, and it was a revelation as great as seeing the works of Michelangelo and Botticelli for the first time. I stood pondering for awhile, then, forgetting all about work, hesitantly entered the building.

Within a few minutes I had added two years to my age and become a member of the party. I was standing in a small room facing a bespectacled, friendly young lady behind a counter. She did not believe my age for a moment but seemed not to care. Over her head a portrait of Bela Somogyi leaned out from the wall, huge peasant moustaches on guard, his eyes, eternally intact, twinkling benevolently down at us.

When I inquired about joining a political seminar, she told me they were all filled and in session but there would be new ones starting in a few months. Disappointed, I suggested that I might join one of the Marxist seminars at my own trade union headquarters. At this she hesitated and gave me a strange look; then, with an urgency that struck me as odd, she advised me to wait. But at seventeen I was incapable of waiting, so I went around to the trade union building on Sass Street where I signed up on the spot for a newly formed study group and lecture series.

I knew that the trade unions were the strongholds of the Social Democratic Party. What I did not know—and this was the source of the young lady's anxiety—was that the illegal Communist Party had ordered its members to infiltrate the unions so as to have a springboard to power in the future. They had little success in unions like the iron workers' or the transport workers', but unions such as my own and the furriers' they had nearly taken over. It seemed that the real proletarians, the industrial workers, generally had enough sense to see through the Communists; the artisans, on the other hand, had risen to the lower strata of the petite bourgeoisie and were apt to share the general affliction of that class, a narrow-mindedness so pronounced that only the most tortuous logic could worm its way in.

The leaders of the Social Democratic Party were, of course, aware of the situation and technically were required to expel any Communists they found in our ranks and publish their names in the paper. But when they did this the expelled member would usually be arrested, charged with conspiracy and thrown into prison. As a result the leadership decided to tolerate the intrigues of the Communists on humanitarian grounds, whatever the cost. The cost, as it turned out later, was high: many Communists who were sheltered by the Social Democrats and who survived the war in this way later become the persecutors and sometimes the hangmen of the very men who had saved them. It took me some time to grasp what was going on, as it was never discussed. And when finally I did understand, I found it hard to comprehend the degree of humane, not to say suicidal, nobility displayed by the leadership.

I joined the Marxist study group together with a newly acquired friend, George Egri, who was two years older than I and had managed to finish school before the anti-Jewish laws. George was unique among my friends in that he shared some of my views, his own being equally energetic and hazy. He came from a well-off bourgeois family and exuded prosperity, with sleek blue-black hair and a pink face that gleamed like a Chinese teapot in a dark corner. He was splendid in an argument, and in place of the youthful insolence I usually relied upon, he lent me some of his own calmer self-assurance.

There were four other young men and two girls in our study group. With the notable exception of a girl named Esther, who shared with me the same tomato-red hair and insolence, they were all intolerable Moscow-oriented Communists. Arguing with them was like talking to a choir of parrots. George, Esther and I went night after night hoping to learn Marxist theory; but instead of political philosophy we were taught Soviet theology.

In our bottomless ignorance we might well have accepted some of it from a more talented instructor, but ours was a small man of indefinite age with a complexion the colour of dishwater and the paper-thin lips of a soured ascetic. He read to us from pages torn out of a book he did not dare to carry about with him. We called him the Bobcat, and he read to us in the unctuous tones of a *cheder* teacher reciting from the Pentateuch, matter-of-factly serving up unchallengeable and eternal truth. His lectures consisted of paraphrasing what he had just read. "Another fifty minutes of tautologies," George remarked to me after the second lecture. (Egri was always using words I had to look up later at home.)

I had assumed that the Bobcat would quote Marx, Engels, Bebel and Kautsky, but except for Marx he mentioned none of them. We were told that human history rose in an endless spiral of constant progress to end shortly in the final victory of the masses in their class struggle against the exploiters. He explained that individuals as such had no role in this struggle, then went on almost in the same breath to assure us that Marx, Lenin and Stalin were the men who turned the wheels of this engine of progress.

In his first lecture the Bobcat asserted that the great Stalin had avoided war by concluding his pact with Hitler the year before. When a few months later Hitler attacked the Soviet Union, he would in the same tones announce that war had been inevitable and Stalin had been preparing for it all along by means of the pact. Sometimes the Bobcat turned to philosophy, propounding the axiom that man's being determines his consciousness, by which he meant that class background dictates outlook. This prompted me to ask how then Marx, a bourgeois, and Engels, an industrialist, had escaped the consequences of this eternal truth. "Great men," intoned the Bobcat, unruffled, "are exceptions." He told us that Plato and Socrates had been the "hirelings of the Athenian bourgeoisie"; he lengthily refuted Kant and Nietzsche in a manner I later recognized as that of the *Great Soviet Encyclopedia*—which has perfected the grotesque art of criticizing views without first stating them.

That it was all the silliest sort of rubbish Egri, Esther and I agreed from the first. After the lectures we retired to the corner of a pub and ridiculed the Bobcat, thereby resharpening minds blunted into stupefaction by his lecture. What disquieted us was that the other five members of our seminar, and evidently many in other seminars, were swallowing it all uncritically. Still, considering the situation, we decided not to be too fussy. We thought of ourselves as Socialists, even as Marxists, and for my part I found myself drawn more and more to the doctrines of Leon Trotsky, whose idea of permanent revolution had thrilled two generations of adolescents before me. At seventeen I did not have the sense to see that a society could survive permanent revolution about as long as an individual could survive permanent surgery. I had doubts as to whether the Social Democrats would accept my Trotskyite views, but Egri assured me that ours was a party of open discussion and freedom. He also told me that one of the leaders was a man called Paul Justus, known as the Hungarian Trotsky.

Even native insolence could not blind me to the fact that I had not yet acquired either the knowledge or the experience to justify an approach to Justus. I continued attending the seminars and through the effort required to refute the Bobcat's nonsense began to give myself a sort of political education. During the day I continued to master the craft of leather-working, basking in the goodwill radiated by Janos and the others; but sometimes, with shame, I found myself longing for Hitler's defeat mostly because it would mean I could go back to being a happy, pampered bourgeois again.

Early in the spring of 1941 I was approached by several colleagues in the Social Democratic Party's youth movement and invited to join them putting up antiwar and anti-Nazi posters around the city. We entered upon this dangerous game for urgent reasons. As a result of Hitler's lightning victories over Poland and France, the Hungarian Nazis had become the second most powerful party in the country. It could be argued, in fact, that they were the most powerful, as a majority of army officers, civil servants and members of parliament were secretly paying membership fees to them.

The Nazis were hardly newcomers to Hungarian politics. They went back as far as 1919, when a group calling itself the Arrow Cross Party came up with a racial theory proclaiming the superiority of something called the Turanian race, by which they meant Hungarian. The leader of the party was an army officer called Szalasi, a man whose fanaticism for Turanian racial purity was rendered comical by his own ancestry, which was Armenian. Szalasi, whose father had borne the ancient Armenian name of Salosyan, was given to historical meditations, during which he demanded total silence, exiling his wife to a stool in the bathroom while he churned out his theories. Among these was the idea that Jesus Christ had not been a Jew but a Turanian. In this Szalasi closely resembled that other great racial theorist, Huston Stewart Chamberlain, who had made the lunatic discovery that Christ, Dante and Michelangelo had been Germans.

In their adulation of Hitler the Arrow Cross were as pathetic as they were dangerous, for the Führer had made it clear in *Mein Kampf* that after a German victory inferior races, by which he meant Jews, Gypsies, Slavs and Hungarians, were to be exterminated or, in the case of the last two, used as slave labour. In 1941 the Arrow Cross were preparing for the takeover they would finally achieve in 1944. They appeared in strength at mass meetings and strikes organized to win over the workers. They were also beginning to control the streets, and one came across their posters and leaflets throughout Budapest. Shopkeepers began to put Hitler's picture in their windows to defend the glass and their own heads. Tenement houses were covered with posters paid for with funds from the German embassy. Before the end of the war it would be discovered that those inexhaustible stacks of crisp British five-pound notes had all been printed in Berlin.

As for us, we printed our posters secretly and at our own expense, and one March afternoon five of us from the trade union took a bundle of them and headed for the working-class suburb of Ujpest. After a long bus ride we got out at Szent Laszlo Street, one of the grimmest industrial districts in all Hungary: an endless row of decaying five- and six-story tenements with families crammed into one-room flats, one toilet for each story at the end of the outdoor passageways. Between the tenements were factories and small workshops.

The horizon was all chimneys and flues, brick and smoke, a Blakean nightmare. Beyond stretched lines of tiny, soot-covered dwellings with a scrap of yard in front. We walked on, passing a plot containing a chicken tied to a fence by a long cord. It was tended by an emaciated child who stood motionless, watching us with large expressionless eyes.

I fell into a depression, horrified by the place. Ujpest, more than any place I knew until I saw parts of the industrial cities of England and Scotland, proclaimed the obvious but generally unrecognized fact that the real tragedy of the heirs of the industrial revolution, the proletariat, lies in the unrelieved ugliness of their surroundings as much as in their poverty.

As we walked quickly through the district toward the meadow that divided it from Ujpest proper, second-shift men on their way to work passed us with quick glances at our clothing: however much we mouthed about our solidarity with them, they knew a bourgeois when they saw one. As dusk arrived we began pasting up our posters in the street beyond the meadow.

During the bus ride I had had a growing feeling that the whole thing was senseless. Why were we taking this risk? What could we do that would have any effect against the force of German arms, money and propaganda? But as we began pasting away on the brick wall of a tenement, even as the sweat of fear and exertion trickled down my ribs, I felt a delirious happiness. Keeping one eye on our two lookouts, we ripped down old Arrow Cross posters and replaced them with our own, feeling that somehow the whole population would read them in the morning and change their views, that all Budapest and all Hungary would wake up to reality and start behaving decently. I was intoxicated with this thought, which became stronger and stronger, at once sentimental and sensual, a transcendental joy that seemed to lift me like an elevator to the top of the building.

Suddenly one of our lookouts whistled the danger signal. But he was too late and came stumbling back to us as a group of ten or eleven Arrow Cross bully boys rounded the corner. Judging from their paste pot, they had been putting up posters on the other side of the same building. My legs trembled and the cold wind chilled the sweat on my body. Each group stared at the other open mouthed, and I was deeply humiliated to hear my own voice, nervously off key, suggest to the Arrow Cross men that we talk, that we let reason, not force, decide which of us was right.

There were loud guffaws, and almost before they stopped laughing they fell on us with shouts of "Stinking Jews!" and "Lousy Communists!" I found myself trying to batter in the soft belly of a huge, pig-faced fellow who towered over me and kept bringing his hammy fist down hard on the side of my head. I was staggering and kept thinking, "How stupid! We're not Communists, and I'm the only Jew." Then through the ringing in my ears I heard the sound of singing. A large group of workmen on their way home from the pub were coming down the street, giving an ear-splitting rendition of an anti-Nazi song. The Arrow Cross heroes stopped battering us and retreated, panting from their exertions. Pigface took his knee off my chest and followed the others shouting, "I'll get you later, Jew!"

The workmen looked down, for by now all of us were on the ground, and studied us with interest. They were all very drunk. Then one of them began reading our poster's text aloud. When he had finished, another ripped down the remaining Arrow Cross posters, and then a youth in filthy overalls leaned over, shook my hand and handed me a bottle. Their show of goodwill warmed me almost as much as the huge gulps of raw brandy I swallowed. When the workmen finally left, we wiped our bleeding noses and finished our work.

Suddenly I was reeling with dizziness and desperate to be alone. Taking all the money out of my wallet, I divided it with the others and told them to take taxis home. When they too had gone, I slumped down against the brick wall. The street was empty and dark except for a single distant lamp. Closing my eyes, I saw my mother lighting the Sabbath candles. I heard the prayers at table, smelled the aromas of goose fat and spices and felt the soft warmth of my eiderdown bed. I was adrift in this sea of nostalgia when a hand shook my shoulder roughly. A policeman was looking down reprovingly. "High time to sober up, young man. You'd better go back to your own neighbourhood." Clutching the brick wall, I climbed to my feet and staggered off in the general direction of home.

"My God," moaned Aunt Lina, "how you look! God forbid your dear mother should see you like this!" After that she shut up, however, heated water and began cleaning my bloodied face, as I told her what had happened. After a hot bath and supper, she tucked me into bed—I had recently graduated from the sofa when her son Zoltan was drafted into a Jewish labour batallion—and tried to sound severe. But for all the bitter hardship of her life, years of slow sinking in society even as she struggled to stay afloat, Aunt Lina was the least severe of women when faced with someone else's troubles. For the time being, at least, I knew she would not tell my family.

That year, 1941, saw Hungary's real entry into the war. Nevertheless Admiral Horthy and his chief adviser, Count Bethlen, were far from enchanted at the prospect of a German victory, Bethlen reportedly saying, "If the English win, we lose; if the Germans win, we're lost." Both men were Anglophiles who thought Hitler a vulgarian and an extremist; they could look the other way when he committed genocide, but on no account could they forget that he had been a corporal. For their part, the Germans sought to mollify Horthy, rightly thinking that he would serve them better than the unreliable and neurotic Szalasi.

In 1938 Hungary had been allowed to annex southern Slovakia; in 1940 Hitler gave Horthy Ruthenia and half of Transylvania. The admiral was delighted to ride into these regained territories on his famous white horse and was especially enchanted that Hitler asked nothing in return. But Count Teleki, the prime minister, had reservations, even though he too had approved the country's signing the Tripartite Pact. Late in 1940 Teleki had concluded a treaty of eternal friendship with Yugoslavia. Then in April 1941 Hitler attacked Yugoslavia and promised Horthy the recovery of ancient Hungarian districts, including Croatia, in return for his cooperation.

The prospect of possessing a seaport was too much for the old admiral, and he agreed to join Hitler in the venture. Count Teleki committed suicide in protest, and the Hungarian army followed the Germans in their atrocity-filled blitzkrieg against the Yugoslavs. When in June 1941 Hitler attacked the Soviet Union, he did not even bother asking Hungary to participate, knowing well that Horthy would not be able to resist. But Hungary had no territorial claims against the Soviet Union and no evident reason to launch itself against that colossus. Then, three days after Hitler invaded Russia, the Hungarian town of Kassa was bombed briefly one morning by planes bearing Soviet markings. That Stalin should bomb Hungary three days after Hitler invaded Russia, that he should seek to provoke Hungary when the Soviet Union was staggering under the blitzkrieg, was too much even for the popular press to swallow with a straight face. Hungarian air force observers testified that, while the markings had been Soviet, the planes were German. Newspapers that reported this were confiscated, and Hungary declared war on the Soviet Union in retaliation for a German air raid. This automatically meant a state of war with Great Britain as well, and a few months later German diplomacy had a further triumph when, for the second time in twenty-five years, Hungary declared war on the United States. It was as if the Austro-Hungarian Empire were still alive. We were still ruled by homicidal cretins in plumed hats.

Suddenly our Communist colleagues in the trade union stopped mouthing about "the three worker states, Germany, Italy and the Soviet Union" and joined us when we put up antiwar posters. With that amnesia communism induces in its followers, they immediately began speaking as if they had always been antifascists and we, the Social Democrats, were latecomers to their cause. Then Stalin dissolved the Hungarian Communist Party (along with many others), and when our colleagues had time to catch their breath they reemerged as the Peace Party, a dovelike organization utterly devoted to keeping Hungary out of the war.

The continuing stream of German victories forced me to realize that the chances of Hungarian Jewry were slim. Yet if I so much as breathed a word of this, those around me scoffed and ridiculed. Everyone, even the Jews, seemed strangely indifferent to what was happening. If you mentioned the mass killings in Poland or Russia to a Jew, he was apt to shrug and change the subject. The non-Jews were confident that Admiral Horthy's wisdom would see them safely through the war. As for the admiral and his government, publicly they spoke about the "common German-Hungarian destiny" and "our iron will to win the war against the Anglo-Saxon-Judeo-Bolshevik plutocrats." Privately they hoped for a speedy Allied victory and not too much in the way of retribution.

I began to break into a cold sweat when I looked into a mirror: my red hair, pale freckled skin and the shape of my head were de facto proof of Jewish origin in Nazi eyes, and I dreaded the day I would be drafted into a labour batallion. I had no doubts that when they decided who would serve on the home front and who would go with the army to clear mine fields in Russia, my red hair would condemn me to the latter.

In the meantime, taking comfort in the fact that what others considered my paranoia was in fact a realistic view of the situation, I went on pasting up antiwar posters, distributing leaflets and reading voraciously the rest of the time. As Belgrade was bombed to rubble and Hungarian officers began the massacre of thousands of Serbs and Jews in Novi Sad, I worked my way through Trotsky's *Mein Leben* under the bedclothes with a German dictionary and a flashlight. The monumental hypocrisy and intellectual dishonesty of the Communists in the Social Democratic Party made me skeptical of even a heretic and outcast like Trotsky. But I was impressed in spite of myself by the man's spirited fight against tyranny. It only occurred to me years later that there was absolutely nothing in Trotsky's character or doctrine that would have prevented him from becoming the tyrant his colleagues became. By the time I finished the book, however, I considered myself a Trotskyite and was thus in the uncomfortable and slightly distasteful position of being on the radical left of the Social Democrats.

One evening after work I received a message to see Sandor Gancz, one of the non-Communist leaders of the union. When I got to his office, Gancz asked me if I would like to enter "a higher course of study." I was overjoyed when he told me that the instructor would be Paul Justus, famous in political circles as the Hungarian Trotsky.

Paul Justus was not an original thinker of the first rank. He was undeniably a brilliant political theoretician and a *rara avis* among Marxists in that he was unwilling, even in theory, to sacrifice human blood on the altars of ideology. He was known and admired in the leftist circles of Western Europe, counting men like Leon Blum and Dennis Healey as his friends. He was charming, enormously erudite, unfailingly kind and blindly fanatical to his cause. It frequently came as a surprise to those who knew and esteemed him to discover that they did not actually like him.

After having made me swear not to reveal a word to anyone, Gancz gave me Justus's address and told me to be there the following evening. I glanced at the paper and was mildly surprised to find that the man who more than anyone else embodied for me the proletariat's struggle for a decent life lived in one of the most elegant districts of the capital.

The day after my meeting with Gancz, I arrived at Justus's building far too early and had to pace up and down the street for nearly an hour before ringing the bell. Then I was admitted by a haughty maid and shown into a book-lined flat. Justus's manner was altogether informal and cordial. He was in his forties at this time, but the dancing eyes behind his spectacles made him seem younger. He greeted me as if we had been friends for years.

Three other students were already there, but I think they noticed me as little as I did them: so overwhelming was Justus's personality when he began to speak that those of us who listened were scarcely aware of one another. He proceeded at once with his lecture and at the end accepted our bumbling questions with good-humoured patience, never condescending in his manner. Looking back on those sessions, I was later to wonder that a man who was in so many ways an embodiment of all that is positive in life could have advocated a philosophy that in its moral aspects trivialized or ignored as beside the point those very virtues that made him what he was. But for the time being I was captivated, and from that first day my life seemed to acquire new meaning under his attentive guidance.

Justus instilled in his students a number of traits. They were usually persuaded to a love of art, of the best thought of Western civilization; they also had it indelibly written on their minds that ideology is the servant of humanity, not vice versa. On the other hand, they tended to fall victim to Justus's latest theories, which were sometimes bizarre even by Marxist standards, as when he decided that the war was essentially between the "proletarian powers" (by which he meant the United States, Great Britain, France and the Soviet Union) and the "upper-class powers" (Germany, Italy and, presumably, Japan).

But for all its quirks, his was the most powerful intellect I had yet come into contact with, and shortly after I met him I was impressed to the point of adulation by his learning, his personal goodness and, perhaps most important of all, his ability to trace with surgical precision the cancerlike evil in minds like Hitler's and Stalin's.

I began to miss work in order to study for the sessions with

Justus, and Aunt Lina—who daily feather-dusted the highly illegal books on my desk without comment—began at last to balk. The household was in desperate shape and my pay packets made a great difference. Finally she had had enough and wrote to my mother, and so it happened that the postman brought me an ultimatum from Putnok one day: "George, my son, you can stay in Budapest if you keep your nose out of politics; if you don't, you must come home." My mother never wasted words.

That evening Justus, noticing my depression, asked me to stay for dinner. When I told him about my mother's letter, he encouraged me to return home to plead my case and to inform my relatives bluntly about the mass killings in Poland and how Berlin was making plans for the total extermination of European Jewry. I told him they would not believe it. He looked at me for a moment, eyes big behind their lenses, then sighed: "I know, I know."

As he saw me to the door, Justus told me gently not to be so loudly insistent in my anticommunism. My ideals were Marxist, and when I came to explain myself to my family I could in good conscience present my case as simple antifascism. He told me to impress upon them that Social Democracy was Hungary's last hope for defeating the Arrow Cross. Then, brightening, he said I ought to be more cheerful: there was no doubt that the Allies would win the war and our cause would triumph. Suddenly it seemed to me that the man before me in this elegant apartment was living in a world of dreams. Hungary was an island surrounded by a rising tide of blood; when it rose a little bit higher we were going to drown in it, whatever our political attitudes.

3

Love and Politics

THE TRAIN JOLTED through the winter landscape of northern Hungary, climbed with difficulty the foothills approaching the Czech border and at last stopped at the dark, icy little platform at Putnok. It was Christmas, and I trudged through the snow-covered streets awed by the stillness, the peace and tranquillity I had almost forgotten. Behind the walls of eighteenth-century houses, lamps cast yellow patches out onto the snow. From an upper story a woman was singing a carol, and a few steps farther on her voice blended with the sound of Mozart coming from someone's piano. At first it seemed that the war had not reached Putnok at all, but as I walked I noted more than one Jewish shop with its windows boarded up, and when I came to the little two-story syna-gogue surrounded by a picket fence I stopped to stare at the swastikas and arrow crosses daubed across the façade and the inscription, "The time of reckoning is coming, Jews! We'll wipe you off the earth!" Pulling my head deeper into the collar of my coat, I hastened home.

Nearly every relative from the whole county was there to welcome me, and in a joyful hubbub I kissed a succession of bearded uncles and pink-cheeked aunts. A family council had been called for the following evening, but in the meantime I was allowed the pleasure of being the prodigal returned and the family pet. But twenty-four hours later as we sat down to dinner I felt like a condemned man having his last meal. It looked like Pesach, except that my father and grandfather were missing. My plate was loaded with delicacies, though I had little appetite.

Finally my grandmother, as reigning matriarch, cleared her throat and without beating around the bush demanded an account of my "political aberrations" in Budapest. In a voice tinged with querulous incredulity she asked how I had come into contact with ideas and people so far removed from our Jewish ethics. Did I think I was Rabbi Ben Akiba to take on the whole gentile world single-handed? "Stay away from gentile politics," she said, shaking her finger at me. "Don't fool yourself; whatever you do for them, you're just a Jew in their eyes."

After the others had spoken, more or less in the same vein, I stood up to face the great circle of reproachful faces across the flickering candles. I told them that what was happening in Putnok was just a small sample of what was going on elsewhere and would sooner or later happen here. I told them all I knew about events in Poland and that they were wrong if they hoped to avoid the same fate by lying low and pretending that all was well. Our choice, I concluded, was either to fight back or else to die like sheep. Then I sat down to complete silence and exchanged looks of embarrassment. They thought I was mad.

The debate went on for hours, and when finally they grasped that I would not give up my activities, I was given grudging permission to return to Budapest. They asked only that I be more cautious and not bring disgrace down on the family or on myself. I sighed, in despair of making them understand what was going on, and agreed. As I climbed into bed my mother embraced me and began to weep quietly; but when she spoke it was only to wish me good night.

Justus had the idea that when the deportation of the

Hungarian Jews began the provinces would be hit before Budapest, and because of this I tried next morning to persuade my mother to follow me back to the capital. She smiled, saying that there would be no deportations; and in any case, whatever happened, it was her duty to be with her family. Then she and my brother, Andrew, accompanied me through the almost empty streets to the station where, as we were somewhat late, we embraced quickly, weeping, before the shrieking whistle forced me to jump aboard.

As the train pulled out, I had a vivid and completely overpowering premonition that I would never see my mother again. Frantically I tried to open the window, but it was frozen, and when I wiped the glass with my palm she was already out of sight. Miserably I huddled in a corner of the coach and in my mind begain pleading with her to come with me to Budapest. I must have muttered aloud, because the only other passenger, a woman sitting across from me, stared in alarm and moved to a seat beside the door.

At Social Democratic headquarters we were told to attend the ceremony planned for the national holiday on the fifteenth of March. During the preceding weeks public opinion had shifted noticeably against the Nazis, and the Communists were planning to attend the celebrations and stir up trouble. Our job was to try to keep them from giving the police any excuse for interference—though how we were to do this was not said.

When I arrived in the plaza before the statue of the poet Petofi there were already at least eight thousand people jammed into the neighbouring streets. First an actor recited the national hymn, a Petofi poem, then another man took his place and began making an anti-Nazi speech. The crowd cheered and the government representatives present began looking uncomfortable. Then chanting broke out here and there, and when it became clear that the slogans were Communist, policemen began moving people away from the pedestal of the statue. When this proved difficult, mounted police moved in and began hitting people at random with the flats of their swords. Thoroughly enraged by this, the crowd shouted obscenities and slogans at the police who, after a slight pause, attacked in earnest, driving people with their horses in the direction of a long line of police vans standing nearby.

One minute I was stumbling backward between a wall of people and the muzzle of a horse; the next I found myself crammed into a black maria. Sirens blared and in no time at all I was giving a desk sergeant my name and address and was then shoved into a room that turned out to be the famous "cell two hundred" of police headquarters. The room was big, but not nearly big enough for the several hundred people already packed into it. Among the last to be brought in, I was near a wall and could lean against it. There was no room to lie down, and although everybody was acutely uncomfortable, arguments soon broke out between Communists and Social Democrats. Somewhere in the middle there was even a Nazi, arrested by mistake, and mirth rippled through the cell every time his voice rose in protest. Nobody came for us, and the arguments went on with increasing hostility until dawn, although by then several people had fainted, a claustrophobic had had hysterics and the latrine buckets were overflowing.

In the morning we were summoned one by one for hours. At last I was taken out, and my stomach contracted in fear as they led me down a corridor reeking of disinfectant and shoved me into a small, dimly lit room. I was just starting to look around when a hand struck me with incredible force in the mouth and sent me sprawling. Dazed, I climbed to my feet and stumbled into the detective who had escorted me; he held me with one hand and slapped me back and forth repeatedly with the other. When he let go I slid to the floor, and the two men who had been waiting in the room began working on me with rubber truncheons, one on either side.

I came to, dazed by the pain in my head and gasping for air as they threw water in my face. One of the detectives was leaning over me, calling me a dirty, red-headed Jew and various other names in a curiously dispassionate voice, as if he were commenting on the weather. They propped me up in a wooden chair and demanded to know the names of my friends, who had hired me for the demonstration and what Communist cell I belonged to. When I declined to answer (my tongue was in any case busy exploring a gap where they had knocked out a tooth and I was nauseated by swallowed blood) they began shouting; so I said that I was a Social Democrat and had had no part in the disorder, quite the contrary. At this one of them pulled the chair out from under me, and even before I hit the floor they flew at me again with the truncheons. I made a great effort to keep silent, but as the pain increased I began to sob, then, losing control when it became altogether unbearable, to scream and to try to crawl away across the floor.

At this point the door opened and they stopped immediately and snapped to attention, still panting for breath. An officer walked over and looked down at me.

"What are you politically?" he asked quietly.

"A Trotskyite, I suppose."

"You suppose, you young fool? How old are you?"

"Eighteen," I replied, then added, "sir!"

"Take his fingerprints," he said in a bored voice to the detectives; then he turned back to me, still lying on the floor, and shouted, "If I ever catch you here again I'll flay you alive! Get out!"

I have had many things to be grateful for in my life, and high on the list is the existence in the back of my mind of a kind of dead-letter box where unpleasant experiences are filed away as soon as they are over. I have also been blessed with a tendency to find in the smaller pleasures of life more than enough compensation for its major horrors. So when they put me in a sort of store room to sleep for a few hours I experienced, not for the last time in my life, the bliss of not being beaten—a pleasure that is, strangely, more intense than the pain of the beating. Finally an old warder awoke me, took my prints and helped me—still unsteady on my feet—to the main gate. I was free.

Raising a stiff arm and wincing, I hailed a taxi. The driver looked at my purple, swollen face and gave a long, low whistle of respect, which cheered me enormously.

"Police?" he asked, tilting his head toward the building across from us.

"No," I replied, "I ran into a doorknob." We both laughed shortly, he with commiseration and I with a gasp as hot needles stabbed my bruised ribs.

When Aunt Lina recovered from her shock, she began cleaning me up—she was becoming expert at that by now—and summoned the family physician. The old gentleman prodded me all over with a marked lack of sympathy and announced that, given a few hours of sleep, I might be expected to live.

"Nothing cracked except his head," he muttered, glancing at Trotsky's *Mein Leben* lying on the bedside table, "and I don't have a cure for that. *Non crescit herba in hortis contra vim furoris*," which even my schoolboy Latin could interpret as meaning there are no medicinal herbs for insanity.

I slept on and off for two days, rousing myself only when Aunt Lina brought in enormous bowls of chicken soup, hot rolls and wine. On the second afternoon of this delightful treatment I finally forced myself out of the warm bed when she told me that Paul Justus and a lot of other people had been telephoning constantly. Until that moment it had not occurred to me that I was something of a martyr at union headquarters. I telephoned Justus, and he asked me if I was feeling well enough to come around that evening.

He was alone in his drawing room when I arrived, and he asked for a detailed account of what had happened, congratulated me for what he called my "noble behaviour" and added, "You're my youngest student, George, and I think you may turn out to be the most useful. But I did not drag you out of bed to pay you compliments. Tomorrow there will be a lecture at your trade union. The title is 'The Progress of the USSR under Stalin and the Leadership of the USSR in the Struggles of the International Workers' Movement.' " We both smiled as he pronounced this Muscovite mouthful; nobody could compete with the Stalinists when it came to fatuous verbiage.

"What do you want me to do?" I asked.

"Everybody knows how you got those dreadful bruises on your face," he went on, "and no one can question your loyalty. I want you to attend the lecture, and during the question period I want you to rip the speaker's arguments to shreds, one by one. Things have gone too far. It's time to separate the sheep from the goats."

Hesitantly, I asked him what good there was in attacking Stalin when the real enemy just now was Hitler.

"Is he?" replied Justus, looking at me over his glasses. "After the war it will be discovered that of the two, the Georgian pervert is the greater murderer. When two maniacs turn to rend one another, it does not follow that one ought to come to the rescue of either."

As I entered the trade union building the next evening, various people came up to shake my hand. Some knew what was afoot and whispered their support; Justus and I were not the only ones who were angry and alarmed at the way the Communists had begun taking over. The great hall was filled to capacity to hear the lecturer, Gyorgy Markos. All I knew about the man was a pamphlet he had written in the usual Soviet style, all superlatives and non sequiturs, called *The Development of Russia from Peter the Great to J.V. Stalin.* After the war he would become one of the leading Communists in the country, rising to ever more lyrical heights in his praise of the Greatest Friend of the Working Man. He turned out to be an extremely able speaker, almost hypnotizing us with phrases which, on examination, meant nothing at all. He spoke for about an hour, and when he finished there was a storm of applause. Here and there throughout the hall groups took up the chant: "Long live Stalin!"

My palms were cold and sweating as I stood up. Gripping the back of the chair before me, I began to speak, scarcely recognizing my own voice in the puzzled silence that gradually fell. But as I spoke real indignation drove away fear, and as acidly as possible I pointed out that the speaker's analysis of Marxist values ought to be applied to the USSR itself. I recited statistics, Soviet statistics, which, however exaggerated, served to show that the USSR was admittedly inferior to the West in industrial technology. It followed, I went on, according to Marxist theory that those employing this technology must work more to produce less—that they were in fact being exploited by managerial incompetence. I went on to mention the show trials, the deportation of unknown hundreds of thousands, the genocide of national minorities, the elimination of all Stalin's former colleagues—those who had known him as he murdered his way to power.

By this time an angry murmuring was going on all around me, but I was enjoying myself telling the truth and went on to ask Markos, sneering now on the platform with one arm raised for silence, what he thought of Stalin's betrayal of the left in the Spanish Civil War when he sold oil to the Fascists and had his commissars massacre their allies, the Anarchists and the Social Democrats. Finally, carried away by my own fury, I shouted that it was ludicrous, not to say obscene, for a country that tolerated a mass murderer as its leader to offer itself as a model for the international workers' movement.

There was hatred in the shouts that broke all around me now. Here and there my friends shouted back and, fearing pandemonium, the president of the trade union officially and hastily declared the meeting closed.

Many of those who had shaken my hand an hour before avoided me as we filed out of the hall. But five or six surrounded me and hustled me down the street to the nearest pub. We were all a little hysterical with excitement and anger and began to relax only well into the second bottle of wine. I was just wondering what Justus had hoped to achieve by my performance, when I felt a hand resting on my arm and found that an extremely pretty girl, whose name I knew was Eva, had moved very close to me. My nervous system responded by channelling all my tension down another and more interesting track.

No one knew exactly why Eva hung around the union. She was obviously not a spy—a spy would not have reserved her interest so exclusively for the young men among us. She was about twenty and possessed a sort of oval-faced beauty that made sustained conversation almost impossible in its presence. As the others talked and drank around us, I returned the pressure of her thigh and agreed to have dinner at her home the following evening.

The next morning at work I received a message that I was to report before a disciplinary committee at the trade union at eight o'clock that night. After work I reshaved carefully and went in search of Eva's house, depressed at the cool reception I received from my workmates who obviously thought I was letting the side down with my attack on Stalin.

Eva's house, when at last I found it, was one of those huge crumbling workers' tenements held together by its own weight and the accumulated filth of generations. The gate hung open, and I picked my way cautiously through a refuse-strewn courtyard reeking of urine and garbage. Sounds of a domestic quarrel, Gypsy music and the hoarse laughter of a woman floated down the dark stairwell as I climbed to the fourth floor.

Eva greeted me with a kiss and led me into her family's one-room flat. At a bare table in the centre of the depressing little room, painted an oily dark green, sat her father finishing off a bottle of wine. A bare bulb dangled above him, showing the stains on his shirt and giving his wrinkled face a greenish tinge. He was completely drunk.

"Daddy," said Eva cheerfully, "this is George. He's having dinner with us tonight. Later he's being expelled from his trade union." I wondered how she knew that but did not have time to ask.

"Don't worry about it, boy!" Her father squeezed one eye shut and examined me with the other. "If they throw you out you can always join us in the Arrow Cross. Have some wine!" At that, Eva's mother scuttled out from the kitchen with another bottle and a cracked glass. She was a haggard little woman and we immediately exchanged sympathetic smiles, like two distant relatives at a funeral.

That was the extent of our conversation, and after a few minutes of excruciating silence we sat down to plates of steaming pork *gulyas* and dumplings. Eva, beside me, pressed her ankle against mine in a way at once innocent and unbearably exciting. Across from us her father transferred *gulyas* from plate to mouth like a steam shovel at an excavation site, beads of sweat rolling down his face. He washed each mouthful down with wine, and just when I had finally thought of something to say, he suddenly looked into his lap and slowly toppled off his chair.

The three of us helped him to the bed. My embarrassment by this time was turning into hysteria, but Eva just laughed at me and in silence we consumed the rest of the *gulyas*, which, it must be admitted, was delicious. At seven-thirty I announced that I had to go, and as I put on my coat Eva's father raised his head off the bed and called after me, "Don't forget, boy, you can join us! If we've got to sell the country, it might as well be to Hitler as to Stalin."

"Mr. Foldes," I replied, weary of the situation, "I'm a Jew."

He wheezed with laughter, coughed and addressed the wall. "I know, little brother. Don't imagine you're the first Jew to join us. We're all together, stinking Jews, stinking workers, stinking Nazis. . . ." His voice trailed off, and Eva grabbed my arm and propelled me out onto the landing above the courtyard.

"I told Daddy you were a Jew," she said seriously. "I also told him you're unlike every other Jew in the world." This sounded like a line in a bad film. Unable to think of anything to reply, I took her in my arms and gave her the sort of lingering kiss I had hotly admired when Rudolf Valentino applied it to Vilma Banki. Then I ran off to find a taxi.

I arrived with two minutes to spare, and as I entered the union building three friends separated themselves from the others and asked me how I was going to defend myself. They were among those who had defended me the previous night, and they too were to appear before the committee. Just then we were summoned, and as we walked past the onlookers several Communists gave us open grins of such delighted malevolence that I could scarcely restrain myself from smashing in a face or two.

The committee was seated behind a long table. In the

centre sat Hugo Nemeth, the president of the union. Nemeth was a tall man; even sitting he dominated the other five with his height and bulk. The overhead lights gleamed off his shining scalp visible under a Prussian haircut. He looked up from his papers, tapping a pencil against the table, and I stared in fascination at the long jagged scar that disfigured the left side of his face, then looked away, ashamed of my involuntary rudeness.

He began with me, omitting the usual "comrade" when he addressed me. They had, he began, ascertained that I was a Trotskyite and a "wrecker" and under the influence of a known traitor to the Social Democratic Party. This, of course, was a reference to Justus; Gancz, who had sent me to Justus and who was now seated beside Nemeth, began to examine his fingernails with sudden interest.

"As far as I know, *Comrade* Nemeth," I began in a voice dripping with all the scorn I could summon, "the Social Democratic Party has never declared any Trotskyite, neither Paul Justus nor myself, its enemy. On the contrary, it is the Communist Party of the Soviet Union that has declared Trotskyites its enemies. There seems to be some confusion, *Comrade* Nemeth, about which party you belong to."

There were sharp intakes of breath on both sides of the table as I spoke. Everybody knew the truth, but nobody ever said it in so many words. Nemeth had turned purple and his little eyes almost disappeared behind their slits.

"We have decided," he continued in a voice that he just managed to control, "that self-criticism will not suffice in your case. Accordingly we have decided to expel—" He broke off as I came out with a laugh that was only half forced. I was suddenly furious at having wasted so much time with people like those around me.

"Really, Nemeth, you people and your endless 'self-criticism.' Do you take me for one of your *apparatchik* robots?" I turned on my heel and walked out. As I closed the door I caught a glimpse of expressions ranging from pure hatred to blank incredulity.

In the foyer I walked straight past the small crowd waiting for the results and stepped into the cold, wind-swept street with my coat still over my arm. Eva was standing before the building. Without a word she helped me on with my coat and we headed slowly in the direction of the Danube, that great sewer of Hungarian sorrows. At last, in a tone I had not yet heard from her, she asked softly, "Where can we go spend the night?" Eva had any number of good qualities, but her forte was undoubtedly her ability to take one's mind off one's troubles just at the right moment.

At eighteen there was only one thing that competed for first place in my mind with politics and that was the increasingly oppressive fact of my virginity. No sooner had Eva spoken than the union, the party and the war itself faded into the background, and I decided to match her boldness with my own, steering us away from the Danube toward Aunt Lina's.

"George, you're a bourgeois!" whispered Eva as I led her across the carpets of my aunt's entrance hall. Aunt Lina, to my dismay, was not in bed but sitting in the living room in a dressing gown. My hopes plummeted as her eyebrows rose; but then with a curious smile she offered us both a late supper, which we declined, and then astonished me by feigning exhaustion and marching off to her room with a cheery good night.

For all our mutual fondness, Eva and I were certainly not in love. But lust mingled with fondness is already lust lifted beyond itself, and to that I added a large element of gratitude. The night that followed was filled with the sniggering blissfulness of two adolescents poring over medical texts in an attic, a hilarious shamelessness that, before dawn, gradually gave way to romantic tenderness. When it was over I stored away the memory of that night, taking it out from time to time long afterward for nostalgic examination.

In the morning I took Eva to the shop where she worked as a sales clerk, then went to my own workshop—where I discovered that I was sacked. Old Janos looked up from his bench as I stood talking with the manager. He gave me a sincerely puzzled look, then shook his head sadly and returned to his cutting board. I had expected to be sacked, but the streets of Budapest seemed colder and lonelier as I headed toward Justus's house.

Justus, of course, was full of congratulations, having heard all the details of my little speech to Nemeth.

"I myself wasted ten years of my youth on the altars of Soviet ideology," he said. "You are both clever and lucky to have extricated yourself from that crowd."

"Yes, but how can I fight the Nazis without an organization behind me?" I asked, though what I was really wondering was how I was going to live without a job.

"My dear boy," replied Justus, leaning forward in his satin dressing gown to pour me a second cup of coffee, "the point is that it was necessary for someone to stand up and tell them the truth. Even in the Florence of the Medici one was not forced to become a disciple of Machiavelli just because one opened one's mouth against Savonarola." I pondered this for a moment. As so often, Justus's logic was impeccable but seemed to concern another situation. "In any case," he continued, "I think we have an organization for you."

He went on to tell me that as secretary of the Social Democratic organization of the sixth district of Budapest, he could bypass the trade union apparatus and keep me active in the party as a member of its musical society, a choir.

"But I sing like a rooster!" I protested, alarmed.

"Dear boy," he said, amused, patting his lower lip with a napkin, "ours is a very special sort of choir. Some sing Palestrina and folk songs, others only pretend to sing while preparing another sort of serenade for the Germans when they arrive—as they assuredly will. The serenade I have in mind will be cacophonic, so to speak, but it will contribute to Western civilization as much as any Mozart mass!"

So a few days later the choirmaster auditioned me. Her eyes grew large with disbelief as I began to sing, and she quickly waved her hand to shut me up. I took a solemn oath never under any circumstances to do more than mouth the words during concerts.

In the months that followed I travelled all over Hungary mouthing folk songs to audiences in provincial towns, gradually assuming the character of a singer to such an extent that I would be soaked with sweat at the end of a concert from my exertions. Only once, however, did I get so carried away that I broke into what I took to be glorious song. The audience shifted uneasily in their seats and the choirmaster's face contorted with pain. Even among the several other nonsingers who were filed away in the choir, for future reference as it were, my voice was something of a legend.

But as the months rolled by I became more and more depressed, despairing of ever doing anything against the Germans. In Budapest I picked up odd jobs for two or three weeks at a time to have something to give to Aunt Lina. I saw Eva from time to time, but things began to cool off between us as she was thinking of becoming a policewoman. Everything, as we say in Hungarian, has its limits. The routine of my life began to seem as dull, pointless and interminable as the war itself.

4

The Coming of the Germans

IN 1942 AN ARMY of two hundred thousand Hungarians had
been sent into the Soviet Union in summer uniforms and with
antiquated equipment, including horse-drawn guns which
had to be heated with burning straw before they would fire in
the Russian cold. As winter frost set in the horses began to die
of exposure and starvation, and soon after them the soldiers.
The wretched men of the Second Hungarian Army were
drafted almost exclusively from the ranks of landless peasants and day labourers. In what they obviously thought a
stroke of genius, Horthy and his new prime minister,
Bardossy, sought to solve a large part of the country's social
problem by the expenditure of these men. They were justified
in their confidence that most Hungarians would never notice
the loss and that Hitler, who was constantly pressuring them
now for more help, would be pleased.

In January 1943 the Germans, retreating from Voronezh, left the Second Hungarian Army behind in a bend of the river Don to cover them. The commanding officer, General Jany, was a quintessentially old-school Austro-Hungarian soldier, combining ruthlessness with imbecilic incompetence. Ordering his troops to hold out to the last man, he took the only available airplane and flew behind the lines to Kiev. The advancing Red Army encircled the hapless Hungarians and cut them to pieces. In a few days more than forty thousand died either of wounds or from the cold, and over seventy thousand were captured and taken to prison camps where thousands more died of typhus.

In Budapest no word of this appeared in the press, and what we knew reached us by word of mouth. Daily we read about "the immortal deeds of our German allies at Stalingrad." Statistics have never been published about those seventy thousand men. The few groups that eventually returned to Hungary five, ten and twelve years later were made up of emaciated ghosts.

In the meantime Bardossy boosted the war effort by bringing in a third anti-Jewish law, this one virtually depriving us of our citizenship. Jewish officers, non-coms and other ranks were immediately thrown out of the army. All Jewish males between twenty and fifty (occasionally up to sixty-five) were drafted into labour batallions. These men wore civilian clothing with a yellow star sewn on the front. I began dreading my twentieth birthday as one by one my friends were conscripted for forced labour. First George Egri went, then a frail boy named Felix Biro, whom we had always called Infelix because his gentle, melancholy nature made him so ill equipped to survive in a society such as ours.

Then Bardossy was succeeded by a new prime minister, Kallay, thanks to whose humanity many Jews were recalled from the eastern front to build roads in Hungary (or, when it amused the local authorities, to carry loads of earth and stone from one place to another and back again, like Sisyphus). Egri was sent away to Transylvania, and I did not see him again until after the war. Most of those who survived the batallions did so by managing to stay in Hungary and, like Egri, escaping at the end of the war. Those who did not escape would during the last days be driven on foot toward Austria where thousands were to be shot along the way by the guards.

A few months after Stalingrad I was awakened about six one spring morning by loud knocking at the door. Felix Biro stood there, so pale and thin I hardly recognized him. He had had the unheard of good luck to be granted two weeks' leave from the front. I hurried him into the dining room, where Aunt Lina, with tears in her eyes as she thought of her own son, ransacked our meagre food supply to give him a magnificent breakfast. I noticed with horror that his fingers were grotesquely discoloured and several fingernails were missing. He had difficulty holding his fork. "A little frostbite," said Felix softly in embarrassment when he caught me staring. I counted the months remaining before I too would probably join the fifty thousand Hungarian Jews in the Ukraine.

Felix looked distinctly more cheerful after breakfast and was staring at his surroundings. I realized that even our shabby flat looked like a mythical paradise to him. I asked him whose lot was worse, the Jewish forced labourers' or the Hungarian soldiers'. "Oh, the army," he replied casually, and I knew he was lying for my sake. Later I discovered that while the army averaged twenty-five percent losses, the figure for Jewish forced labourers was over seventy-five percent.

When I pressed him for information he tried to change the subject but finally gave in and wearily, in the same uncannily mild voice I had heard him use once to discuss the philosophy of Spinoza or the poems of Rilke, he told me about his comrades and their commanding officer, a former classical scholar much hated by his fellow officers for the way he tried to protect the Jews under his command. The previous commander, he said, had been an animal, a sadist who boasted that he had confidential orders from the high command to bring his Jews home in his attaché case, as death certificates.

He told me they were constantly hungry—which was painfully obvious from his almost skeletal frame—and that they had bartered fountain pens, watches and rings with the Hungarian soldiers for bread. But it sometimes happened that a non-com simply took a Jew aside and shot him, thus acquiring the goods and keeping his bread. During the retreat from the Don the Germans and Hungarians used the roads, while the Jews marched in snow-filled ditches alongside. At night the Germans had slept in the houses, the Hungarians in stables and pigsties, while the Jews sat in village squares huddled around fires when they could find kindling. When a

Jew was wounded or stricken with typhus he was simply left in the snow to freeze.

When I asked him if none of them ever tried to give themselves up to the Russians, he laughed bitterly and told me that he had seen such an attempt when their line was less than two hundred yards away from the Russians. Six Jews were sent out to bring back the Hungarian dead. They crawled through the snow for a long time, then jumped up and began running toward the Russians waving their scarves. The Russians opened fire, killing them all except one man who stayed on his knees; a Hungarian sharpshooter took care of him. That same evening, behind a hill, the hundred and sixty Jews of Felix's unit were lined up; sixteen were chosen at random and shot where they stood.

Two days after our breakfast Felix came to dinner, after which we went to a pub. He drank glass after glass of wine, but it might have been water for all the effect it had on him. I had realized how cruel it was of me to question him so decided to talk about something cheerful. But as I chattered away he voluntarily brought the conversation back to the war, telling me how when his batallion was at the Soviet-Hungarian border station of Verecke they camped near the stockyards where hundreds of Jews were herded together by Hungarian gendarmes. These were a few of the fifteen thousand Jews who had sought refuge in Hungary when the Germans occupied Poland. Bardossy's government expelled them, and when Felix saw them they were being handed over to German *Einsatzkommandos* for transport to extermination camps. Infants, the insane and those whose strength had given out were shot in the stockyards by the guards.

Farther east they had marched through the ghetto of Stanislawow, where the cobblestones were still slippery with blood. Near the city walls were piles of tiny corpses, the children whose heads had been smashed against the stones. At Kolomya they had passed a huge mass grave in a forest clearing: thousands of intertwined bodies lay beneath a flutter of yellow birch leaves. Beside the pit was a windmill; on each of its four blades the Germans had hung a bearded corpse. As they marched past, the four dead Jews revolved slowly, black caftans flowing in a *danse macabre*.

Still farther east, as they approached Kiev, there were no Jews at all except for themselves. They were walking through a part of the world where some five million Jews had been living five years before. German units passing them on the road would stare in amazement and ridicule the Hungarian soldiers for keeping them alive. An SS officer, incredulous, had asked their commander if he was keeping them alive as a zoo exhibit.

"But there was one thing more terrible than all the rest," Felix went on, then stopped, noticing the man at the next table who had been staring at us for some time with a strange expression on his face. I stared back at the man, but he ignored me, his eyes glued on Felix. Shrugging, I urged Felix to continue.

"It was less than a month ago," he said, looking around at the miracle of finding himself in a pub. "We were camped in a beautiful grove of trees, just like a hunting scene out of Turgenev, near some little tributary of the Dnieper. It was about an hour before sunset and we were sitting on the grass. Our commander had been gone most of the day, and some of us were singing, when suddenly a lieutenant from another labour batallion arrived with two sergeants and three Jews. The lieutenant began boasting that he was the best bird hunter in Hungary. Then he ordered the three Jews to climb a tree about fifty or sixty paces away. They were just pulling themselves into the middle branches when he took aim and fired. A man screamed and fell. "One Jewish bird down," said the lieutenant and immediately shot the second man. But when he fired at the third man he missed, swearing loudly. "You might as well come down," he shouted. "A gentleman doesn't waste two bullets on one Jew." Then he and the non-coms marched off, followed by the trembling Jew.

I saw Felix once again during his leave. He was staying with his mother on Mexico Street and told me he had decided to go into hiding with friends. Whether or not he succeeded I never found out.

After Stalingrad, El Alamein and the beginning of the German retreat in Russia, the more-or-less secretly pro-British elements in the government, including Horthy himself, began to take heart. Prime Minister Kallay was a conservative who in his detestation of all popular movements loathed the Nazis as much as the Communists. All Budapest knew by the grapevine that he had secretly sent envoys to negotiate with the Allies in Italy. Unfortunately the Germans had their own sources of information, and Hitler knew all about it. Pressure increased, but we began to take heart as

Kallay refused to hand over a single Hungarian Jew to the Germans. He and the minister of war, Vilmos Nagy, even went so far as to try to alleviate the misery of those in the labour batallions. But in this they were hindered by the fact that the Hungarian officers' corps had become increasingly Fascist as the war went on, as had a majority of the middle class and a large number of workers. There was an atmosphere of lunacy: the more obvious it was that the war was lost, the more loudly these people predicted final victory.

Budapest itself was strangely calm. As Jews we suffered abuse, an increasingly meagre diet and a lot of public humiliation, but we were only too aware—those of us with our eyes open—that alone of almost all the Jews between Denmark and Bulgaria, we were alive.

Then finally Hitler lost patience with the Hungarian government, and one winter morning early in 1944, with the rest of the population I watched the long columns of German troops march along the Danube to take up the centres of occupation. Most watched in silence, but others were jubilant. What few knew was that with the Germans arrived a special *Kommando* under an officer named Adolf Eichmann, whose task it would be to wipe Hungarian Jewry off the face of the earth. Nor did we know that Gestapo plain-clothes men had arrived the day before and commandeered the Majestic Hotel, the cellars of which they were already turning into cells and torture chambers. Within a few weeks the Gestapo were to receive more than thirty-five thousand denunciations of Jews, Communists and liberals—more cooperation than they were accorded in any other city in Europe. And, finally, we did not know that Nagy, the minister of war, had urgently summoned the chiefs of staff to order resistance to the Germans and that not one general showed up.

That same afternoon the Germans closed the offices of the Social Democatic Pary, arresting the leadership and deporting them to Mauthausen. Those of us in the choir met secretly and sadly agreed there was nothing to do but disband. We had waited for months to act, and now that the Germans were here there was nothing we could do.

The next morning Aunt Lina read that Horthy had returned from his visit to the Führer and had appointed a German collaborator named Sztojay as prime minister. The members of the new cabinet were all Nazis. Then on the second and third pages of the paper we read the new regulations aimed at the Jews. We were to wear the yellow star at all times; this included all Christians of Jewish origin. All remaining Jewish businesses were immediately confiscated. No Jew would be allowed to practise in any of the professions. We could travel only with special permits (which, as we soon discovered, were unobtainable). Our food rations were reduced still further. We had to surrender all cash except for three thousand *pengo* (about a hundred and fifty dollars) per person. We were forbidden to own cars, horses, bicycles, radios, telephones, typewriters or jewelery. We were henceforth forbidden to use cafés, bars, restaurants, buses, streetcars, theatres, cinemas, museums, hotels, baths or public parks.

When Eichmann's plans became known, as they soon did, the reaction of many was to go into hiding. Yet there were many, including religious leaders, who urged calm and patience, utterly refusing to see the evidence written in blood in all the countries surrounding us: the Germans were going to kill us and the Hungarians were going to help them do it. Immediately people came forward, however, Christians and liberals who offered to hide their Jewish friends and acquaintances at the risk of their own lives. Others were willing to do so for a price. But most either shrugged or else actively helped in the tragedy that now began to unfold.

About three days after the beginning of the occupation I pinned on my yellow star and went around to Justus's house, afraid that he might have been arrested. Although he was half Jewish, Justus turned out to be in no immediate danger. When not teaching the doctrines of Trotsky, he was director of one of the largest steelworks in the country. As long as Horthy remained in power, he would be considered an "honorary Christian."

Justus offered me the choice of escaping to Yugoslavia or else taking my chances in Budapest. Personally, he considered it would be safer for me to be drafted into a labour batallion; the death rate among Tito's partisans was even higher. I thanked him, promising to return the next day with my decision. But when I reached home I was greeted with the notice that I had to report immediately for induction. Frantically I paced up and down the living room, trying to decide whether to return at once to Justus's to hide or else to show up at the railway station as ordered. At last I packed a rucksack and a blanket, asked Aunt Lina to let Justus and several other friends know what had happened, and after a tearful embrace I left for the railway station, where under the great steel and glass roof I found myself lost in a sea of hundreds of yellow stars, Jews young and old obeying the summons.

"I thought Jews didn't eat pork," sneered a voice as I sat on the floor of the packed cattle car eating smoked bacon and bread from my rucksack. The young man, powerfully built with long blond hair and blue eyes, was sitting directly opposite me with his arms folded on his knees. He looked like an SS man or a Viking, a character out of the nightmares of a Ukrainian rabbi. I continued eating, studiously ignoring his stare.

"I am a Jew who eats pork," I replied at last. "What sort of Jew are you?"

"I'm not a Jew!" he said furiously, but when I made no response and went on eating, he said more calmly, "They're trying to tell me that my mother was a Jewess. She and my father are dead. It's my uncle who's done this to me, to get his hands on the house." There was something in the young man's voice that told me he was mad. As for his story, however, I did not doubt that for a minute; that sort of thing was going on all over Hungary just now.

"So you're a Christian?" I asked.

"Do you take me for a stink . . . for a Jew?" he snapped back, staring at my yellow star. I fought down the urge to tell him how nice it was to see Christian anti-Semites being deported along with the rest of us. When I failed to reply, he put his head on his knees and stayed that way as we rocked along for about three or four hours.

Finally the train stopped at Jaszbereny. We were unloaded, formed up outside the station and marched to the great labour camp outside the town, camp number 301-3 in the universe of Jewish labour batallions. There the guards put us into a long row of sheds and issued us filthy straw mattresses, which we placed on the ground as there were no bunks. The tall blond, whose name was Paul Gedeon, stuck with me although the cold hatred he displayed toward everyone but the guards certainly did not exclude me. By the time they had fed us and sent us back to our rotten straw pallets I was becoming tired of the man.

Clustered along both walls of the shed sat little groups of men and boys, most of whom had never done heavy manual labour before and were nervous about what was in store for them. Some of the anxiety had worn off at supper, however, when it became clear that for the time being the guards were inclined toward nothing more than verbal abuse.

"It makes me sick," Gedeon muttered, "being penned up with a lot of money-lenders and old-clothes dealers!"

"And it makes me sick," I shot back, slamming closed the book I had taken out of my rucksack, "sleeping next to a stinking anti-Semite! Go on, get out!"

He stared at me, then in tones so abject I thought he was going to cry, he said, "I'm sorry. I don't mean to be uncivil. It's just that I was brought up to despise Jews and now the whole world is telling me that I am one. You're a good fellow. I'm sorry."

I pondered this for a while, trying without success to imagine myself in the same situation; but it made me relent somewhat.

"Look, Gedeon, you don't look anything like a Jew. Eventually they'll let us out of here, or if not, perhaps we can escape. For you it's just a matter of getting your hands on new papers, then you'll be safe."

"I know that," he said, "but don't you see? It's not a question of papers. If it's true that my mother was Jewish, my life is ruined anyway. This is where I belong."

I found the stupidity of this breath-taking and turned back to my pocket edition of Stefan Zweig's *Erasmus*, squinting in the fading light. I remembered that my grandfather had once told me that the poet Heine had said that a baptismal certificate was the only passport into Western civilization. Gedeon's case showed clearly that the Germans did not accept this logic—which was in any case false. The fact that the Vatican, the hierarchy of Hungary and all the surrounding countries, with few exceptions, found little or nothing to protest about in what was happening to us was enough to show that Christianity played little part in what I, at least, meant by civilization. And what *did* I mean by civilization? I tried out various Marxist-sounding definitions, but all rang false. The one I finally formulated and stuck with was "a dogged preference for the decent and the agreeable in the face of all opposition." Not wholly adequate, perhaps, but it had the virtue of excluding Hitler, Stalin, our guards, the pope, and poor Gedeon sitting beside me; and of including my grandfather, a priest I knew to be hiding Jews in Budapest, Paul Justus and, I hoped, myself. Immensely cheered by my solution, I fell asleep.

The week that followed was one of endless rain, of being marched out into the mud for roll calls and meals of watery soup and mouldering bread, then marching back to sit on sodden straw, listening to the rhythmical thumping of the rain of the roof. Someone, clearly, had made a mistake. There was no work for us to do at Jaszbereny. Decks of cards were produced and men spent hour after hour gambling away whatever money they had on them; others slept as much as possible, conserving energy for whatever was ahead. Rumours flew: Hitler had been assassinated, Hungary had signed an armistice with the Russians, the Americans were at Vienna; or, we were going to be sent to Auschwitz, we were going to the eastern front to clear mine fields, New York had been destroyed by Hitler's famous secret weapons.

Then one day soldiers ran in, someone blew a whistle and we barely had time to stuff our few possessions in our rucksacks before they marched us back to the station at Jaszbereny.

'Come on, old man," I said to Gedeon as we stood in ranks before the cattle cars. "Who knows, you may get your chance to escape wherever we're going."

They loaded us into the wagons, the tiny windows of which had been boarded up. Panic ran through us in a sickening wave. Men who had been laughing or quarrelling two hours before over cards now turned pale as death. Gedeon, wild-looking in his fear, suddenly became hysterical and in a tone of shrill merriment shouted, "It's off to the gas chambers, gentlemen! Better collect the interest on your loans while you can!" At this a tiny, withered old man opposite us leaned forward, studying Gedeon. Then without a change of expression he slapped Gedeon on the face so hard that it made me wince to hear it. Gedeon covered his face with his hands and began weeping quietly.

After several hours the train stopped and shouting broke out at the other end of the car. Those who could peep through a crack in the planks announced that we were at Rakos, the freight station of Budapest. A great sigh of relief went up, and when after another hour of stop-and-go we pulled into the West Station of the capital men were singing patriotic Hungarian songs in their gratitude that Hungarians were not yet turning us over to the Germans. In my disgust, for a second I came almost to share some of Gedeon's anti-Semitism.

Trucks took us to the grounds of the Hungarian army's

chief quartermaster depot, where we settled down on the inevitable straw mattresses, though this time in stone barracks with real wooden bunks.

At five the next morning we had roll call, were given an inedible breakfast and assigned jobs. Some unloaded trucks, others worked in the bakery, the kitchens, lumberyard or warehouse. We worked twelve hours every day, and every day conditions deteriorated as the pressure increased for us to work harder. The guards showed a surly hostility that often erupted into savagery, as when we stood helpless and watched an old man beaten because he could not lift the sacks from a truck or when, as sometimes happened, one of us failed to salute a Hungarian private. Then we stood in the barracks' courtyard with a hundred-pound sack on our shoulders for two hours and were kicked and beaten if we fell, as the old and sick frequently did.

One morning I met Gedeon working in the kitchens. He had come across a corporal who was a former schoolmate. The man had promised to help him escape. Rather unexpectedly, Gedeon offered to take me along. I accepted on the spot and spent the rest of the day in a fever of excitement. The quartermaster depot was not Auschwitz, but I had had enough of it all the same.

After lights-out that night I crouched with Gedeon beside the huge pile of lumber stacked along one length of the wall surrounding the depot. We were invisible where we were, but I was terrified of climbing the lumber, where we could be seen by anybody for a hundred yards. Suddenly a voice called softly out of the darkness behind us, "Is that you, Pali?"

"Right!" answered Gedeon.

"Go on, take your time, there's nobody in sight," the man said. Then, to my dismay, he began whistling, and I was afraid that it was a trap. But when Gedeon, no hero as far as I knew, started before me up the lumber pile, I quickly followed. The barbed wire at the top was ancient, rusted and badly strung. We slipped through with only minor damage and dropped heavily to the street beyond the wall. Hastily we tore off our yellow stars, shook hands and went off at a fast walk in opposite directions.

5

Going Underground

"MY HUSBAND IS OCCUPIED, I'M AFRAID," said Mrs. Justus anxiously. She started to close the door, and would have, had my foot not been in it. The city was blacked out, but the moon was bright and my red hair and freckles were all too visible to passers-by, so I had no intention of being turned away. Slowly I forced the door open.

"Forgive me," I apologized, "but I'll wait in the kitchen." I brushed past her and startled the maid by sitting in a corner on a stool without so much as a word. From the drawing room beyond came the sound of several voices, including Justus's. Some time later his guests departed and Justus fairly ran into the kitchen.

"Dear boy," he beamed, taking me by both hands. "I thought you'd never arrive. How thin you are! Well, I'm entering the army in two days and there's someone I want you to meet. Come on, we've a rendezvous in just a few minutes!" Going outside was the last thing I wanted to do, but Justus waved his hand airily and handed me a beret, which, he declared, made me look like a gentile, a working-class gentile at that. A few minutes later he guided me to a table in his neighbourhood pub and began looking around impatiently. There were twenty or thirty customers.

"It's not like Tony to be late," he began, and at that moment the doors were flung open and four men and a woman in police uniform came in. I groaned inwardly and stared at the table.

"Identity check!" one of them shouted superfluously. Another was standing just inside the door with a submachine gun at the ready. The only papers I possessed were the labour batallion ID, which marked me as a deserter. Silently cursing Justus, I thought of making a break for the door, but that was clearly suicidal. Then my heart leaped as the policewoman turned and came toward us: it was Eva Foldes.

"Papers," she said simply, showing no sign of recognition. Slowly I handed her my ID. She looked at it closely, then murmured, "Is your friend a deserter too?"

"No," I said quietly, trying not to show my relief too visibly lest her companions notice. She scrutinized Justus's papers for a while, then just as one of her friends was approaching handed them back and said just a trifle too loudly, "Everything all right here." As they all trooped out, having arrested no one, my eyes followed her with what must have been a look of doglike gratitude.

"Friend of yours?" asked Justus after a long pause. I nodded. He was clearly shaken, as well he might be.

As we headed back toward his flat a man wearing a dark trench coat and a wide-brimmed hat crossed over and joined us. He looked like Hollywood's idea of a Gestapo agent except for the wide grin as he shook hands with us. "I would have joined you in there," he apologized, "except it looked a bit crowded!"

Tony, whose surname I never learned, was about thirty, one of those Asiatic-looking Hungarians, a strain left over from the days of Arpad, if not Attila, short and wiry with high cheekbones and deep-set, slightly slanting eyes. But in Tony (who was an architect by profession) the gravity and reserve that usually accompany such features in Hungary were replaced by a permanent air of half-repressed mirth. A mischievous, ironical smile was likely to appear on his face in almost any situation. He looked like Genghis Khan playing Peter Pan.

"Of course you must stay here tonight," said Justus as the three of us entered his drawing room. Then he left me alone with Tony, who immediately started questioning me about my background, about the labour batallion and about my political views.

"Have you had any word about your family?" he asked after a while. I said I had not. "You know about the deportations?" I nodded. All Hungary knew that Eichmann was deporting Jews from every place except Budapest itself, just as Justus had predicted many months before. "Well, let's hope for the best. In any case, you're going to have a chance to fight back from now on—if you want it, that is." He looked at me questioningly, and again, more vigorously, I nodded. "Very well, I'll be here for you tomorrow at six in the evening, and we'll begin. By the way, while you were at Jaszbereny the Red Army advanced. They're about thirty-five kilometres from the border now. Our German friends are bringing in all the equipment they can find to stop them. We're going to destroy as much as we can."

The next morning I awoke on Justus's sofa to a concert of air-raid sirens and distant explosions. Justus and his wife, the latter still leery of me, invited me to join them in the cellar, but I preferred to take my chances where I was. After a little while the all-clear sounded and we had lunch, Paul and his wife forcing great helpings on me. I was skin and bones after even a short time at Jaszbereny.

Promptly at six Tony arrived in a taxi and took me to 51 Elemer Street, where we climbed to the third floor. "Here's the pigeon!" he announced, shoving me before him into an elegant little flat past its proprietor, who greeted us beaming. I was nearly overcome with shyness as we shook hands. Her name was Irma, and she was beyond doubt the most beautiful woman I had ever met. She and Tony both laughed, and I blushed as I found that I was still holding her hand.

Irma bustled about serving us real coffee in china cups. Then she leaned back in a huge chrome-and-leather Bauhaus chair, crossed her dazzling legs and lit a cigarette. She was inspecting me casually, as if trying to decide what role to play with me: surrogate mother or something else. I had already decided on "something else" and could hardly take my eyes off her. Silky black hair fell to her shoulders, and beneath her dress her slight plumpness was so enticing that I think she must have worked to maintain it the way other women diet.

As if to banish the mist of sensuality that was slowly filling the room, Tony cleared his throat and turned to business. Irma, he told me, had at one time been a make-up artist for the National Theatre. She was going to change my appearance. He himself would come back the next evening with a set of identity papers for me, and once I was photographed and had learned my new history, we would begin.

When he left, Irma took me into the kitchen and fed me cold cuts and wine. I was feeling a little queasy from the surfeit of food, wine and excitement, when an air-raid siren, evidently on the roof of the building we were in, made us jump to our feet. "Oh God," moaned Irma, "not again!" Then a worried frown creased her brow. "What are we going to do? I can't take you to the cellar before we've made you up!"

"It doesn't matter," I replied. Actually this time I wanted very much to go to the shelter. Still frowning, she ran about turning off the lights, then dashed out. I sat in the dark beside the kitchen window and waited. In the distance searchlights came on and swept across the almost cloudless sky. Suddenly Irma ran in again, snatched a blanket from a closet and shouted, "I forgot! Open the windows so they won't get broken." Then she ran out again.

As I opened the last window, letting a cool breeze flow through the flat, the first explosions went off in the distance. Nervously I lit one of the cigarettes Irma had left on the little table. The explosions came closer and then the whole building shook. I crawled under the table and puffed away furiously on the cigarette. Bombs were falling all over the neighbourhood. I had the bizarre thought that an airplane had stopped directly above us to empty its cargo of bombs. There was a short pause, then several ear-splitting detonations occurred in quick succession and through the doorway I could make out the furniture dancing and sliding. Pictures fell to the floor, and as the table jumped above me cups and saucers shattered beside me.

There was a long silence broken finally by the all-clear and the roar and crackling of a fire. I crawled through the debris to the window sill and peered out. The opposite side of the street was a block-long wall of flame. Houses were sliced in two and flames were licking their way up to rooms in which all the furniture was exposed. In the distance other fires lit up the sky with reddish-orange bonfires. Hastily I leaned out as far as I dared and vomited. Irma's Gold Flakes were the first cigarettes I had ever smoked.

I was put to bed on the sofa, too sick to mind, and fell asleep to the sound of the fire brigade's futile efforts across the street. When I awoke Irma immediately set about making me up. As she scrubbed my hair, which had grown very long, she talked about her early morning shopping expedition. "If the Americans keep up these raids there won't be anything for the Russians to conquer when they get here." She sounded quite cheerful about this, so I asked her what people were saying about it. "Well, my sister Zsuzsa says it's all the Nazis' fault—who would have thought she had that much sense?—but most people are complaining that we're innocent and the Americans should leave us alone. Stupid, no?" She laughed, spilling cigarette ash down my nose, and put a shower cap on me. A little later she began combing out my hair.

"Watch closely now," she said. "You'll have to do this part by yourself from now on. Every morning!" She began rubbing cold cream into my face, applied a smooth, thin layer of dry make-up, then touched my eyebrows and lashes with brown mascara, finishing up with a film of beige powder. I could not believe my eyes: the man staring back at me from the mirror was, in spite of a slightly more than Roman nose, anything but Jewish.

When Tony arrived in the evening he too was flabbergasted. "Here," he said, handing me a wallet with worn-looking documents in it, "your new name is Gabori. I must say, you look the part." As Irma made coffee he took me aside and said softly, "You know, her husband's a prisoner of war. Somewhere in Russia. You can trust her completely, of course; but for her sake don't tell her any more than necessary about what you'll be doing from now on." He handed me a card with the address of an electrical supply shop on Nagymezo Street printed on it. "Be there tomorrow morning at nine. Just one other thing"—he looked at me uncomfortably—"some of those working with us are Communists. I know how you feel about them; I feel the same way. But we've got to get along together, so ease up a bit on the anti-Soviet line."

"I'll do everything you say," I replied, "but don't expect me to get along with those traitors. The Arrow Cross have sold us to the Nazis and the Communists can't wait to sell us to the Soviet Union. I fail to see the difference."

"Remember this," Tony said stiffly. "If any of those deported come out of this alive it will be because the Russians get here in time. Doesn't it strike you as strange that with your family almost certainly in Auschwitz you spend so much time hating the Soviets?"

Taken aback, I stammered that I was as willing as he was to fight the Germans; and when the Russians arrived and behaved more or less the same way, as they undoubtedly would, then I would fight them as well. Seeing that his thrust had gone home, Tony at once relented. "I ought not to have said that—about your family, I mean. But remember, we've got to work with the Communists. Look out there!" He waved his arm toward the window. "Who the hell else is there in this country with the guts or the inclination to help us?"

At breakfast next morning Irma questioned me like a drill sergeant about my new identity, and when at last she was satisfied she kissed me softly on the cheek and sent me out to face the world as George Gabori. The other side of the street was cordoned off. People were poking through the smouldering rubble at the edges trying to salvage what they could. The sun was hot and the air filled with dust and acrid smoke. I was afraid the sweat would make the light make-up run down my face, but when I stopped at a tobacconist's for cigarettes—having liked the Gold Flakes in spite of my sickness—a glance in the mirror reassured me. The woman behind the counter muttered complaints. "Why do they bomb us?" she whined. "It's the Germans they're supposed to be fighting!" I grunted assent and left in wonder. Everybody knew that the Americans had promised to bomb Hungary only if the country actively helped the Germans. We had helped the Germans but there was little bombing. Then Roosevelt told Horthy they would bomb only if we allowed the deportation of the Jews. Now Roosevelt was keeping his promise. If Hungarians did not like being bombed, they knew how to stop it.

I entered the electrical supply shop feeling a bit ridiculous as I said the code words Tony had given me to the clerk: "I'd like to have some batteries in exchange for cigarettes." "We sell only in exchange for money," the clerk replied, smiling slightly. Then when I repeated the first phrase he led me to a door behind the store room and down a rickety flight of stairs into a vaulted cellar. There was a long table against one wall, three mimeograph machines against the other and nothing else except for three lumpy sacks in a corner. Four men were working with Tony on one of the machines, and all gave me a quick glance as I descended, then ignored me to continue tinkering on the broken machine. With nothing else to do, I looked again at the sacks, realizing with a start that they contained not potatoes, as I had thought, but hand grenades.

Tony beckoned me over and introduced me to the others, first names only. All wiped their ink-covered hands first except one, a lanky youth about my own age. "This is Fritzi," said Tony in a tone that gave me to know that Fritzi was the Communist I was forbidden to antagonize. Fritzi's cold eyes, set in a pallid, pimply face, announced quite clearly that he was collaborating with Social Democrats only because Moscow had ordered it.

Except for Fritzi, it was like old times, all the other men being Social Democrats in hiding. We printed leaflets to be left surreptitiously in public places and posters to be put up at night. Early in the afternoon I took off and went searching high and low throughout Budapest until at last I found some coffee for sale. Irma was addicted to the stuff, which was becoming impossible to find, and I wanted to please her after all she had done for me.

I was just starting to climb the stairs when a middle-aged man startled me by thrusting a piece of paper in my face. "Are you Mrs. Nagy's new tenant?" he asked, punctuating his question with an obscene wink. I remembered just in time that Irma was Mrs. Nagy, and taking the papers, I signed them against the wall.

"It's just a formality," he added. "The whole city is lousy with Jews trying to hide."

"Well, uncle," I replied, "it won't help them, will it, with people like you on the lookout!" He happily accepted the Gold Flake I offered him and wandered back to his little outpost at the entrance. I had become a more-or-less legal resident in the house.

Irma, distraught with worry about me, ignored the coffee as I held it out and launched into a flood of down-to-earth Hungarian abuse. My nerves were still taut from the encounter with the concierge, however, and I was in no mood for this. Gradually she stopped shouting and a look of concern crept over her lovely face.

"Poor George," she said, "I'm not helping, am I?" Then she embraced me and gave me the first of many succeeding lessons in the art of kissing. Grabbing my necktie (which in any case belonged to her husband), she pulled me into the bedroom like a poodle on a leash. In the hours that followed I

was bothered only occasionally by the thought of poor
Lieutenant Nagy in his Russian prisoner-of-war camp, each
time reminding myself uneasily that the man was after all a
Fascist. When the air-raid sirens went off and we slipped into
our clothes and headed for the cellar we had not even realized
that night had fallen.

Several days later I arrived at the electrical supply shop and
found Uncle Horvath, the senior member of the group except
for Tony, ready with the news that my old friend Esther was
on her way over. "It's all right, lad," he added, seeing my
puzzled look, "they're the Budaorsi Cell. Tony's going to lend
them some stuff." He nodded toward the sacks in the corner,
and I tried without success to imagine Esther hurling hand
grenades. "By the way," Uncle Horvath went on, pointing the
mouthpiece of his pipe at me, "you're going to be our liaison
man with them." He stuck the pipe back in his mouth as if to
say, as he frequently did say, "Well, who would have
thought?"

A little later Esther came tripping down the cellar steps
with the air of a hostess greeting guests in her sunken living
room. There was no trace left of the rather gawky girl of the
trade union seminars, and if it had not been for her
memorable bosom I might not have recognized her. She was
dressed in a way that suggested that she was quite above such
nuisances as World War II and austerity. Her features,
formerly a little harsh, had been softened by prosperity.

"Darling George!" she intoned, clacking across the stone
floor in high heels. Uncle Horvath stood watching, pipe in
hand, mouth agape. She held me dramatically at arm's length
and stared. "My God, it is you after all. You're better at
make-up than I am!" She laughed at my blush, and a few
minutes later we were in a taxi crossing the Danube by the
Margaret Bridge. Where the bridge touched the island in the
middle of the river we watched a column of German troops
descending the stone steps to the gun emplacements below.

"You'll like Bela," she said firmly as we stopped before a
hillside villa and she slipped me the money for the driver.
"He's a bourgeois. Not at all like *us*, but very, very nice." I
had not realized she was married, and although we had been
more like brother and sister in the past, I felt a little pang of
disappointment.

Bela was unpacking boxes of books as we entered, a tall,

thin, sandy-haired man at least ten years older than either of us. Smiling broadly, he approached us with a book in each hand, stumbled over a carton and went sprawling with a crash. Rubbing his shin, he sat on the floor and looked up with a wry expression. "Now I ask you, how the hell am I going to blow anything up successfully when I can't even cross my own living room?" Laughing, we helped him to his feet. Esther was right, Bela was certainly a bourgeois—exactly, in fact, like *us*—and very nice.

They were just moving in and the flat looked like a battlefield. We sipped wine, sitting on packing crates. Far away across the Danube the domes and spires of the parliament building gleamed in the sun. Half of Pest was visible from their windows. I looked around the room in fascination. Among the thousands of unpacked books were strange objects such as a medieval astrolabe, a globe that looked genuinely Renaissance, glass cases filled with stuffed birds and, already hanging, a tapestry of a hunting scene.

"But this is the room of an alchemist!" I exclaimed, delightedly remembering Sarkozi's translation of Thomas Mann.

"Merely an engineer, I'm afraid," laughed Bela. Then he turned to the operation I was to take part in. Tony had promised them hand grenades, dynamite and detonator caps. Everything, it seemed, had been planned down to the last detail, and as he went over it with me I could scarcely believe my ears. We were going to blow up a munitions train on a siding almost in downtown Budapest.

Tony was a mechanical engineer and I had the impression that his Budaorsi Cell consisted entirely of similar professionals. I asked him what my role was going to be.

"Well, old man," he said, "there's been a change. We hoped to use detonator caps, but for various reasons — one of which being that we don't know exactly when they plan to move the train — we can't. We'll have to light four fuses, and since your people are supplying the stuff the least we can do is let you light one of them." I opened my mouth to say thank you, but nothing came out.

Fritzi was folding leaflets when I arrived at the shop the next morning. Curtly he informed me that Tony was not coming in but had ordered Uncle Horvath and himself to plant leaflets in Zuglo District beyond the City Park. I rejoiced silently: Esther and Bela were coming at ten o'clock for the grenades. Clearly Tony did not want Fritzi to know what was going on, and neither did I — though at that time I could not have said exactly why.

After the two of them left I sat chain-smoking Irma's Gold Flakes while Peter and Fatty, two former members of the trade union youth movement, sat at the table chewing pen nibs, thinking up the text of our next leaflet. Finally Esther and Bela arrived carrying string bags of vegetables. Esther picked through the sack of hand grenades like a housewife shopping for lettuce, holding each up to the light for defects. When they had two paper bags full, Bela tucked them in among the groceries.

"We'll pick you up at eleven-thirty *sharp*," he said as they departed. It sounded like a death sentence, and when they were gone I too went out to have one last look at the world. Trams rumbled down Lajos Kossuth Street as I strolled toward the Danube through the midday crowd. I looked casually over the left shoulders of passing policemen as Tony had taught me to do. A suspicious look might lead to interrogation, and interrogation for a Jew in hiding would almost certainly have fatal results. Turning onto Snake Street near the university, I slipped into a café and over bitter ersatz coffee pondered the fates of my mother, my brother, my aunts, uncles and cousins. If they were dead was I doing this to revenge them? And if not for that, then what? Patriotism? I watched the people passing by inches away on the other side of the plate glass. I was as Hungarian as they were, more so than some of them. Their national poet, Petofi, had been a Slovak; their next leader, the Hungaromaniac Szalasi, was about as Hungarian as Chiang Kai-shek. But I was a Jew, and a majority of them would cheerfully tear me limb from limb if they got the chance — or, to be accurate, would turn me over to some German to do it for them.

In the WC I carefully applied more powder to my face, then left and headed toward Irma's. At the corner of Rakoczi Street and the Great Boulevard I passed Paul Gedeon coming the other way. I stopped myself from greeting him just in time. Our eyes met briefly, and it was clear that he did not recognize me. His blond head passed out of sight and I began examining the coiffeurs of passers-by, wondering how many like me had dyed hair. Homosexuals and certain classes of criminals were said to be able to recognize each other on sight. Jews, I concluded, could not.

In spite of my agitation, when Bela knocked at eleven-thirty I was dozing beside Irma, one hand still holding open *The Magic Mountain*, the other resting on the twin moons of her silken backside. She was snoring softly as I slipped out of the flat with Bela. Esther was in the back seat of an old Mercedes sedan at the curb. Behind the wheel sat a tough-looking young man to whom I was not introduced.

"Really, darling, making love at a time like this?" Esther laughed lightly as I finished tucking in my shirt tail and began a monologue of party patter while we drove toward Vaci Street. She was as nervous as I was.

After some time the driver turned off onto a side street and parked about three blocks from the Rakos switching yard. Bela turned to me in the dark.

"Note carefully exactly where we are," he said. "When we run for it, head straight back to the car. Our friend here will let us off at various points. After that you're on your own." I was aching to point out that I still did not know what was expected of me but kept silent.

Bela and the driver led us through the almost completely dark courtyard of a tenement, then through a door in a wooden fence at the far end. It was pitch black all around us, but beyond the steep enbankment just ahead came the faint glow of the lights in the yard. Esther took my arm and we began climbing the damp grassy slope of the embankment. Halfway up Bela stopped to listen, squatting behind some bushes. Just before the summit there were more bushes, and all four of us, crawling now, huddled behind them. Bela crawled on to the top and quickly returned.

"Everything's all right, children!" he whispered, by which I took him to mean there was no one on the other side. Then he reached into his pocket and handed each of us a little metal box containing kitchen matches. I do not know what sort of elaborate sabotage devices I had been expecting, but I peered at the matches and thought: it's not true; this is not happening to me!

"For heaven's sake, don't strike one now, but open the box to make sure you can get at them when the time comes."

Then Bela crawled with each of us, one by one, to the top to brief us. When it was my turn, nose in the wet grass, I peeped over and saw the long rows of silvery tracks. On the second row stood two flatcars and six freight cars. On the flatcars the sinister shapes of Panzer tanks were sharply etched against the dull glow of the Budapest sky.

"The guards won't be along for about ten minutes," Bela whispered, looking at his watch. "Yours is the first flatcar on the right. Now look closely"—I looked and saw what I had seen before—"just above the first wheel of that car, and slightly to the right, there is a fuse fastened to the undercarriage. It is a ninety-second fuse and it loops back almost to the charge. When we go down, carry the match box in in your left hand. Crawl under the wheel and feel for the charge — we're not using your dynamite after all, by the way — it'll feel like a cigar box. Then feel your way along the fuse until you find the end. Whatever you do, don't light anything except the *end* of the fuse or you'll blow us all to hell. Got it?" I was still staring at the outline of the Panzers. Absolutely nothing else was visible. But I whispered yes, and we slid back to the others.

After a little while we could hear the tread of boots on gravel. At least two guards were passing. Then there was silence and we waited what seemed like an eternity. My legs were paralyzed from staying huddled up and I kept yawning, my usual response to fear. Then Bela looked again at the luminous dial of his watch.

"Any second now there will, I hope, be some explosions up the line. When that begins keep your eyes on me, and when I say *run*, head over the top at full speed and light your fuse." Bela slithered back to the top and waited. From far away came the muffled sounds of explosions, brief pops like dud firecrackers. Then came the sound of boots again, running on the gravel bed this time.

"Now, run!" said Bela hoarsely.

I dashed to the top and passed Esther and Bela on the way down the other side. At the bottom I paused to look both ways. Far to the right lights were flashing in all directions as people ran in the direction of the explosions. But at this end there was no one in sight. Were the Germans crazy, I wondered, to have so few guards?

I slid painfully to my knees at the wheel of the flatcar, tearing cloth and skin against the cinders. I felt around furiously for the charge, banging my head badly in the darkness. I almost sobbed with relief when at last I found it and delicately began feeling along the fuse. The end dangled about two centimetres and I dared not let go of it, so I held the match box in my mouth while I struck the first match, which splintered, then another, which set the fuse hissing and sputtering.

As I darted back toward the embankment I was going to

call out to Esther and Bela to my right when I tripped and
went sprawling in the cinders. Cursing my own stupidity for
having forgotten the first row of tracks, I went on, limping
from the atrocious pain in my ankle. When I found the
doorway in the fence there was no sign of the others. Then
from beyond the embankment came an ear-splitting roar
followed immediately by lightning-like cracks; then more
explosions in quick succession. Flames and debris shot into
the air and fell clattering all around. Window glass from the
back of the tenement was falling next to me and I hobbled
quickly through the opening only to find, not the courtyard,
but a sort of vacant lot with bare walls on either side and a
solid line of stone-wall fence in front. Evidently there was
more than one doorway in the fence. Going as fast as I could, I
felt my way along the wooden hoarding that stood out from
the building on my left, but there was no opening. Ignoring
the pain in my ankle, I jumped and pulled myself over the
top, falling heavily on the other side. I was in a long cul-de-sac
not much more than a yard wide. Before me was a metal-
covered door in the wall of the building, but it was locked. In
despair I slumped down beside the door.

"You'd better come inside, son," said the voice of an old
man, invisible behind the flashlight that was blinding me
from the doorway. I followed him and he closed and relocked
the door behind us.

"You'll be better off down there," he said, shining the light
on what was obviously a cellar door. "I've been waiting for
somebody to do that," he said. "Congratulations!"

I felt my way down the steps into the dank cellar. There
were chairs and benches everywhere, and I lay on a plank
bench to take the pressure off my ankle, which, I could feel,
was swelling like a melon. Half expecting the old man to
return with the police at any moment, I closed my eyes and
found that I did not care very much. I was still lying like that
when, hours later, the door opened above me and the same
voice said quietly, "It's just after dawn, young man. I think
it's safe for you to go now."

When I reached the top, he gave me a long, cool look.

"You a Communist?" he asked hopefully.

"No, uncle."

"Well, whatever you are, you did a good job last night. By
the way, you almost had visitors. Tenants thought it was an
air raid. I had the very devil of a time keeping them out of the
cellar!"

I shook his hand and looked long at his gnarled old face so that I would not forget it.

A block away I bought a newspaper, folded it under my arm and limped toward the last station of the tram line where I joined a small crowd of sleepy workers. There was a little talk about the explosions but less than I expected. Some seemed to think it had been an air raid. An hour later I was home with Irma.

I slept until long after dark, and Irma awakened me with coffee and the news that she had been to see my Aunt Lina. Several times I had been on the verge of going myself, but it would have been insane and suicidal. I sat up in bed, all ears.

"They came looking for you about a week ago," Irma said, "but it seems they believed her when she said she hadn't seen or heard from you. They poked around a bit and left. She's fine and she knows you're all right. She sends you her love." Irma cleared her throat and looked past me. "She says to tell you that your brother, Andrew, is alive. There's no word about the others."

"You shouldn't have risked it, going there," I said angrily to cover up the emotion that threatened to spill over. "Promise me you won't go to the ghetto again."

She nodded and covered her face with her hands, tears trickling through her fingers and down her cheeks.

The next day I made my way back to the cellar. Tony had cleared the cellar table of its leaflets and ink bottles and spread a clean cloth, where I found him eating salami and bread with a man he introduced as Uncle Szabo. The two Asiatic faces with a candle burning between them reminded me of a Soviet painting I had once seen of Lenin and some other conspirator plotting their 1917 revival of the Byzantine Empire. Uncle Szabo turned out to be head of a small group of workers operating in Ujpest, and again I was to be our liaison man. I winced as we shook hands, partly from his bearlike grip and partly because I was beginning to know what "liaison man" meant to Tony.

At first sight I thought Uncle Szabo the most typical proletarian I had ever met, with grease permanently imbedded under the skin of his face and hands. But as he began speaking, I realized that the man's education far surpassed my own. His words came slowly and carefully, each one examined in the light of the thought it was meant to convey.

"I understand you're a Trotskyite?" he said, and I looked at him to see if I was being patronized, but that was far from the case.

"Yes."

"I don't hold with Marxism, myself. They tell me I'm on the right wing, whatever the hell that may mean. But Tony tells me you're a good man in a scrape, and if that's true it's enough for me."

Swallowing a chunk of salami, he cleared aside the cloth and spread out a stained, home-made map. Oh, God, not another train, I prayed.

"What's it going to be?" I asked.

"German fuel barges on the Danube," said Tony happily. "By the way, congratulations on the other night. Quite a lot of damage, as I imagine you heard."

We went over the plan until dawn, and three nights later, as agreed, I made my way to Ujpest and met Uncle Szabo in a down-at-heels sort of pub where conversation stopped as I entered. I was wearing an old trench coat belonging to Irma's husband and stood out like a sore thumb in the roomful of workers in shabby overalls and mended jackets. Uncle Szabo got up as I approached his table.

"We've got to leave right now. There are three barges instead of two," he said in a low voice, "and they've already started unloading them. Let's go."

We drove through Ujpest in Uncle Szabo's broken-down old Opel, arriving shortly at his house, a little cottage not far from the Danube. A girl of about fifteen was sitting at the kitchen table as we entered. She smiled as I greeted her but said nothing, just nodded toward me over and over again.

"She can't hear you, boy," said Uncle Szabo. "She's been that way since she was ten. Her mother's dead, but I took her out of the institution anyway. It's just a matter of time before they start killing them off with injections the way they do in Germany. Go to bed now, Kati." The girl went on nodding, twisting the cord of her nightgown around her fingers. Uncle Szabo very gently took her arm and led her to the bedroom. When he returned it was with a briefcase into which he was stuffing a length of fuse.

We set out on foot for the Ujpest railway bridge. At the edge of the bridge was a sidewalk for pedestrians and below were strung high-tension wires. I remembered Irma telling me in fascinated horror how a drunk had urinated off the bridge one night and had electrocuted himself. We reached the steps leading down to the island and descended. The yellow lamps of the bridge cast down long, eerily beautiful pools of light on the white sand beneath our feet. Silently we passed rows of boathouses, locked up for the season, following a path filled with the decaying leaves of the plane trees overhead.

When we entered Uncle Szabo's boathouse I was filled with awe as he lit a candle and showed me his motorboat, a sleek craft nearly twenty-five feet long.

"It's a pity to destroy this!" I said. One of my boyhood dreams had been to own just such a boat.

"It's just a pleasure boat," Uncle Szabo replied stoically, "and for me there's far more pleasure in blowing up a German barge than in racing up and down the Danube. Anyway," he added, chuckling, "it's not mine!"

He removed a panel in the nose of the boat and I could see bundles of cellophane-wrapped dynamite. He began attaching the fuse from his briefcase.

"Why don't you use detonator caps?" I asked, remembering Tony's untouched supply.

"I'd like to, but think of it: if we miss the barge, the boat might end up in the mud on the other side—undestroyed. We don't want anyone tracing it, do we? This way it'll be blown to smithereens no matter what happens."

Then we sat on the deck of the boathouse, playing cards by candlelight. I took a shoe off and soaked my ankle in the cold Danube water. The swelling had gone down but it was still painful beneath Irma's bandages.

Uncle Szabo kept checking his watch, and finally he put the cards away and started the motor of the boat. It roared to life for one alarming instant, then he cut it. We poled our way out of the boathouse, then rowed slowly toward the head of the island, keeping close to shore and overhanging branches. Once around the bend we no longer felt the pull of the open Danube. In the distance on the opposite bank were the lights of the dock area, and when finally we were across from the docks Uncle Szabo headed us into a sort of tiny cove almost completely covered by the overhanging trees.

"Take your shoes off and roll up your trousers," he said as we scrambled ashore.

I obeyed, then held the boat steady while he reached underwater and secured the device he had rigged up to hold the rudder. Only now did I realize the purpose of the sandbags stacked behind the wheel of the boat—they were ballast to make up for his own weight. I could see Uncle Szabo had experimented more than once, timing the trip from here to the docks.

Now we stood knee deep in the water, holding the boat steady, waiting. Suddenly there was the sound of hand grenades and rifle fire, exactly as at the switching yards, except now it echoed dully across the water, becoming hollow and flat. Then there was a louder plopping sound, like a hot-water bottle exploding, and at this Uncle Szabo started the engine while I held the boat pointed toward the outline of the three barges about a hundred yards across from us.

"Light the fuse," he said loudly above the noise of the motor. I did so with trembling hands; then the boat jumped away, darting across the nearly mirrorlike surface of the river.

I hopped like a bird through the undergrowth, carrying my shoes and trying to stay off my sprained ankle, and headed toward the bridge. In spite of his age, Uncle Szabo was far ahead of me and turned back to help me. Just as he reached me there was another explosion from across the river, and panting for breath, we both stopped and waited. But we did not need to wait: a second later there was an even louder explosion, a boom that shook the plane trees and drowned out all other sounds. The barges had gone up, or at least one of them had.

As we reached the pathway on the bridge the first orange of dawn appeared, and we stopped to look beyond the railing with several workmen who were watching the fireworks at the docks. None of them said a word, and it occurred to me for the first time that there were not only German soldiers there at the docks, but Hungarian workmen as well. Sobered, I limped on at Uncle Szabo's side until we reached his cottage, entering through the kitchen garden.

He went in to check on his daughter, then came back, and in silence we ate breakfast, washing it down with large swigs of brandy. It was broad daylight when finally there was a knock on the kitchen door and Uncle Szabo sprang up to admit six men, all looking tired but happy. Everyone had escaped without a scratch, the Germans having been frightened half to death with explosions behind them and a wall of rifle fire before them. The men had easily made their way back to the shed from which they had started, left their rifles there and melted in with the crowds of other Ujpest workers going to their factories. To my astonishment, after quick swigs of brandy, they all shook hands and went off.

"Where are they going?" I asked Uncle Szabo.

"To work, of course," he replied, giving me a puzzled look.

6

A Prisoner of the Gestapo

IT WAS THE MORNING OF OCTOBER 15, 1944. Irma was shaking me awake violently, shouting in my ear, "For God's sake, wake up! The Germans are overthrowing Horthy. Wake up, George. The Arrow Cross are in power!" My first reaction was to head for the shop, but then I decided to stay by the radio. All Budapest was doing the same. Finally, after lunch, we were startled to hear the admiral's voice on the air. The Germans had kidnapped his son the night before, and we expected the old man to crumble before their blackmail.

"Today," said Horthy in the heavy German accent left over from imperial days, "it is clear to any sober, thinking person that the German Reich has lost the war. All those governments who feel themselves responsible for the destiny of their countries must draw the pertinent conclusions from this fact;

for, as the great German statesman Bismarck once said: 'No nation ought to sacrifice itself on the altar of an alliance.' In full awareness of my historical responsibility, I have the duty to undertake every step in order to prevent further unnecessary bloodshed."

We were dumbfounded, never having expected such courage from Horthy. We stared at each other, knowing he would not get away with it. By eight that evening it was clear that Horthy was no longer in power. The radio station changed hands, captured by the same Emil Kovarcz of the Arrow Cross—a man I loathed in the way one loathes certain reptiles—who had gouged out Somogyi's eyes.

We slept little that night, and early the next morning I phoned the shop several times but received no answer.

"I've got to go see what's happening with the others," I announced to Irma, half expecting her to object. She nodded and served me breakfast. As I left the flat the air was thick with the apprehension we both felt. Outside, Budapest was ominously silent, and all my instincts were to stay home.

There were fewer people than usual in the street, and those few did not dawdle. Turning a corner, I heard the sound of distant gunfire, punctuated by the abrupt roar of tanks firing their guns. I stopped a man coming the other way.

"What is it? What's going on?" I asked.

"It's the Arrow Cross. They're shooting up the ghetto. They've got a couple of German tanks with them. Better stay away from that district, friend," he added, giving me a curious look.

Wild thoughts flew through my mind, the first of which was to run to the shop, get the remaining hand grenades and head for the ghetto. Then common sense took over and I realized that my suicide would not help Aunt Lina. I had to find a way to get her into hiding. I headed toward the City Park, beyond which Uncle Horvath, the only member of our group whose real name and address I knew, lived on Uzsoki Street. If anyone knew what to do, he would.

I was just about to turn into Csokonai Street, the red-light district, when to my right I saw a long column of people— men, women and children—herded down the centre of the street by men in Arrow Cross uniforms, guns at the ready. There were over seven thousand people in that line. They were being taken to the racetrack, where many of them would be shot. Admiral Horthy was indeed gone; the real scum had come to power.

Paralyzed with horror, I stood at the corner as the endless line of misery walked past. As they entered Csokonai Street, prostitutes lined the curb to watch. Here and there the guards kicked or smashed with rifle butts those who could not keep up. Not ten yards from me an old woman was sent sprawling into the gutter. Painfully, biting her lower lip to keep from crying, she pulled herself to her feet. Just then one of the prostitutes in high heels and a housecoat darted forward and kicked her over again, her groans accompanied now by shrieks of laughter from the prostitutes. Sweat poured off me and something was prompting me to take several steps forward and join the marchers. I felt filthy posing as a gentile while the hand-picked dregs of Hungary were tormenting my people. I backed into a doorway, closed my eyes, then forced them open again to examine all the faces as they passed. But Aunt Lina was not among them.

Giving up the idea of finding Uncle Horvath, when the last Jew had been driven past I turned back toward town. On Nagymezo Street I slowed my pace, walking very casually past the shop. Our danger signal was to overturn a spool of insulated wiring that stood in the window. It was upright now. I continued on to the next corner, bought a packet of cigarettes and, inhaling deeply, turned back toward the shop. The door was unlocked, though no one was behind the counter.

"Hello in there! Are you open?" I called into the dark entrance passage and was about to turn back when suddenly a hand grabbed my collar and a fist smashed into my face, sending me flying all the way into the shop. Blood was spurting from my nose, and as I tried to protect my face two other men emerged from the shadows and began sending me back and forth with their fists like a punching bag.

Then I was on the floor, gasping, and one of the detectives was asking me my name. Trying to reply, I succeeded only in spitting out a mass of blood.

"Go wash up," he said, helping me to my feet.

I spread my palms, indicating I did not know where the washroom was. They laughed ironically, but one of them led me by the arm. When I had vomited and washed my face, the first detective, a paunchy, badly shaved man, looked speculatively at my now clearly revealed freckles.

"Are you a Jew?"

"What the hell else could he be?" said one of the others when I failed to reply.

"What are you doing here?"

"I buy flashlight batteries here," I replied through swollen lips, "in exchange for cigarettes."

I went on to tell them that I lived near the synagogue and made my living by selling the batteries.

"We know you're a Communist, little Jew," said the first man. "Your life will be easier, maybe even longer, if you tell us the names of your friends, those with whom you've been selling the country to the Russians!"

"I don't know any Communists," I replied.

"This is your last chance," he said with unexpected, almost fatherly concern in his voice. "When we turn you over to the experts you'll wish you were back with us. Come on, the names!"

I shrugged helplessly and closed my eyes, waiting for the blows to begin. But instead they pinned one arm behind my back and hustled me out of the shop, one pushing me, the other holding a pistol to the side of my head. The first detective remained behind in the shop, and as they pushed me into the back seat of a sedan that glided up to us, through the throbbing of my head I experienced a strange feeling of relief. I remembered Paul Gedeon moaning that if he was a Jew the forced labour camp was where he belonged. I was a Jew; for all my nineteen years I had tried to live as Hungarian, which I also was. Whatever they were going to do to me, at least one thing was now clear: the victim no longer had to walk among the murderers disguised as one of them.

A few minutes later the car turned onto my aunt's street in what was now the sealed and guarded ghetto. From the corner of my eye I glanced at Aunt Lina's house as we sped by. It was undamaged by the tanks. Everything looked normal except for the fact that almost no one was in the street. We stopped before the Institute of Rabbinical Studies.

Other guards took charge of me at the entrance, and I was led into a great hall. On the floor sat three long rows of men with their hands, untied, behind their backs and their heads bowed. Three policemen strolled up and down the rows, and in front, at what had been the rabbi's lectern, sat a Hungarian officer. The guards left me standing in the doorway.

"There!" shouted the officer at the lectern, pointing. "Begin a fourth row. Hands behind and head down, or we'll kick your balls off!"

Trembling, I passed the three rows. The faces of many were purple and swollen. Some were barefoot and had monstrously swollen feet. All was silent except for a steady low moaning. As I sat down I saw just opposite me one of the two pamphlet writers from the shop, the fellow we called Fatty.

From time to time the double doors at the side would open and a name would be called, summoning one of us for interrogation. Then briefly we could hear distant shouts and screams down the corridor. As the doors closed again a sigh went up all over the hall: "Not me, not yet!" Then my name was called, or rather the name on my papers. A detective led me down the corridor and shoved me into a room.

The detectives who had brought me in were standing beside a large desk behind which, outlined against the window, sat a man also in civilian clothes. He looked like my high school geometry teacher, with wire-framed spectacles tottering precariously on a bulbous nose.

"Please take a seat," said the man.

Licking my swollen lips, I looked around to see if he meant someone else. The detective who accompanied me kicked me so hard I landed on all fours in front of the desk.

"Now, now, lieutenant," said the schoolmaster, "no impatience with the prisoner."

As I dragged myself onto a wooden chair, the man held out his cigarette case to me. I reached out my arm and froze as my eyes caught his. The smile on his face only half concealed the hatred radiated by his eyes.

"I advise you to start by telling the truth. We will take your age into consideration. Your name?"

"George Grosz," I replied.

"Your papers say Gabori."

"I bought those papers from a man in the Emke Coffeehouse. I don't mix in politics. I'm a student. I deal in batteries and cigarettes. I know I'm breaking the law, but what am I to do?"

One of the detectives started to laugh but was cut off by the schoolmaster.

"Shut up! Now, George Grosz, who is the leader of your cell? What did you do besides print these stupid leaflets?" He waved a piece of folded paper at me, then threw it down on the desk.

"I can't answer your questions, sir. I don't understand them."

"How old are you?" he asked, standing and peering out the curtains.

"Nineteen, sir."

"If you want to live to see your next birthday you can start telling the truth now! Are you a member of the Communist cell on Nagymezo Street?"

"No," I replied, looking him in the eye.

At this he walked past me and left the room. Even before the door closed behind him the chair was pulled out from under me, and I grunted as one of the detectives kicked me sharply in the ribs.

"Take your shoes and socks off!" he shouted.

One man held me down and two others set to work with truncheons on my feet. As the pain mounted I began to weep, silently at first, then losing control, I started to scream. A strange thing happened then. It was almost as if I were standing across the room witnessing my own agony. My mind retreated to some still-intact point at its centre, and I saw myself, very clearly, standing beside my father's grave wanting to weep but unable to—as had indeed been the case. I knew that now, belatedly, I was weeping for him.

When they were tired they put down the truncheons and rested a minute, chatting about one thing and another as I groaned at their feet. Then they took me under the arms and ran around the room with me.

"Like this your feet won't swell up," explained one. "We wouldn't want to have to carry you to your execution, would we?" he laughed.

"Ready to talk now?" the other asked as they dumped me in the chair.

"I've told you all I know," I replied.

Then they made me extend my palms and they began again with the truncheons, one on each hand. I closed my eyes and again my mind retreated to another time and place. I was in my grandfather's sleigh riding through the hills around Putnok. Beautiful blue rings arose from grandfather's long-stemmed pipe, crystallizing in the frozen air. Then I was standing before my father on my thirteenth birthday, wearing long trousers for the first time and earnestly promising him that I would follow faithfully in his footsteps. There is no telling how long this would have gone on if one arm had not involuntarily jerked away from the truncheon, and one of the men struck me full force on the back of the head.

I came to on the tiled floor of a washroom, my face lying in a soothing puddle of cold water mixed with blood. Just before my eyes were the brown shoes of one of the detectives.

"Awake?" he asked. "We're going to give you a little time to think."

When they dragged me back to the great hall the lights were on overhead. Food was being distributed, each man being given a dixie cup. My hands were already swollen, and I could scarcely hold the dixie cup as a guard ladled hot soup into it. The warm liquid spilled down my shirt, but my numb and tingling hands managed to direct some down my throat. Immediately the warmth flooded through me, and with it, hope. Justus had been right when once he had called me one of nature's Epicureans. My eyes met those of Fatty down the way and we smiled, though he must have been as horrified by my appearance as I was by his.

I do not know how long I had been sleeping when a boot nudged my ribs and two guards took me, one under each arm, back down the corridor, stopping this time before a padded door. One knocked politely on the frame. My blood froze when the reply came from within. It was in German.

The room was softly illuminated by shaded lamps. Behind the desk sat a man in a silver-trimmed black uniform.

"Komm, komm näher!"

I pretended not to understand even this much German, and when I did not move a guard shoved me roughly forward on my battered feet. As I leaned against his desk for support, the German came around, held his desk lamp up and examined me. He grabbed my hair and twisted my head sideways.

"You idiots," he said to the Hungarians, "can't you see that his hair has been dyed? Cut it!"

On a stool in the adjoining washroom another German hastily cropped my head with hand clippers, leaving only stubble. I stared at the tiled floor. Blood was splattered everywhere, on one wall almost to the ceiling. Before my eyes the spots transformed themselves into the shapes of amputated limbs, heads and buttocks. Then they led me back into the room, where the officer looked at the red roots of my hair and without warning slapped me twice across the face.

"This is your last chance," someone translated as the officer began shouting at me in German. There was a pause; then they took me to a chair in a corner and I found myself being strapped by the arms and legs. Suddenly my whole body convulsed, straining against the straps. A million wasps were stinging me, and as the voltage was increased I felt myself vibrating like a violin string, emitting a high-pitched screech. Then I heard an animallike howling, my own voice; blood-red figures danced before my eyes and I was falling into a dark pit.

When I came to I was in the great hall. Pale autumn light was coming through the windows. There was a cold wetness on my thighs and with disgust I realized it was urine. It was dark when they came for me again, and this time the two detectives had almost to carry me. The German was in a lounge suit, from which I concluded that I had been unconscious at least twenty-four hours.

"I very much hope you have come to your senses," he began as I slumped into the chair.

"What can I confess?" I muttered, overcome with weariness. "I can't tell you what I don't know."

A Hungarian was still translating this when the door opened and they brought in Fatty. I looked up, silently begging Fatty to have the courage to hold out.

"Do you know this man?" asked the officer.

I dug my fingernails into my palms, waiting for Fatty to speak.

"I've never seen him before, except out there," said Fatty, nodding his head toward the hall.

A few minutes later they took Fatty out, having slapped him around a little; then I stared in horror as they brought in Fritzi. He looked frightened but was untouched as far as I could see.

"Is this one of them?" asked the officer.

Fritzi peered at me, knotting his brows. It was the first time he had ever looked at me without hatred.

"I'm not certain, sir, that I've never seen him before, but he's not one of them."

"What are you saying?" shouted the officer, his voice rising in incredulity.

"I beg you to believe, sir," said Fritzi in quite excellent German, "that I am telling you the truth now as before."

At first I thought that Fritzi really had not recognized me without my long brown hair and make-up. Later I began to doubt this but had no way of finding out as I never saw him again. They took Fritzi away, and the German turned to the interpreter.

"*Die Wolldecke!*" he snapped. (The blanket.)

Then I was back in the washroom, lying on the tiles. They were soaking a blanket in the bathtub, after which they rolled me up tight in the wet wool and attached electrodes to it.

"For God's sake," said the interpreter to me, "tell them what they want to know."

I shook my head and closed my eyes. Then the needles of electricity tore through me and a deep humming began in my throat to match the humming of the transformer. The voltage increased, my teeth chattered, tears sprang from my eyes, and then I began screaming. Violent hammering began in my brain, and if I had been able to talk I would have told them anything. The hammering continued as I banged my forehead against the floor, and at last unconsciousness came.

I awoke in a bed, with a blanket pulled up to my chin. I tried to move, but at first my limbs would not budge. The numbness in my hands and feet had spread throughout my body, combined with tingling. My head throbbed and I felt I was dying of thirst. A physician came and took my pulse.

"I almost gave you up," he said. "You've been out four days now. Well, never mind. We'll soon have you back on your feet." Evidently sensing that I might not find that such welcome news, the man frowned and began spooning soup into my mouth.

For the next week the doctor arrived at my bedside three times a day to feed me and nurse the various cuts and bruises I bore from head to foot. Beside the door of the otherwise empty little ward sat a Hungarian soldier. Sometimes I attempted to speak to him, but he gaped with peasant suspicion and looked away.

On the afternoon of the eighth day the doctor returned with one of the detectives who had first arrested me. The man reached down and tore the blanket off me.

"Come on! Up!" he said.

I had already rehearsed this scene in my mind, so when the doctor helped me to my feet and then let go of me, as I knew the good man would, I rolled my eyes dramatically and fell at their feet with a thud rather harder than I had planned. In fact I was weaker than I had realized.

"As you see, sir," said the doctor, injecting as much professional authority into his voice as he dared, "he's in no condition to be moved. I won't take any responsibility."

"All right. Three days, but not a minute more!" agreed the detective grudgingly.

On the third morning he returned, flinging my clothes and—to my astonishment—my watch, wallet and briefcase on the bed. A few minutes later, supported on both sides, I was put into a large black automobile and taken to the Majestic Hotel. The elegant façade was draped in Nazi banners. Now I was in the hands of the Gestapo.

In happier days the cellars of the Majestic had, I am told, housed the best wine in Hungary. Now there were rows of cells. An almost comically brutal-looking young German nodded as he unlocked the door, signalling me to enter.

The cell was about the size of a pantry, but there were already four men in it, sitting on three bunks. In the corner sat Hugo Nemeth, the man who had expelled me from the trade union. Nemeth seemed untouched, unlike the other three men, all of whom bore traces of beatings. A middle-aged man offered me a place beside him, so, leaning my head against my rolled-up trench coat, I stared across at Nemeth. His ugly face was rendered more sinister than usual by the light of a single caged bulb overhead.

"Ignoring me, Comrade Nemeth?" I asked.

He looked away and said nothing.

"Are Stalinists not allowed to talk to Trotskyites even in the cells of the Gestapo?" I persisted.

Nemeth maintained his silence, and the only sound in the cell was a low, murmured complaint from the man beside me: "I gave them my factory, I gave them my money, now you let them do this to me. Just a modicum of justice, God, that's all I ask. . . ."

The man beside Nemeth introduced himself as Dr. Pesti Pista, editor of the humorous paper *Pesti Posta*—a conjunction of phonemes which was far from being the funniest aspect of his publication. There was something comforting about Dr. Pesti. Good humour emanated from his rotund body, and no one in the same cell with him could take the Gestapo altogether seriously. Life, his attitude seemed to say, may be nothing but a joke in poor taste, but there is no reason not to enjoy a good laugh over it in the meantime. He had been arrested for printing a satire against Szalasi. "A humourless people, the Armenians!" he chuckled through bruised lips.

Beside Dr. Pesti sat a former staff officer of the Hungarian army, a tall, ascetic eagle of a man with iron-grey hair and bloodshot eyes, one of which was swollen half shut. He extended his hand toward mine and bent in a short bow as I shook it.

"Tandori!" he said, introducing himself, each syllable

coming out like a heel click. This was not, to say the least, the usual behaviour of staff officers toward a Jew forty years their junior, but I knew I was not being patronized.

"Why are you here, uncle?" I asked him.

"Why am I here? I am here, my young friend, to avoid, so to speak, the dishonour of not being here. If you follow me."

I nodded, and he looked at me gravely.

"Since arriving here," he continued, "I have begun to understand the slogans of the French Revolution at long last. *Liberté, Egalité, Fraternité.* You will think, of course, that I would have done well to learn such things earlier, and you will be right."

All of us in the cell, except Nemeth, had been badly beaten, and partly because of this we trusted one another and talked quite openly. The man who had been sending up a litany of complaints to the Almighty turned out to be a Jewish industrialist. Uncle Eugene, as I called him, noticed the ill feeling between Nemeth and myself and asked me what I had against the Communists. By way of reply I gave him a long lecture concerning the Communists, the USSR, and their Hungarian followers.

"We want a real socialism for Hungary," I concluded, "one that has swept away superstition, not merely substituted the latest dogmas from the Muscovite Vatican."

"I have often thought," replied Uncle Eugene, "that revolution itself can become as addictive as that other opiate, religion. You speak very passionately, my young friend. What is your passion for?"

"For justice," I replied without hesitation.

"And what do you think justice is?" he went on.

"Justice is—justice!" I said, at a loss.

"Justice, it seems to me at least," he replied modestly, "is a sort of passion for dealing decently with people. It almost seems to me to be a form of charity sometimes."

I must have raised my eyebrows, because he hastily went on.

"Be that as it may, my friend," he said rather more sternly, "I can assuredly tell you what justice is not: it is not a political issue, and the absurd supposition that it is, that ideology put into practice can bring it about, is the same sort of idiocy that has caused us to be placed in this cell. Good God, boy! You're sitting in the cells of the Gestapo and you still think that politics is a solution to anything at all?"

I was about to reply when the door was thrown open and a

young German private summoned the staff officer, who came to attention before the boy without the least sign of irony. A few minutes later the same private returned and took Nemeth away, not for interrogation, but to serve food to the other cells in the corridor. Nemeth was a trusty. If there was an informer among us, I had no doubt who it was.

We were given mess kits, and Nemeth ladled watery soup into them from his cart, setting aside one for the staff officer, who a short time later was brought back by two Germans and thrown onto the floor. Uncle Eugene made room for him by moving himself onto the stone floor beside me, and we lifted him gently onto the bunk and tried to get some of the now-cold soup down his throat. He was conscious but trembling violently, and one side of his face looked like raw liver. Then Nemeth returned, having secreted a bit of potato for each of us in his pockets.

"Tell me, Mr. Nemeth," I said, my loathing for the man temporarily replaced by anxiety, "you must hear things on your rounds. What are they going to do with us?"

"Our liberation is a matter of weeks at most," he said. "The Soviet army is executing a pincer movement around Debrecen. The military genius of Stalin, you can be quite sure, will shortly liberate us from the Fascist hordes."

"Information, Mr. Nemeth, not slogans, if you please," said Uncle Eugene. Nemeth blinked and his eyes lost their flash of a moment before.

"I think they mean to hold Budapest at all costs," he said. "Before the Russians get here, they'll probably have deported us to Germany or else shot us."

The next evening I thought they were coming for me, but it was Nemeth they took away. When they brought him back it was obvious that they had not touched him. I was almost asleep when they returned and called my name. I was marched up the cellar stairs and taken down the endless carpeted corridors of the hotel, which, though it was well past midnight, were filled with uniformed Germans coming and going. The part of my mind not paralyzed with apprehension wondered if the Russians were not already in the suburbs.

The room they took me to made no pretense of being anything but what it was: a torture chamber. In the corner stood the chair with straps dangling; beyond the open door was the washroom; the carpets had been rolled up and taken away, leaving the wooden floor bare and stained with blood. Behind the desk sat an officer who, without looking at me even once, read out my previous statement from a German text, simultaneously translated by a Hungarian plain-clothes man standing beside him.

"Do you have anything to add?" the officer asked, finally looking up.

I shook my head.

"We have definite information that you were involved in the underground—though 'underground' is perhaps too strong a word to categorize the little resistance we have met with here," he added with a glance at the plain-clothes man, whose expression did not alter.

"As far as I have heard, sir," I replied, "the only resistance is Communist. Whoever told you that I did, or ever would, work with the Communists is trying to save his own skin. That is the whole truth."

"Your file says you call yourself a Trotskyite. I'm afraid I haven't time for such subtle subclassifications," he said, tapping a pencil on the green desk top beneath a lamp. "We'll give you a little more time to think about it."

"A crazy country!" he said to the plain-clothes man as the guards led me out. "This is the first time in my career that I've been forced to mix Jews with politicals. It's disgusting!"

In the morning we sipped the bitter mixture they gave us in lieu of coffee, and my spirits sank as I felt my cellmates' reserve toward me. I wanted to shout out that Nemeth was the informer, if anyone was; that they had left me untouched on purpose so that I would suffer their suspicion. But there was nothing I could say. Even Nemeth, with incredible hypocrisy, looked at me with disgust. Knees drawn up, I sat in the corner on the stone floor, burning with resentment.

Everyone in the cell except for Nemeth and myself was taken for interrogation that day. Dr. Pesti was brought back scarcely recognizable, his face battered to bloody pulp. At midday we were given four pieces of bread, although we were five. Each of the others broke off a small part of his share and tossed it to me, except for Uncle Eugene, who handed it to me.

Two more days passed like this, and even Uncle Eugene began to regard me with suspicion. Then, late at night, they came for me again.

"How does it feel to be considered an informer?" asked the same officer.

"I have no objections," I replied, infuriated.

Before I knew what had happened, a man standing behind

my chair came around and began slapping me back and forth, then took out a truncheon and began smashing it into the back of my neck and head. Blood trickled out of my mouth and down my shirt.

"Confess now or you will be shot immediately," said the officer.

"I'm ready to die now," I replied, immediately wishing I had said something else. Of all the lies I had told them, that was undoubtedly the greatest.

My hands were tied behind my back and I was taken to a cellar where three others were already standing, facing the wall with their hands tied and blindfolds over their eyes.

"Anyone ready to talk has ten seconds to do so," said one of the four or five uniformed Germans behind us. His voice echoed around the vaulted ceiling; then there was silence.

As they blindfolded me a weird calm descended upon my mind, completely at odds with the violent trembling of my legs. As I awaited the bullet that would end my life I tried to pray, but instead saw my grandfather's face again. He was telling me some tale from the other war, and as he spoke my father appeared as well, urging me to read the classics. Then my aged Aunt Julia replaced my father, insisting to the others that I was basically a good child even though I had just been caught inserting hot peppers into the anus of a dray horse, which had run off spilling wine into the gutters of Putnok.

"Fire!" shouted the same voice.

Ear-splitting cracks reverberated from the ceiling, the acrid smell of gunpowder reached my nostrils, and through the ringing in my ears I heard the man beside me fall to the floor in a faint. The Germans laughed uproariously and then fell on us with their rifle butts. I was being kicked in the ribs; then I screamed as a boot caught me in the groin and went spinning off into unconsciousness from a blow to the head.

They must have kept it up for some time, however, because when I awoke Uncle Eugene told me I had been out for nearly two days. He had covered me with his own blood-stiffened trench coat.

"Don't move, George," he said as I opened my eyes to see his face above mine. "Just lie still, boy."

My skull had obviously sustained a fracture. It ached so badly that I almost wished they had finished me off in the cellar. I began to weep, though more as a reaction to Uncle Eugene's tenderness than from the pain. I closed my eyes, trying because of the pain in my ribs not to breathe deeply.

One by one the others, except for Nemeth, came up and whispered into my ear, apologizing for their previous suspicions.

The next day Nemeth returned from his rounds with three nearly intact boiled potatoes for me in his pockets. To everyone's astonishment, I could already sit up to eat them. Our family physician had been right when in my childhood I had fallen out of a tree and broken my leg. "Oh, don't worry about him," he had told my mother. "He's got the constitution of a fighting cock." The next day I could make it to the end of the corridor with only slight help from Uncle Eugene when they let us go to the latrines.

The day after that we were sitting around, speculating on the Russian advance. Our breath was visible in the cold air. Winter was arriving outside. Then the door opened and my name was called. They took me down the now-familiar corridors but into a different room, where I found myself before an officer whom I stared at. His jaw retreated toward his neck just below his lower lip, the almost total lack of chin making him appear at once foolish and sinister.

"Ready to talk?"

"Ich habe nichts zu sagen," I replied, not waiting for the interpreter.

He signalled to the others, and I was taken off to one corner where they began punching me back and forth silently, as in an old movie. This time, I thought, they're going to kill me. I was still conscious and on my feet when they sat me in the chair, strapping my arms and legs. One of the two men was blond and strangely effeminate for one in such a profession. He regarded me for a moment, holding his right elbow in his left hand, leaning his face against the palm of his hand. I closed my eyes, then grunted and lurched as the current hit me. This time, however, the red shapes barely had time to flash on the screen of my mind before I passed out. The last thing I heard was the animal noise of my own howling.

Uncle Eugene was beside me when I awoke. I tried to speak but could not. I heard the staff officer advising him to massage my arms and legs, which he did. Sensation began to return, and with it, pain. I determined to stay awake at least for a little while, but Uncle Eugene's voice crooning softly over me lulled me back into the soft blackness from which I had just emerged.

The cell doors crashed open down the length of the corridor, and we were driven up to the lobby of the hotel. I had done nothing but sleep for a week, but Uncle Eugene still had to support me as we stood in ranks before tables where our names were checked against a list and we were handed back our few possessions. Then we were put into trucks. I tried to climb onto the tailgate but fell back, hitting my head on the pavement.

When I came to it was on the floor of a cattle car. The temperature was nearly freezing in spite of the fifty or so bodies packed together. Uncle Eugene had put my head in his lap.

"I've got your rations for you," he said with steaming breath. "Look! They've given each of us a whole loaf of bread, some margarine, a chunk of horse-meat sausage and some carrot jam. Do you know what that means, boy? That means they intend to keep us alive, at least for now."

We were still standing at a siding, and two German enlisted men brought in milk cans filled with water, a tin cup to drink from and a lidless barrel for a latrine. Then the doors were locked, and we all breathed a sigh of relief: we were locked in, but they were locked out. The train gave several jolts and began moving off into the unknown. The only thing certain was that they had to take us westward. Everything to the east, including Auschwitz, had fallen to the Russians by now.

"Is Nemeth here?" I asked Uncle Eugene.

"No," he replied, puzzled. "They called out his name after you fell. He was already in the truck, but they took him back into the Majestic."

For the time being no one was afraid of informers, and men began boasting about their exploits in the resistance. To my amusement I heard several men hint that they had had a hand in blowing up the barges at Ujpest. I looked up at Uncle Eugene and asked him if he had done anything against the Germans.

"Resist? Me? The only resisting I did was to try to save a few things when they confiscated my factory. But speaking of resistance, there's a fellow over there by the doors who tells me that there has just been an uprising in Warsaw. It seems the Red Army waited on the east bank of the Vistula and just watched while the Germans exterminated the Polish underground." I listened, not at all surprised. In its fathomless cynicism, the Soviet mind no doubt found it logical to let the

Germans kill off that part of a population with the guts to resist. It would save them trouble later on.

"When the Allies have finished off the Nazis," I said, "if they have any sense they'll do the same with the Stalinists. Surely they can see that there's no difference between them?"

"The difference, my boy," said Uncle Eugene, still cradling my aching head, "is that for the moment we are in a German cattle car heading for a German concentration camp. Do you really think life consists only of mouthing about politics? George, George," he almost whispered, "in my sixty years I have learned this much: the only thing that makes life worth living is beauty, and in politics there is no beauty. Look, boy! We're alive, we're still breathing, and here you are wasting this precious gift. Who knows how much longer it will be granted us?"

"What beauty?" I interrupted, astonished that Uncle Eugene could think of beauty while we sat freezing in this filth.

"Have you no memory, then?" he countered. "Have you never seen anything beautiful? What I am talking about is contemplation. All you have to do is close your eyes, fill your mind with all the beauty stored away in it, and transcend all this—this shit!"

I had never heard Uncle Eugene use a vulgar word before, and it lent an odd force to what he was saying.

"You're a great reader, aren't you?" he continued. "And why do you read? I'll tell you why. You keep hoping that in some book or another you'll find the magic solution to the world's woes, some political formula, or some metaphysical key to the universe that once put into practice will render us all happy forever. Well, it doesn't exist, boy. There is happiness to be found in books, but you'll never find it the way you're looking."

"How then?" I asked.

"By absorbing the beauty in them, the beauty of descriptions, of the human mind struggling with human destiny, always climbing higher and higher. And if you're lucky, once in a while you'll find a book whose author has really climbed, who has transcended the rubbish of life and stands on some peak, holding his hand out to any reader with the strength to climb up after him. If civilization has any meaning, that's where it lies."

"And do you think there are no civilized men among the

murderers?" I asked. "These animals listen to Mozart and read Goethe, don't they?"

"Yes," admitted Uncle Eugene after a thoughtful silence. "It puzzled me for a long time. It's true, they weep over Mozart; as for Goethe, he's what the Germans love most, a sentimental windbag, albeit a genius. Music lends itself to anything. But show me a great book built on moral courage, and I'll show you a book they've burned!"

I thought about how puzzled I had been by *The Magic Mountain*, moved by the fierce debate between Naphta and Settembrini, pained by the fact that politically I had to think the villain, Naphta, basically right. Yet it had been the gentle, humanistic buffoon, Settembrini, who found a place in my heart. I closed my eyes, trying to think.

The next thing I knew it was dark. The train had stopped and there was shouting and the barking of dogs outside. The latrine barrel was emptied, and Uncle Eugene helped me get to it when the doors were shut again.

"You've slept almost thirty hours!" he said as we made our way over the sprawling bodies and slumped back down in our corner.

"Tell me more," I asked. "More of what you told me before."

"What shall I tell you?" he asked, sitting beside me wrapped in his filthy overcoat.

"About art, anything," I begged.

We sat in silence for a while, listening to the clicking of the wheels just below us and the soft curses of men stepped on as others tried to get to the barrel. Then he said he would tell me parts of *The Divine Comedy*, which he knew both in the original and in Mihaly Babits's Hungarian translation. "*Nessun maggior dolore che ricordarsi del tempo felice nella miseria....*" he began; "there is no greater pain than to remember in present misery the happy days of the past...."

And so we rolled through the snow-covered landscape of western Hungary and into Austria that night. Several of those closest to us also listened to Uncle Eugene. Nobody protested. In spite of the numbing cold and the ever-present dull ache in my head, some corner of my mind rejoiced in what he was saying.

———————

It took three days for us to reach Vienna, where we sat two more days at a siding on the outskirts. An overpowering stench filled the cattle car as the latrine barrel filled and then overflowed. Our rations were long gone and only a little water was left. Uncle Eugene was put in charge of this by common consent and now sat beside the two milk cans, rationing out tiny gulps of water in the tin cup. All talk had ceased. Some wept quietly, but most sat in silence, huddled against the biting cold.

"Death is prowling close now," said Uncle Eugene once when I woke up. At the other end of the car a man had died and they were putting the body beside the doors. Finally at night the doors were opened, and I could scarcely believe my eyes: there were Wehrmacht soldiers outside with cauldrons of what must surely be soup.

"How many dead?" asked a German, wrinkling his nose in disgust as he peered into the car.

Uncle Eugene told him there was only one. Two men were detailed to remove the corpse. Then we were given a little bread and mess tins of thin soup, which I sipped with more pleasure than anything I had ever eaten in my life. Suddenly Uncle Eugene went over to one of the middle-aged Wehrmacht conscripts and began a low, intense conversation. He returned, saying to everyone in Hungarian that they should put any rings or other valuables into the hat he was passing around. In a few minutes the hat came back containing a vast assortment of wedding rings and other bits of gold. Uncle Eugene dipped his hand in and gave a fistful to the oldest Wehrmacht soldier, who went off only to return a few minutes later with a burlap bag of bread. We stared, holding our breath.

"Sausage," said Uncle Eugene in a businesslike voice I had never heard him use before. "Then I'll give you the rest."

I wondered why the German simply did not grab the hat; but Uncle Eugene knew his customers. The old Wehrmacht man and Uncle Eugene understood one another perfectly. They were, in their different ways, gentlemen. Snow was falling in the pale light beyond the doors as the soldier trudged off down the tracks. Then, just minutes before the SS came by to lock us in again, he returned with several lengths of horse-meat sausage wrapped in greasy brown paper. Uncle Eugene gave him the rest of the gold. A few minutes later the doors slammed and we began rolling again, evidently toward Munich.

Five more men, those who had been worst tortured by the Gestapo, died before we reached Munich. And later when I found out how lucky we had been after all, it seemed hard to believe. Other prisoner transports from the east, especially those from Russia and the Baltic countries, frequently arrived at the same destination with no one alive, having travelled for weeks in sealed wagons without food or water.

I was also to learn that four months earlier, in July 1944, fifteen hundred political prisoners from France were sent to the same suburb of Munich without food, water or ventilation. At stops along the way the SS had covered the corpses in the boxcars with chloride of lime. Four hundred and eighty-three men died during the journey and about six hundred more died shortly after arriving at the camp. We were indeed a privileged group.

7

Dachau

THE DOORS BANGED OPEN and an SS man shouted at us to line up in columns of five. Stiffly we climbed down to the snow-covered siding, those too slow receiving kicks and blows from rifle butts. It was dark except for a single light over the platform some distance away; it illuminated the name of the station: Dachau.

With guards on either side, we were marched along a road in the predawn darkness. Soon we saw the lights of the huge concrete guard towers between which ran a tall concrete wall surmounted by barbed wire, which even at a distance we could tell was electrified. Beyond the wall rose the chimneys of the crematorium. Above the sound of shoes crunching in the snow, Uncle Eugene whispered to me, "Yes, but there are no gas chambers. This is not an extermination camp!"

We were halted before the iron gate with the inscription *"Arbeit Macht Frei"* (Work Makes Free). I remembered Justus telling me that the same slogan was used in Soviet forced labour camps, where it was equally cynical and meaningless. Suddenly several SS men strolled out of the gatehouse and began using their riding crops on those of us in the outer ranks, lazily lashing out without apparent anger or purpose. There was nothing we could do but stand at attention and take it, and when at last the roll call and chit signing were over with and the gates opened, we marched into Dachau almost eagerly to escape the lashes of the guards.

As the cold winter dawn rose above the huge, sprawling camp, we formed ranks in the snow before the long central administrative building and waited to be processed. It was late in the afternoon when my name was called. By that time I was reeling. My body had only begun to recover from the beatings and electric shocks, and none of us had eaten since the day before. There were five desks side by side, behind each a prisoner-clerk who checked us against long lists and then collected such belongings as we had. The penalties (whippings or hanging) were read out to us for various crimes, beginning with the hiding of valuables. Then we were handed our "triangles," patches of cloth of various colours: yellow for Jew, red for political, pink for homosexual, and so on. For some reason mine was red, not yellow. For the time being I was officially an Aryan.

They took us off in groups to have our heads shaved, after which we were herded into a large wooden-floored room and told to strip. Shivering in the cold, we next entered an enormous shower room. The floor and walls were covered with white tiles and from the ceiling a long row of shower heads projected. A German in the doorway ordered us to stand in groups of four beneath the showers. Then the door was closed, and I noticed for the first time that it was a metal door, and insulated. Beside the door was a small window, obviously for observation. It too was insulated.

As the bolt clicked shut and a face appeared in the window I began to tremble violently. A great moan went up throughout the room, heads craned up toward the showers, and several men fainted in their terror, landing with soft thuds. Some lifted their arms in prayer, and I began to wonder if God would accept our martyrdom as compensation for our misdeeds. Then, as always when death was close, I began to hallucinate, seeing scenes from my own childhood.

This time I saw my mother standing before me for the last time at the station in Putnok; I saw myself in the synagogue, reading from the Torah in a prepubescent voice. My eyes were shut tight, when suddenly hot water shot out of the showerheads with a roar and rattle of pipes.

Uncle Eugene came up to me and grasped my hand. He was laughing and tears were running down his face. In the window the SS man was peering at us with amused irony. We had barely begun to wash the accumulated filth of weeks off ourselves when they turned the water off.

We were each given a towel, a pair of wooden clogs and a blue-and-white striped uniform of coarse twill, then directed to fasten the triangles on our smocks. Still damp, we marched out and formed ranks on the huge expanse of the parade ground, where they counted and recounted us endlessly. Ice formed on our eyebrows and in the stubble on our heads. Hours passed; the sun sank red in a haze of coal smoke.

At last an SS officer arrived with a block elder, a prisoner in charge of an entire block. We were selected, two by two, and taken away to various barracks. Uncle Eugene and I were sent together to block twenty-three in the long avenue of barracks, each containing over a thousand prisoners.

The first room of the barracks was empty except for a swarthy young man standing before a stove.

"Welcome to twenty-three," he said in heavily accented German, and we made our way down the centre aisle past tiers of wooden bunks. "I am Miguel, your barracks elder."

One look at the man was enough to tell us that we were in luck. He was clearly tough, but just as clearly humane. Uncle Eugene and I came to attention and reported. A slight smile played about the corners of his mouth, and he beckoned us over and handed each of us a tin of ersatz coffee.

"The even-numbered barracks are for those prisoners who work; the odd-numbered are for those who do not. Today, however," he said, waving vaguely toward the three tiers of bunks on either side, "my men are working. What are you?"

"I?" asked Uncle Eugene. "I was a rich Jew!" he said in a tone of friendly irony. Miguel laughed and turned toward me. Suddenly not trusting him, I hesitated.

"He's a Social Democrat," said Uncle Eugene. "In spite of his age he was a leader in the resistance."

I flushed with anger, but Miguel's face lit up and, as Uncle Eugene went on in the same vein, Miguel came over and shook my hand.

"There are other Hungarians here. They told me there was resistance in Hungary, but I didn't believe it. It's true then?"

I nodded.

"Jewish?" he asked.

"Me? Yes," I replied.

"Ah, then I believe you. These Hungarians I have here . . . " he broke off and turned his head as if to spit on the floor.

Uncle Eugene was if anything more exhausted than I was, and when Miguel told us it was permitted to sit on the bunks, I helped him up and he immediately fell asleep. Then Miguel sat me down beside the stove and questioned me closely about the resistance movement, about Hungarian trade unionism and the Social Democratic Party. Still mistrustful, I hedged until finally he laughed, slapping his thigh with pleasure. Then he reached over and tapped me lightly on the shoulder.

"Yes, yes! You are right to be cautious. There are informers here. You talk politics and you get twenty, twenty-five lashes. But I am not an informer," he said, his expression becoming grave.

He was in fact a Spanish Social Democrat. He had headed a battalion in the civil war and was filled with bitterness from his experiences in Barcelona. He finally escaped across the Pyrenees into France, having discovered that both sides in the civil war were murderers and liars, as he put it.

"I have been here five years," he said. "You are lucky. Things are much better now; not many people are dying. Last year they were burning bodies day and night in the crematory. There are two kinds of camp, if you don't know it," he said, staring at me, "crematoria and sanatoria. This is a sanatorium. Even the Red Cross comes sometimes to inspect us. On the other hand, it's not difficult to die here either. Take care."

Soon the lights came on and the occupants of the other bunks returned from their work *Kommando*. Some looked quite fit, others were almost skeletal. Even on that first day in Dachau it was obvious to me that conditions varied greatly from block to block and from section to section. One man thrived and beside him another man died of malnutrition and exhaustion. A few prisoners had been here nearly ten years and apart from thinness showed no signs of being in bad condition; others were close to death after a few weeks or months. It all depended on whom you knew, what rations you managed to get and whether or not you managed to avoid punishment.

We ran out for another roll call, again standing endlessly in the snow as they counted and recounted us. Silently I thanked God for having made Miguel a Social Democrat; with his goodwill Uncle Eugene and I might last out the war. When we returned to the barracks they gave us more ersatz coffee, watery soup with a single cabbage leaf floating in it and the twelfth part of a loaf of bread.

In the days that followed there were no more work details, only roll calls, barracks inspections and the meals that kept one alive but permanently hungry. There was one prisoner, an old man who slept just below Uncle Eugene, who had been there since the camp was opened in 1933. He was a German Communist and he had recently been thrown out of his job in the camp administrative offices, where he had worked for ten years, for stealing a newspaper. Cut off from outside rations, he too was becoming hollow cheeked. But he told us that things were very much better now than before. In the past, for instance, the SS were sometimes given to shooting prisoners for sport, a thing that seldom happened now. "Legality" was the rule now, he said. Heinrich Himmler, in Berlin, had decided to use Dachau as a show camp for the Red Cross inspectors.

"I think, however," said the Communist, "that they are going to kill us all before the Americans arrive."

After a few days Miguel took me through the partition into the next section and introduced me to another Hungarian, a young man named Lajos Dalnoki-Miklos, the son of the commander in chief of the Hungarian First Army. When we had shaken hands I could not help commenting that the policies of his father were not exactly the sort that usually got people sent to Dachau.

"Well, there are honest people even among our kind, you see!" laughed Dalnoki. He was not at all put out when I told him that until now I had strongly doubted that. He invited me up to his bunk, the Dachau sign of social acceptance, and for a long time we huddled there, going over everything that had happened in Hungary during the past year.

"What astonishes me about you," said Dalnoki in his languid aristocratic drawl, "is that though you are a Jew and a Social Democrat, you are so furiously anti-Communist. Now I am not one of those who think that a Jew cannot be a Hungarian, but still it seems to me that you might have some right to hope for a Soviet victory, some right to be a Communist. How is this?"

I thought for a while, then told him that Bela Kun, a Jew who had led the short-lived Hungarian Soviet Republic of 1919, had been executed in Moscow. On the other hand, Count Karoly, an aristocrat who had tried to maintain a liberal democracy, would have met the same fate, murdered by his own class, had he not escaped to the West after the fall of his government.

"And is there a moral to be drawn from that?" asked Dalnoki.

"The moral is this," I replied. "For me to become a Communist because the Russians are approaching and because it might give me an opportunity for revenge would be the same thing, morally speaking, as if you had joined the Arrow Cross to take revenge because your class and its privileges are being swept away—as they are in fact. Have you ever stopped to think of the meaning of the word 'reaction'? We are not reactionaries, you and I. I am a Social Democrat because I think ethics is confined to personal relationships. With a group of people ethics no longer works; you enter politics—whatever Uncle Eugene might say to deny it—and in the realm of politics I can find nothing that will keep us above the filth of Dachau or of Budapest except Social Democracy."

Dalnoki gave me a long, hard look, then asked, "Did you get all this from your Trotsky?"

"Oh, no," I lied haughtily, "it's all in Aristotle."

The atmosphere in Dachau was not one of comradeship. On the other hand, we did not live there in the permanent state of terror that dehumanized those in the extermination camps or in the despair-filled rage I would later experience in a Communist concentration camp. We were miserable, but not so miserable that we could not form friendships among those who seemed worthy of trust.

Gradually Miguel introduced me to several other men, among whom was a young Pole named Marek whom I invited up to my bunk to tell his story. About three years older than I, Marek was one of those large-boned, angular Slavs whose cropped blond hair looked like sun-dried straw. He had been an art student in Warsaw, and after the German invasion his family had fled to Lwow in the east while he remained behind in Warsaw. When Hitler and Stalin decided to divide Poland between them, he set out at last to join his family.

It was easy to cross the border, he told me in his fluent though heavily accented German, and near the town of Chelm a truck driven by Russian soldiers stopped to give him a ride. Before they drove into Chelm the Russians had stopped for ten or twelve other hitchhiking Poles. The truck had stopped before the NKVD headquarters in Chelm, where all of them were thrown into a cell. A few days later they were taken to Kiev, and after some months in another cell Marek found himself before a tribunal, sentenced to twenty years' hard labour for being a German spy, as were all the other hapless Poles who had been hitchhiking that day.

From Kiev they were sent in a transport of thousands of political prisoners to the Kola Peninsula on the Arctic Ocean. According to Marek, the guards were as miserable as the prisoners. When they arrived there was no camp waiting for them, and to survive they had to scrape dugouts in the frozen earth. When winter arrived with full force many died; they were on starvation rations and dressed in the light clothing they had been arrested in.

After Hitler invaded the Soviet Union, an order reached the camp one day that all Poles were to be freed to join a Free Polish Army to fight the Fascists. He was released along with several others and joined a contingent of Red Army men travelling by rail, stopping here and there to recruit others, issuing them uniforms and giving them food. Nobody knew where the Free Polish Army was located, or even if it existed at all. Near anarchy reigned throughout the northern USSR, and week after week they travelled from village to village, drilling with dummy rifles along the tracks, watching as new faces were recruited and old faces, having had enough, deserted.

Finally orders reached them to head back north, and when they arrived there he too deserted. What followed I found hard to believe. Marek, the frail art student, had walked from Murmansk to Finland early in the spring, wrapped in his army blanket, through snow-covered forests, past patrols, border guards and a hundred other hazards, eating nothing but the mouldy bread he started out with and then bark, moss and melted snow. He walked nearly three hundred kilometres, mostly in snow, always at night. He did not stop until he reached the shores of Lake Inari, deep inside Finland. From there, with the help of various Finnish farmers, he crossed into Norway and some weeks later became a member of the Norwegian resistance.

"And then?" I asked.

"Then," he said, "they caught me, as you see." He grinned, revealing several missing teeth. "Two years in Dachau, so far. It could be worse. You won't freeze to death here. It's very different from a Russian camp. As a Pole I dislike Russians on principle. Still, as a rule they don't shoot you for the hell of it. Here they might, though the chances in Dachau are slight if you watch your step. When we first arrived in the Kola Peninsula we were marched down the coast of the White Sea past a town called Lesnoy. When we got to the place where we had to build our own camp, there weren't enough guards to surround us, and no fences of course. So the guards drove us out onto a sort of jetty, a tongue of rock and ice sticking out into the sea. That way we couldn't escape. They hadn't counted on the tide or the waves, and both rose as the night went on. We were packed tight together, clinging to each other. But as the water rose and the wind whipped up the waves, men began to fall into the water. We pleaded with the guards to let us move back, but they sat by their fire and threatened us with their guns. It's not that they wanted to kill us, you understand. But for them it was better that a few of us should freeze to death in the water than that any of us should escape. If a man escaped a guard would have to serve out his sentence for him! Now with the Germans, of course, such things never happen. If you die here, my friend, it will be when they decide it's time for you to do so."

In the mornings we were awakened by shrill whistles before dawn and immediately set about making our bunks with the hospitallike perfection demanded by the SS for inspection. If they singled someone out for their disfavour, his bunk never passed inspection and he was liable to spend days, sometimes weeks, in "the box"—an enclosure in which a man could neither sit nor stand completely upright, and where after some hours he wept, then screamed, then lapsed into mad whimpering. After preparing for inspection there was roll call. Aside from our uniforms and wooden clogs, we had only a sort of smock of thin twill for a coat. The first half hour was tolerable, but after a whole hour men began to hop from one foot to another to keep warm, and the weaker prisoners began to sway. Then those on either side would take hold of them to keep them upright. When at last the count was satisfactory, the SS would have the block elders select men for various fatigue duties—always the same men, those who had earned or bought the privilege. These had a certain freedom of movement around the camp, picking up food, bartering and hearing the latest news.

One morning after I had helped Uncle Eugene back to the barracks and up to his bunk—he had a slight fever that I was afraid would turn into pneumonia—I stopped in my tracks as they brought in another middle-aged prisoner and laid him in the bunk beside mine. He stared out of huge eyes like a man who has seen something so terrible that merely closing his eyes would not shut it out.

"He is a priest," said Miguel, with just a hint of respect in his voice. He may have been a leftist, but he was also a Spaniard.

"What have they done to him?" I asked quietly.

"He heard someone's confession, which is forbidden of course, and someone reported him. He's been in the box for ten days. He'll be all right though, you'll see. An *extraordinary* man, that one," he added, this time with unmistakable respect.

Not far from us was a block containing no one but priests, about a thousand of them from all over Europe. Sometimes, however, the Germans decided not to recognize clerical status, especially that of East Europeans, and put priests in with the rest of us. This man, a Lithuanian, had been studying in Paris at the fall of France, and when the Gestapo finally caught up with him the archbishop of Paris had made no effort to protect him.

Father John, as we called him, was a man of formidable strength, both physical and moral. Twenty-four hours after he was brought back he seemed quite recovered, although when Miguel introduced us I noticed a tremor in his hand. What was astonishing, though, was that the man addressed me in fluent Hungarian.

"I'm sorry I don't speak better," he said, "but I learned the language in Paris from a Jew who was also my Hebrew teacher. He was a Hungarian, you see, so I decided to get two languages for the price of one!"

"And you know Hebrew as well?" I asked, incredulous that a priest might speak the language of the Talmud.

"Oh, yes," said Father John, running a wrinkled hand over his stubbly white head. "Perhaps as you are a Jew, I believe, it would interest you to know that in my youth I briefly considered leaving the faith of my fathers and converting to

Judaism. Quite a novel idea in Lithuania, I can assure you!"
He chuckled. "It would have been a mistake, I now think—do
not be offended— and it now seems to me that a Catholic
must in some sense be a Jew whether he likes it or not. Christ
was after all a Jew, and we are his followers, or so we fondly
think."

"I don't think many Catholics would agree with you," I
mused.

"Obviously not!" he laughed. "During my second trip to
Paris," he went on, "I studied Hebrew in the mornings with
my Hungarian friend; then sometimes in the afternoons I
attended the lectures of another Jew, a great philosopher
named Bergson. Have you heard of him, my friend?"

I admitted I had not.

"Well, you ought to be proud of him!" he said reprovingly.
"Because of his fame the Vichy government was afraid to
deport him with the other Jews, but he refused the exemp-
tion. Refused! They tell me he is dead now," he sighed. "In
the city of lights the greatest light I saw emanated from that
Jewish agnostic."

Being a secular priest, attached to no order and coming
from a well-to-do family, Father John had studied at his
leisure in Paris, and for two years during the occupation he
and his Hungarian friend, Gelber, had inhabited a tiny room
on the rue de Rennes. Gelber, having no documents and
looking very Jewish, never went out of doors. Father John left
each morning for one library or another, carrying his Hebrew
grammars and notebooks of Aramaic commentaries. Among
other things, he was trying to establish the Aramaic originals
of certain idioms in the Greek New Testament.

"I went out one morning," he continued. "It was in June of
last year. I said mass at my old seminary, where they always
put an altar at my disposal. But I had forgotten some papers I
would need in the Bibliothèque Nationale so I returned home
afterward. In the entrance stood our landlady, wringing her
hands. She said nothing when I asked her what was wrong,
and then two French policemen came up and arrested me.
They had already taken poor Gelber away, God have mercy
on him. Do you pray, young man?"

I opened my mouth but could find no reply. Father John
looked at me with his gentle, steady gaze.

"Well, if you do, my boy, pray for the Germans. Of all of us
they need it the most."

Miguel called me aside one afternoon. For some reason the SS were in a particularly ferocious mood and had beaten one man unconscious on the parade ground earlier. We were all apprehensive, expecting them to storm into the barracks at any moment and begin on the rest of us.

"Listen, George," he began, "in a few days there are going to be openings for workers in the airplane factory near Augsburg. Conditions there are better than here. One man from each block can volunteer, and I'm offering you the chance."

Nearly every night we heard the Allied planes flying over to pound Munich, and there were few German planes left to defend the city. Apart from Hitler's famous—and mythical—secret weapons, Germany's only hope now was to get enough planes in the air to stop the Russians long enough to make a deal with the Allies, something we all dreaded might happen. I looked at Miguel and nodded.

"Good," he said. "Volunteer for the job. I'll tell you when and I'll see to it that you get it."

I hesitated, miserable because of what I knew I had to say to him.

"I'm grateful, Miguel, but I can't leave Uncle Eugene behind. Won't you let him volunteer with me?"

For a few seconds he stared at me, then paced up and down thinking aloud in Spanish. One did not make conditions with block elders in Dachau, but it was typical of the nobility of Miguel that he never noticed such things. The Germans, I thought, must have been soft in the head the day they made a man like that a block elder.

"I'm sorry," he said at last, "but no. Only one man per block; no exceptions."

He held out his hand and, reluctantly, I shook on it, then went to my bunk dejected. A louse moved on the blanket and I pounced, crushing it between my fingernails. The older prisoners said that the camp had been kept scrupulously clean not long before; but as Germany crumbled the SS paid less and less attention to such things. The camp was so overcrowded now with transports arriving almost daily from the east that lice were common and typhus was beginning to break out.

Uncle Eugene came and sat beside me, mistaking the cause of my depression.

"Don't worry, George," he said patting me on the shoulder.

"If things go on like this we're bound to be alive when the Americans get here."

He had become frighteningly thin and pale, and more than anything in the world I wanted to tell him about the jobs in the airplane factory where, according to Miguel, both the food and the treatment were better. Then Dalnoki, cheerful as always and wearing his striped uniform with the air of someone on his way to a masquerade, came and sat beside us.

"I was listening to you and the priest the other day," he said. "I can't say that I've ever given much thought to the subject of Judaism, but while you were speaking it occurred to me—forgive me for putting it this way—that you are really altogether Hungarian except for this question of religion. Are you religious?"

"Not very," I replied. "Are you?"

"Me? No, not at all, really."

"Then what exactly do you mean by 'this question of religion'? If Father John were to baptize me and make me a Catholic, I'd still be a Jew in your eyes, wouldn't I?"

"In a way, I suppose," Dalnoki admitted slowly.

"So it's not religion at all, is it?" I persisted.

Dalnoki found nothing to reply to this, but Uncle Eugene began to lecture us both, giving a capsule history of Hungary and the place of Jews in it. He praised King Matyas Corvinus, the Renaissance monarch who raised the cultural level of his court to almost Florentine standards. He told us about the eleventh-century King Kalman the First who was so tolerant that he even forbade the persecution of witches, who, he insisted, "do not exist." He related a number of things neither of us had ever heard about before, showing that from time to time during a thousand years of horror there had been Hungarians who had stood on the side of humanity, little islands of tolerance and civilization.

When at last he began speaking about the twentieth century and the role the Jews had played in the modernization of Hungary, Dalnoki finally interrupted. "Surely you are not going to claim that what my people call the Jewish Curse—with exaggeration, I admit— surely you don't maintain that that has done anything to bring us into the modern era?"

Before Uncle Eugene could reply, the lights went out and we headed for our bunks in the darkness. When we got there I made up my mind to tell Uncle Eugene about the Augsburg camp. Whispering in his ear, I told him everything except that Miguel had insisted on my volunteering alone. Overjoyed, he pumped my hand and promised that we would see the liberation together. Climbing onto my bunk, I watched the searchlight from the watchtower sweep by. The stove had gone out, and I pulled the dirty army blanket close against the cold. But when at last I fell asleep it was with a clear conscience.

At roll call the next morning there were fewer SS than usual, and afterward Miguel told me that a huge transport had arrived from the east. There was no more barracks space and they were going to live in makeshift tents of blankets and whatever was available.

"But they're lucky," he added in a grim voice. "Have you noticed how few Russians there are here? Usually they take them straight to the firing range outside the camp. They shoot them there and then cremate the bodies."

"Why do they bring them all the way here to shoot them?" I asked, not sure I believed him—though later I found out it was all too true.

"Who knows why the Germans do anything?" He shrugged and walked off.

Dalnoki, who had been watching, came over and together we leaned against the window sill between the bunks and watched the soft snow falling between the blocks.

"Is he a Communist?" he asked, meaning Miguel.

"No, just a Marxist. A Social Democrat, like me."

"Tell me," Dalnoki went on, "why is it there are so many Marxists among the Jews? It strikes a chord of response, you know, when they go on about Jewish bolshevism."

"Have you ever heard of an unbaptized Fascist?" I replied in annoyance. "The phrase 'Christian Nazism' has a certain ring to it, too, don't you think? But as to your question, I don't know. Uncle Eugene's certainly not a Marxist. He says that a lot of Jews are looking for a new Messiah because they've abandoned orthodoxy. Marx is the latest false Messiah, a sort of Sabbatai Sevi. Father John says that one thing Jews and Christians now have in common is a passion for shouting about the truth and absolutely no interest in discovering it. He says we both lost our taste for wisdom the day we killed the last surviving pagans in Rome and Byzantium. Then, when we began to abandon superstition in this century, we found ourselves empty and the prey of false Messiahs and false religions. Mind you, I don't consider Marx a Messiah of any sort. I admit I'm not interested in wisdom, only in justice."

"Your Father John is a decent enough fellow," said Dalnoki, "but he doesn't strike me as much of a Catholic."

"My dear Dalnoki," I replied, "if all your Catholics were like Father John you and I wouldn't be here."

A party of prisoners came into view, slowly sweeping the snow off the pathway with rush brooms. Among them were long-timers reduced to near skeletons by overwork and undernourishment. They shuffled forward under the direction of a kapo. One man who barely had strength enough to lean on the broom, let alone use it, was suddenly kicked by the kapo and went sprawling in the snow, where he remained on all fours with his head down. We looked away.

Several days later my "inner clock" told me that the whistle had blown earlier than usual. Everyone else noticed it too, and as we scrambled in the dark to make our bunks there was an uneasy silence. The snow had begun to fall again and it filled our wooden clogs as we ran out to form up on the parade ground. The searchlights slowly swept over the thousand men of block twenty-three and then over the other blocks, one by one. As roll call went on and on endlessly, even Miguel began to curse under his breath. A single SS man strode back and forth before us with his dog straining at the leash. Then four more SS men arrived, and soon after them a truck turned onto the parade ground and roared slowly through the snow, its headlights in our eyes.

At last the count came out right, and a non-com came up and shouted that anyone with experience in aluminum work should raise his hand. Miguel, cap in hand, came to attention and reported. A great silence fell over the parade ground. The thousand men of block twenty-three stood and waited. Then Uncle Eugene, ahead of me in the front rank, raised his hand, and I quickly followed. The SS man shouted for us to fall out.

We stood before them, and my heart beat fast as Miguel turned to the non-com and whispered something to him. The non-com strode over with an officer, who raised Uncle Eugene's chin with his riding crop, then felt his muscles and examined his teeth as if he were a horse.

"Back into formation," he said at last.

I closed my eyes, tears running down my cheeks. I wanted

to call after Uncle Eugene but stood rigid in the snow, a pillar
of salt even though I had not looked back.

"God be with you," I heard Father John whisper from the
first rank as they ordered me to get into the truck.

Balling my fists, I strode toward the truck, glaring at
Miguel, whose eyes blinked and looked away as they met
mine. I was enraged that in his attempt to save me he had
deprived me of my only real friend.

Eventually there were about thirty of us in the bed of the
truck, crowded as far away as possible from the SS guards.
We drove through the enormous, empty parade ground and
out the main gate. Through the half-opened canvas flaps I
read once again the great sign: *Arbeit Macht Frei.*

8

Lessons in Survival

WE WERE FORBIDDEN TO TALK. As the truck roared down the highway, I watched the winter landscape of Bavaria unroll like a white carpet behind the truck, framed on either side by the SS guards. Thin wisps of smoke rising from chimneys filled me with nostalgia for Putnok. As we approached the industrial suburbs of Augsburg I saw the first signs of war, gutted houses and factories, lonely smokestacks rising out of vast fields of rubble. One of the guards pulled the canvas flaps together, leaving only a chink of light.

A little later we were ordered out and formed up in the centre of a quadrangle surrounded by new-looking buildings. There were the inevitable barbed-wire fences and watchtowers, but before us stood a quite different building, a huge, snow-covered shell that appeared to be an airplane hangar but turned out to be our barracks.

Roll call for the first time in my experience went quickly, and soon we were inside the cavernous building and were turned over to the camp elder. This man, like all of his kind, wore a prison uniform; but in his case the uniform was tailored, and beneath it he wore a white shirt and a scarf of yellow silk. As we stood at attention, he joked with the SS in what was obviously native German. I gaped at the spectacle of a prisoner laughing with the SS. It was unheard of. The camp elder, with long blond hair and a relaxed air of confidence, resembled the SS in everything except the uniform.

"I'm just a prisoner like the rest of you," he announced to us. "For the past nine years I have seen many camps, but none better than this one. The reason for this is that the Red Cross visits from time to time; also, they're desperate in Berlin to get more planes built."

I glanced at the SS men not far away, but if they heard what he said they were not interested. He went on to tell us that we would be working in the Messerschmidt factory, travelling to and fro every day by train. We would work twelve-hour shifts. Our work would begin that same evening, and if we overful-filled the quota we would be paid in Reichsmarks with which we might buy whatever was available—which was not much, he added.

Everything in the camp was clean. Along the walls were radiators that steamed day and night, as if Germany had all the fuel it needed. Throughout the great expanse of the hangar stretched row upon row of two-tiered bunks separated into "colonies" according to nationality. Explaining this, the camp elder ordered the Poles, Russians and Ukrainians among us to step forward. He led about fifteen men away to their bunks, then came back and asked for West Europeans. Finally there were only eight of us left: three Yugoslavs, two Czechs, two Rumanians and myself.

"You're Jewish?" asked the elder, slightly surprised.

"I'm also Hungarian," I said, trying to be helpful.

"Well, whichever you are, at the moment you're the only one. You'll go in with the Ukrainians."

I was about as eager to join the Ukrainians as to join the SS; the Ukraine is probably the only area in Europe that has consistently outdone Poland in pathological anti-Semitism. I followed the camp elder reluctantly and was brought face to face with a bulky man with an enormous pumpkin-shaped head. His bushy eyebrows knitted together, and beneath them he examined me with the tiny eyes of an enraged pig.

But when he spoke it was in an incongruously deep, melodious voice. His German was almost incomprehensible.

"*Bist du tovarishch?*" he asked. "*Kommunist?*" he tried again when I did not reply.

I admitted that I was a student of Marx.

"*Ein Jude!*" he said, as if it were something unpleasant he had found in his soup.

Relieving himself of a long string of curses, the man spat and pointed to a bunk. All around me the Ukrainians sat playing cards and talking. Conversation stopped as I walked by, men exchanged looks and I knew I was in for serious trouble. I watched the Ukrainians for a while. They had made decks of cards out of paper bags and seemed obsessed with gambling. After a while I strolled elsewhere in the hangar. There were no guards in sight. Finally I found myself in the West European section. I stared at the sight of men reading books. Others lounged about, smoking and talking.

A little farther on was a shower room, and with no one to stop me, I tore off my clothes and turned on the water. It was hot! Suddenly a hand touched my arm, and when I spun around I was face to face with a diminutive Frenchman, shorter even than I was. He looked like Largillière's portrait of the young Voltaire, even down to the mole on his cheek. Smiling, he handed me a sliver of soap and indicated by signs and broken German that I should visit the French section after my shower.

The French had set themselves apart from the others. They had not actually moved their bunks, but their casual air of natural superiority made it seem as if they had. What struck me most about this air of superiority was that it was not only accepted as natural by the other groups but no one was offended by it. At first I thought this was due to the long, historically-induced inferiority complex of East Europe; but then I noticed that even some of the other West Europeans reacted the same way to the French.

But for all that, when I arrived at their area they were friendly. François, who had given me the soap, called his friend Claude and the two of them gave me a feast of bread and marmalade. It was soon revealed that they were Communists, and when they began questioning me it was all I could do to play down my own political views not to offend them—

whatever they were politically, they were decent types. I told them about the Ukrainians.

"Ah, the Ukrainians," said Claude, whose German was fluent. "Of course they are anti-Semites. Why not? They are also Fascists, deserters from the Red Army mostly. They thought Hitler would give them an independent Ukraine so they went over to him. When that did not happen, some deserted. Those who have a line shaved down the centre of their heads are Soviets—or at least the Germans think so."

Claude and François were both on the night shift, so they told me that when we arrived at the factory I should try to join their group. When I admitted that I knew nothing about aluminum work they stared a moment.

"Then you *must* get away from the Ukrainians," said Claude. "They won't help you fake it, and you'll be sent— elsewhere. Whatever you do, get into our group as soon as we form up at the factory."

When the gong rang for supper I ran back to the Ukrainian section to queue up. I was given a mess kit, and when at last I reached the great steaming cauldrons I saw food more delicious-looking than any I had seen since my last meal with Irma. As I walked toward the benches blissfully smelling the soup, one of the Ukrainians behind me began tripping me at every step, finally sending me sprawling. But I had not spent my youth playing soccer for nothing, and as I fell I spun around and hurled the entire dixie cup of hot soup straight into his face.

Groaning, the man wiped the steaming liquid out of his eyes, then balled his fists and headed toward me. At a table before us the camp elder put down his spoon and narrowed his eyes at the scene. Just as the Ukrainian reached me, still on the floor, a command rang out.

"Fill his mess kit again!" shouted the camp elder, pointing at the Ukrainian. "Then clean up the mess you made."

We went back and I looked away as the man filled my mess kit. I knew I was going to pay for it.

After supper there was still an hour left, so I curled up on my bunk with the blanket over my head. If they were going to kill me, I preferred to die in my sleep. Suddenly a hand grabbed my shoulder and I jumped up ready to defend myself. Looming over me was a broad, smiling Slavic face. Through his straw-coloured hair a furrow had been shaved from his forehead to the back of his neck.

"Nyet! Nyet! Nicht Ukrainski—Russki!" he laughed, backing away a little from my still-raised fist.

Sergei, as he introduced himself, sat beside me and congratulated me on the soup-throwing incident, adding that if I had any more trouble with the Ukrainians he and the other Russians would take care of it for me. Then he extended one finger and lightly tapped the side of my nose with it.

"A brave Jew," he said, laughing again. Then, with formal politeness, he handed me a quarter packet of tobacco and showed me how to roll a cigarette, my first in weeks.

Sergei could not have been much older than I was, but he told me that he had been secretary of the Leningrad Komsomol. He was Russian to the point of caricature: pale skin stretched tight over high cheek bones, changes of mood so sudden and violent that one was perpetually off balance with him and, not least of all, an open goodwill toward everyone he did not consider wicked—such as Ukrainians and capitalists.

He was so outspokenly and naturally a Communist that each time I opened my mouth to argue with him I closed it again. He told me that he had been promoted to captain in the Red Army during the siege of Leningrad and had been captured during a counterattack against the German lines. He considered himself very lucky: many of those captured with him had been shot out of hand and others had died of starvation or typhus later. He had already escaped once and been recaptured, but he had not been shot, he said, because the Germans were so desperate for skilled labour.

"Watch!" he said. "I will escape again. I'll kill a lot more Germans for Stalin and for Russia before the war is over!"

He asked me about myself, and when I got to the part about the trade union and the resistance he slapped me on the shoulder with a bear paw of a hand and announced that he knew it all along, I was a Communist. This endeared me to him even more than the soup throwing, and it was with some reluctance that I pointed out that one did not have to be a Communist to be anti-Nazi.

"Ah, you're a bourgeois, is that it?"

I nodded, and to my astonishment Sergei beamed proudly at me, as if I were his own private bourgeois and how amusing it was.

One aspect of Marxist thinking that has always puzzled me is the tendency to file things away in air-tight mental compartments. Sergei was trying to find the right slot for me and began questioning me about books. I admitted that my favourite novel was *Crime and Punishment*.

"You see! You betray yourself! Only a bourgeois likes Dostoevsky. If you were a worker you would love the novels of Katayev! Well, no matter. Any trouble with the Ukrainians and you tell us."

He gestured toward the Russian area, then grabbed my shoulders and kissed me on the mouth, stood up and moved off, glaring at the Ukrainians. When the shock wore off I was moved. Nervously I glanced toward the Ukrainians to see if they were laughing about the kiss. But it must be one of their customs as well, because they did not look amused; they were watching me with unconcealed hatred.

When the gong began to ring I slipped on the greatcoat they had issued me and wrapped my towel about my neck as a scarf. After a quick roll call we were marched in columns of five toward a railway platform nearby. Suddenly the man behind me, the same man I had thrown the soup at, began treading on my heels in his clogs. I bit my lip, but there was nothing else I could do. There was no question of breaking ranks with the SS guards on both sides. By the time we reached the train the pain was nearly unbearable and my clogs had filled with blood.

Two Ukrainians reached down from the freight car and grabbed my coat to haul me up, but at the same moment Claude and François came up behind me and jerked me away. Sitting on the floor beside them and other Frenchmen, I tore strips off my towel and bandaged my ankles.

"We'll see to it," said Claude finally, "that you escape from those animals."

At the Messerschmidt factory we entered a large workshop with an enormous round table in the centre. SS guards sat on raised platforms in each corner of the room, and foremen came around handing out stacks of aluminum. We had to take the small sections and work them smooth with a wooden mallet and a form. The quota, I heard with dismay, was forty-eight pieces per shift.

"Watch closely and don't worry," whispered Claude as the whistle blew and we began, a dozen pieces before each of us.

German overseers paced back and forth behind us, and I began sweating as I realized that I had not finished the first piece at the end of an hour. Claude and François on either side of me had finished six or seven, however, and each slipped two pieces onto my stack.

When the whistle blew at seven in the morning I had managed only twenty-eight pieces, so Claude and François contributed enough of their overproduction to bring me up to the quota. On the way back the Ukrainians again tried to get me in their car, but this time I wrenched myself loose. An hour later I had moved my things and found a bunk in the French section. Claude and François had bribed the camp elder by promising him the chocolate from all future Red Cross parcels.

"When the Red Cross parcels arrive," said Claude, "we also bribe the overseers at Messerschmidt with them. The poor bloody Germans are beginning to have less than we do! In exchange they credit us with a dozen extra bundles of stabilizer pieces. We split up the money. It ought to make for a good Christmas."

Shortly before Christmas Red Cross parcels did in fact arrive, but only for the French, Belgians, Danes and Norwegians. The majority of us, East Europeans, stood in the formation as the names were called out, feeling sorry for ourselves. But the idea of a Red Cross parcel arriving from east of the Danube was laughable. Back at our bunks the French spilled out a dazzling profusion of cigarettes, candy, milk powder, vitamins, coffee and chocolate. It seemed impossible that there could be so much luxury left in Europe. Claude and François forced food and cigarettes on me, and in an outburst of childishness I strolled slowly through the Ukrainian section exhaling the delicious smoke of real manufactured cigarettes. My attitude toward them at this point was such that I actually absorbed strength from the looks of hatred they turned on me.

At the approach of Christmas Day (which would also be my twentieth birthday) rumours reached us that the great German counterattack in Belgium was being halted by the Allies. Liberation could not be far off. The guards reacted to imminent defeat in different ways. Some resorted to kicks and blows now as we marched to the train every evening; others became almost friendly. The SS commandant, to everyone's surprise, announced that lots would be drawn among the "guest workers" on Christmas Day, with loaves of army bread as the prizes.

When the great day arrived we awoke to find a fir tree being set up in the centre of the hangar. Claude, François and the other Frenchmen solemnly shook my hand, congratulating me on my birthday, then gave me a tiny German-French dictionary. There would be no work that evening, and throughout the great shell of the hangar little groups of men sat in their zebra-striped uniforms singing carols in a dozen languages. I had to admit the Ukrainians sang more beautifully than any of the others. At supper we were given double rations of bread, soup with real meat in it and a small chunk of sausage. Before lights-out Sergei came over near the French section and watched us, smiling. I flushed, realizing that the French were not going to ask him to sit down. They might be Communists, but they showed great reserve toward East Europeans, and it would never have occurred to them to ask him over.

"Here," I said, walking over to him with some candy and tobacco. "They've given me far too much."

Sergei gave me a shrewd look and selected two pieces of candy and gave the rest back.

"Captain Sergei Alexeiev of the Red Army wishes his Jewish friend George Gabori a happy Christmas!" he said stiffly, having learned the German perfectly.

Then I received another Russian bear hug and kiss, after which he turned and walked back to the Russians. I blushed furiously as Claude and François gave me curious looks beneath slightly raised eyebrows.

We had been asleep some time when suddenly the air-raid sirens outside began howling. In spite of the size of the hangar, there had been no air attacks on it, and we all assumed that the Allies knew it was a camp. Bumping into each other in the dark, we formed up and marched out into the snow-covered quadrangle. Guarded on either side by SS men, some of them half dressed, we headed for the shelters at the double. One, very deep, was for the Germans and the West European prisoners; the other, partly above ground, was for the Slavs and other East Europeans. As we entered we could see the searchlights in the distance scanning the sky. So far the Allied planes had not been able to destroy the Messerschmidt factory, well concealed beneath miles of wire netting and artificial foliage.

I sat beside Claude when we reached the bottom of the deep, long shelter, and immediately the rumble of anti-aircraft guns began above us. Then the shelter shook as the first bombs landed, the overhead lights were swinging and bouncing violently, and we crawled beneath the benches as dirt and cement began falling on us. Explosion followed explosion, and I found my face inches away from that of a pale, terrified SS man crouching with me.

By the time the first wave passed the lights were out, and there was absolute silence as we waited for the all-clear. After a minute or so the guns began firing again, and just as I was telling myself that lightning never strikes twice, I was thrown off the bench as the whole shelter heaved and shuddered. The earth all around us was being torn apart, and I waited for the direct hit that would bury us all.

At last the noise and motion stopped. Men coughed and spat, choking in the dust-thick air, and near me some hero of the Reich was muttering a prayer in German. We climbed up the stone steps, SS and prisoners holding onto each other in the darkness, and breathed deeply as we stepped out into the frozen night. Emergency generators whined and the spotlights came on. The entrance of the other shelter had completely disappeared and the first room of the shallow bunker was laid open. There were muffled, distant screams and cries for help; but when we automatically started to run toward the shelter, the SS drove us back with their rifle butts and marched us to the hangar, which, miraculously, was untouched.

We sat dazed on our bunks. From time to time the doors opened and groups of men came in, exhausted and filthy. They told us there were still many dead and dying in the bunker.

It was nearly dark the following evening when the SS commandant entered the hangar with an escort. Shrill whistles announced a formation.

"Well, gentlemen," he began in a low, angry voice, "those you have been waiting for finally came. They came to kill us, but they did not. Aside from two barracks, all they succeeded in doing was killing a number of you. One hundred and twenty-nine of your comrades perished last night. One hundred and nine have been taken to hospital. Consequently there will be no sick call from now on. If any of you fall ill you can either recover on the spot or you will be taken to another sort of camp, if you follow my meaning. Eight of your comrades have escaped. They will be caught and receive the punishment they deserve."

At this he turned and walked out, followed by the escort. I quickly learned that among those who had escaped were several Russians, including my friend Sergei.

Next morning we were turned out before dawn, loaded onto trucks and driven to the centre of Augsburg. As the tarpaulins were thrown back and we climbed out, the sight before my eyes made me forget my hatred of Hitler and his followers. The raid had left the city a field of smouldering rubble with nothing more than a few chimneys sticking out here and there to relieve the endless desolation. Claude pointed out part of a wall, whispering the name of a palace he had visited in his student days. Just before us the road came to an abrupt end where the debris had not yet been cleared, and all around there were German civilians—old men, women and children—picking over the mounds of rubble. They carried boxes and shopping bags, anything into which they could put the fragments of their belongings as they unearthed them from ice and brick.

Nearby an enormous dining table protruded from a pile of masonry, and the SS had us chop it up to build a fire where they sat and warmed themselves as we began clearing the road. Within a few minutes our gloveless hands were bleeding from the attempt to separate the rubble from snow and ice. The SS officer in charge shouted over that if we found anything of value we must inform him immediately; otherwise we would be shot on the spot.

After three or four hours another truck arrived and the SS summoned us to the fire, where we each received a tin of hot soup and a piece of bread. I warmed my hands on the cup, watching as two small children, wrapped in blankets for coats, approached the SS men in the company of a very old woman, probably their grandmother. The woman held her hand out, begging. Beside me Claude caught his breath as an SS man aimed his rifle at them and ordered them away. The woman did not move, but from all sides other Germans began to come nearer, staring at the SS and at us. I could not believe it: they were watching us with envy because of the soup! As pity welled up inside me I tried to connect these people with those who had deported my family, but could not.

A few minutes later we began work again, and the SS ate their own vastly superior rations. The ring of civilians around them now grew larger and included a number of children who began pleading for food. Finally the officer in charge stood up and fired his rifle into the air. The crowd backed away slowly; when they had gone about fifteen yards they stopped again and began shouting. Then lumps of ice and rubble began to fly toward the SS around the fire. We stopped work to watch.

Suddenly an SS man was hit in the face and stood up, clutching one cheek to stanch the flow of blood. Very slowly he shouldered his rifle, aim and fired. There was a scream, and a woman wearing the large coif headdress of Bavarian peasants fell backward on the rubble. Claude swore under his breath and we turned back to our work. If they were shooting their own people now, there was no telling what they might do to us.

The civilians scattered out of sight and a little later a small truck roared up with its siren blaring, closely followed by another truck out of which a platoon of Wehrmacht men poured to face the SS. We heard little of what the angry Wehrmacht officer said to the SS, but in a few minutes we were sent to the trucks and driven straight back to the camp. No one said a word when he got there; there was no need. Even more than the bomb damage, the dead peasant woman told us that Germany was finished.

The Americans had damaged the Messerschmidt factory so badly that there was no work for us, and for a few days we were left in peace. I played chess with Claude, studied French with François and three times a day queued up for meals that were diminishing alarmingly in quantity. Suddenly there was less to eat than there had been in Dachau.

On the fifth day of this the doors flew open and a platoon of SS came in. Whistles blew and we formed up at the front by nationality. The commandant then entered. He was followed by two columns of guards who were surrounding four of the escaped Russians, now recaptured. They were stumbling under the weight of tall, heavy wooden posts. An order was given, and the four Russians came forward, almost staggering under their burdens, and placed the posts in the deep holes in the cement between us and the SS. I closed my eyes, realizing now what the holes were for. When I opened them again I saw that the last Russian was Sergei.

When the gibbets were in place, the Russians stood perfectly still. Sergei, pale but with a calm expression, put his hands behind his back as an SS man came forward to bind them. A hand grabbed the back of my uniform and jerked me sharply.

"Steady!" said Claude.

Sergei was about three yards away, looking straight at me, still expressionless except for the flashing of his steel-grey eyes. The commandant himself helped each Russian up onto a stool in a grotesque parody of politeness, then adjusted the nooses from his own stool. Then he stepped back to survey his work and four SS men came forward, one behind each prisoner.

Sergei shouted in Russian—words that meant "long live the Soviet Union," Claude later told me—and was still shouting as the stools were pulled away. I tried to close my eyes but could not. The four bodies thrashed wildly in the air, eyes bulging. My gorge rose and I was soaked in sweat. Claude tightened his grip on my smock, whispering something over and over in French.

"Two hours!" shouted the commandant to the camp elder. "They will stand here two hours and look!"

The SS clattered after him as he strode out. The camp elder, pale and sick-looking above his yellow silk scarf, cursed as the doors banged shut and immediately posted two Ukrainians at the windows to stand watch. Then he told everyone to stay in formation but to turn away from the four bodies, now still. He looked silently at the Russian group, standing in front just beside us, and waved for them to go back to their bunks. I noticed he avoided looking at their eyes.

"Take him to the showers," he said to Claude and François, and a few minutes later I finally vomited under the cold water and came back to my senses. Then we returned to await the end of the two hours. A few men were kneeling on the cement floor praying, and there was a low buzzing of French, Ukrainian, Polish and a dozen other languages. I wanted to sing Kaddish for Sergei but realized that I could not—the other Slavs would consider it an insult.

It seemed days later when at last the SS returned and ordered the corpses cut down and thrown into a cart, where they landed with sickening thuds. The formation was dismissed, and we were heading back to our areas when all at once the whistles blasted again and we were told to form up outside. Panic rolled through the hangar like a wave as word spread that there was to be a selection. Running, I grabbed my little dictionary and tucked it under my waistband, threw my towel around my neck and raced after the others.

It was dark now and the searchlights swept across the quadrangle. SS with leashed dogs prowled back and forth in front of the formation. Desperately I looked for the French section but could not find it, finally falling in with a group of Bulgarians and Rumanians.

The commandant arrived, followed by a large number of SS men we had never seen before. A searchlight swept slowly over us and in it the breath of hundreds of prisoners rose like steam from tea kettles. Then the first group was ordered forward, and as they reached the SS they were sent either to the right or to the left.

Desperately I tried to ascertain which direction meant work and which meant death—that one group was going to be gassed or shot no one doubted. Then I too was being prodded by an SS man, who jabbed his riding crop in my ribs and sent me off to the right, where perhaps a hundred men were already standing. To my horror I realized that there was not a single Frenchman among them.

But at least I am the only Jew, I told myself as we climbed into trucks and drove out the gate. Perhaps I am going to live after all. Two men crouched beside me were whispering in what I took to be Spanish. But when I spoke to them I had a surprise: their language was indeed a kind of Spanish, but it was the dialect of the Sephardic Jews of Greece. They were brothers, Saul and Isaac Pereira, survivors of the Jewish community of Salonica.

For about two hours the trucks droned along slowly, lights extinguished: the Allies were bombing again behind us, though after the sight of Augsburg I wondered why they were bothering. When the little caravan stopped we emerged on soft earth before a row of wooden barracks in a forest clearing. The brothers and I were sent to the same barracks, and our spirits rose at the sight of a stove burning at the other end. There were straw mattresses on the two-tiered bunks and prisoners were awaiting us with a cup of soup and piece of bread for each.

Before we had time to ask questions an SS non-com entered with the block elder, a tall stocky German who introduced himself as Ludwig. We remained at attention when the SS man left and Ludwig inspected us one by one. There were about twenty new men in the barracks besides Saul, Isaac and myself.

"At ease!" said Ludwig. "You can sit down."

Immediately I took out my tiny pouch of tobacco and rolled a cigarette.

"Offer him the tobacco, all of it!" whispered Isaac urgently, and I saw Ludwig glaring at me.

I knew I ought to do it, but something made me resist. Slowly I lit up and exhaled, but before I had time to pass the cigarette on to Isaac, Ludwig had run up and suddenly slapped me across the mouth.

"Next time," he said very quietly, "you will know who gets the tobacco first around here."

He picked up the tobacco and papers from where they had landed on the floor and disappeared behind the blanket partition that was his private room.

"He's a psychopath," explained an older prisoner, taking me to the far end of the hut. "He wears a black triangle, right? He's in here for murder."

Then Saul came up with more information he had just gleaned: Ludwig had already beaten more than one prisoner to death. First he marked you down, then he tormented you awhile and finally accused you of something before the SS and gave you a beating that you might or might not survive, depending on your condition and his mood.

Every night a charcoal-burning bus arrived and drove us about thirty minutes to another branch of Messerschmidt, this one built low into the surrounding pine forest and entirely camouflaged with wire nets and foliage. When we arrived German engineers chose some of us and set us to work. Overhead cranes moved back and forth on trolleys carrying sections of fighter planes. Each night I was selected by the same engineer, whose work force, apart from me, consisted entirely of Frenchmen.

"*Un hongrois qui parle français? Bizarre, ça! Viens.*"

For some reason my second group of Frenchmen adopted me as readily as the first group had, and this time I had the advantage of speaking a little French—just enough to keep them laughing. The five men headed by the German engineer—who was in reality an Alsatian who preferred to speak French—worked by themselves in a large room off to one side assembling tail sections. In a corner sat an old Wehrmacht reservist half asleep over his rifle, depending on us to tell him if anyone was coming. The SS almost never entered and the atmosphere was freer than any I had breathed for months.

I had not had a full stomach since Christmas morning, and the last time before that had been in October. I was thin as a rail, and when they saw that I barely had strength for the work, one of them, Jean-Pierre, an ardent Gaullist who never stopped preaching politics except in front of the SS, warmed a tarpaulin over the radiators, wrapped it around me and put me in the nearly completed tail section of a Messerschmidt, where I slept blissfully until they called me for lunch at one a.m.

Gradually they let me help them with lighter work, but more often they let me sleep or else dragged me out to argue politics with Jean-Pierre and his arch-enemy, Louis, a Communist. Mangling the language of Ronsard and Molière, I pleaded the case for social democracy.

One night as I handed Jean-Pierre tools the door opened, and we all stared as a creature, recognizable as a woman only by the fact that she wore a skirt, crept in with a broom in her hands. With painful slowness and frightened glances in our direction, she swept up the trash piled in a corner into a tray and emptied it into the barrel. All work and conversation had stopped. It was impossible to tell the woman's age. Her hair was cropped short and her face was haggard. Her arms were so thin I wondered that she had the strength to lift the broom.

"Gunther!" said the Alsatian engineer to the guard, "I've got some tobacco over there in my briefcase, if you want a bit."

The old Wehrmacht man blinked, then understood and went over to the briefcase, turning his back on us. Quickly Jean-Pierre went to the woman and gave her several pieces of dried bread that all of us had extracted from our smocks. She looked unbelievingly at him, then snatched at the bread and stuffed some into her mouth, tilting her head to one side to watch him as she chewed it. When she was gone a depressed silence hung over the room. Louis told me that there was a camp for Jewesses nearby in the forest. Typhus had raged there for months and few were left alive. There were no barracks and the women lived in dugouts covered with branches. Sometimes they were sent to Messerschmidt as cleaners.

"Don't worry," said Louis, misinterpreting my dejected look, "as long as you're wearing that red triangle they won't do that to you."

As it turned out, he was wrong about that too.

January gave way to the still colder February of 1945, and it was clear that the war could not go on much longer. As the American army fought its way across the Rhine and into Germany, some of our guards became almost human as they

lost heart; others in their fury and despair became unpredict-
ably murderous. The same was true of the kapos and block
elders. We waited tensely each day for Ludwig to emerge from
behind his blanket partition. Some days he was listless and
offhand; other days impending liberation filled him with
animal fury—though in retrospect this was strange, as he
certainly had no idea of the fate that awaited him.

One bitterly cold February night I was late for formation.
Ludwig, standing in the doorway, started screaming at me
and several others who were tardy, and when we ran to the
door he brought the club he always carried straight down on
my head. The first blow sent me flying on all fours out into the
snow; as I tried to stand more blows landed on my head and
shoulders, and as I reached the formation I was still crawling,
blood streaming down my face. Several feet away Ludwig
stood, holding the club at his side, horrible little panting
noises coming from his throat.

The world was spinning before my eyes, and those on either
side of me had to hold me up. When we reached the factory
my head had cleared somewhat, but when I took my hand
away from my head blood poured out in alarming amounts.
Jean-Pierre and Louis took one look at me and set me in a
corner on a pile of rags.

"We have to stop the bleeding," said Louis, and with a blow
torch he began heating a metal rod.

When the rod was red-hot the others turned me over and
held me down while Louis, apologizing for the pain he was
about to cause me, cauterized the gash on the back of my
head. With the sleeve of my smock stuffed in my mouth I just
managed not to scream. Then they put me in a tail section
and I fell asleep, determined to take revenge on Ludwig. Saul
and Isaac had already told me that they meant to kill him, one
way or another, whatever the outcome. Now I was going to
volunteer my help.

In the morning as we were driven back to the camp the sun
suddenly came out, sending sodden snow falling to the forest
floor; then clouds arrived and with them heavy, freezing rain.
We emerged from the bus to find the entrances to the
barracks blocked by SS men while others herded us with
shouts and blows to the centre of the parade ground, where
we formed up in the icy downpour, clogs freezing to our feet in
the mud.

Shouting to make himself heard above the rain, an SS
officer read a list of fifteen names, all the Jews in the camp,

and a few minutes later Saul, Isaac and I were squatting on the floor of a truck with twelve other men. All of us wore the red badges of political prisoners, but it made no difference. The bureaucratic machinery of the Germans had finally remembered that we were Jews after all.

9

A Trip to Hell

SOME HOURS LATER THE TRUCK STOPPED and the guards jumped down from the back and told us to get out. The minute our feet touched the ground other SS began kicking us in the direction of a long row of dugouts. Isaac, who was beside me, fell and I paused just long enough to grab his hand and drag him with me. The rain was coming down again in buckets.

"Move!" screamed a German voice behind us as we stood at the top of the steps, muddy boards leading down to the dugout.

Not waiting for another kick, I jumped down and opened the door, afraid the SS would follow. At first I could see nothing in the near-darkness, aware only of the nauseating stench of vomit and excrement. As my eyes adjusted I made

121

out two tiers of what I thought were bunks but what turned out to be tree trunks extending the length of the dugout. Hastily cut branches still projected from them, and as I made my way cautiously down the centre white faces peered over the trunks with no expression at all coming from the eyes, faces so shrunken and parchmentlike that I could not believe they were attached to living bodies. Urine and feces dripped from the upper tiers to the lower and the floor was slippery with it.

"Typhus!" whispered Isaac, following close behind me.

"Almighty God," moaned Saul behind him, "we've got to get out of here!"

At the far end, as far away as we could get, we found vacant places and sat on the edge of the trunk, overcome with horror. Then a man somewhat less skeletal than the rest lowered himself to the floor and approached us.

"Welcome to Turckheim," he said in Yiddish in a voice that conveyed no emotion whatsoever. "Who are you?"

"Jews," said Isaac simply, in German. "Who are you?"

Suddenly the man grabbed Isaac's smock and snarled, "I ask the questions here!"

Before I had time to think I had pulled the man off Isaac and pushed him hard against the tree trunk.

"If you're a Jew," I said, "stop acting like a German."

"What kind of Jews are you if you don't speak Yiddish?" he asked complainingly as I let him go. He was far too weak to play the bully.

"What is this place?" I demanded.

He shrugged, but then in singsong German told us the facts of life and death in Lager Turckheim. Most of the several hundred prisoners in the dugouts had come from other camps farther east. The gas chambers could not keep pace with the advances of the Red Army, so they were sent to Germany to die.

"We lose at least a hundred a day from typhus," said the man who we now realized was the block elder, the kapo. "You get three pieces of potato every day—more if you're clever," he added, giving me a sharp look. "But it doesn't matter. They're going to kill us soon, before the Americans arrive."

"What about work? What about the SS?" asked Saul.

"Give me tobacco and I can try to get you on a work detail. That way you can get out of here during the day at least. The SS? You don't have to worry about them when you're in here!" He gave a dry little laugh. "They're scared to death of the typhus."

Behind the kapo a man slowly stretched out a sticklike arm in our direction, begging. Without so much as a glance, the kapo brushed the arm aside and it dangled loosely in the air while its owner continued staring at us over the trunk he was lying on.

"How much do you want?" I asked.

"I'll talk to the chief kapo," he replied slyly. Then he left, briefly letting in grey light to illuminate the rows of living corpses. Rain hammered on the roof and dripped down in pools at our feet.

As tired as we were, and in my case still half sick from the beating Ludwig had given me, there was no question of sleep. We had been in the dugout less than thirty minutes but already lice were crawling on us. Some time later, toward noon, the kapo returned and took us outside. A whistle blew, and behind us the other prisoners, those with the strength, made their way down the row of dugouts toward a cookhouse. Several cauldrons of potatoes steamed as they were brought out and set in the mud.

"The chief kapo says eight packets of tobacco," he told us as we made our way through the mud and rain. "Two for me and four for him."

"Two and four make six," I replied.

"So? You went to school? Here two and four make eight."

"Six or nothing," said Isaac angrily.

"Then nothing," said the kapo, turning aside from us.

Between the dugouts and the cauldrons was an open-air latrine, nothing but a pole stretched over a pit. As we passed it a man hesitated before the pole, his trousers down, then slowly he turned and fell backward, hitting the pole but making no effort to grab it. Isaac swore and the three of us automatically started to run toward him to pull him out.

"Idiots!" said the kapo, already some ten feet away. "He's better off drowned in shit. Besides, the guard will shoot."

He tilted his head, and we looked to see a lone SS man standing beside the cookhouse, watching impassively.

Hundreds of men were approaching the cauldrons now, some upright, others on all fours doggedly crawling through the mud. Each man who made it that far received three pieces of potato in his bare hands. To the right was a water tap set into a cement block. Those who had eaten clung to it to fill their bellies with water.

Schmuel, the kapo, gave in the next day and accepted the tobacco we had. Two of us would go out on *Sonderkommando*, work detail, each day, one remaining in the dugout.

With each passing day the SS were more reluctant to enter the compound itself, let alone the dugouts. Roll call was perfunctory and sometimes was not even held. Each morning the dead were stacked outside the dugouts, naked, maggot-white under the sodden sky. I felt myself growing weaker and knew that one day soon I would join that ghastly pile of rotting flesh.

The chief kapo put Isaac and myself on a *Kommando* of our own, cleaning two unused buildings, a former orderly room and a hut near the cookhouse. We spent the morning sweeping out the orderly room, already spotlessly clean; then, under the eyes of the SS man who was almost always at the cookhouse, we cleaned out the hut. The second afternoon we were set to work in the cookhouse itself. Scraps of potato were stuck to the bottom of the cauldrons, and as fast as we could we filled our pockets with the soggy pieces, devouring some and saving the rest for Saul.

Each time out we tried to discover the source of the electric power for the fences that ran the camp's perimeter, but it soon became obvious that the generators were somewhere outside. Next, cautiously, we examined the whole area between the orderly room, the dugouts and the cookhouse, making mental maps of the distances.

The nearest fence was directly behind the cookhouse, and we had been warned not to go anywhere near it, but each day I went a bit closer anyway, trying to find a route toward it that was less obvious than the others. I was doing this one morning, broom in hand, when I saw a prisoner perhaps a hundred feet before me shuffling slowly in the direction of the fence. At first I thought he was dazed and did not know what he was doing, but then I realized that he was going to throw himself against the electrified wire. I opened my mouth without thinking, meaning to shout at the man, but Isaac quickly covered my mouth with his hand.

"Don't," he said. "It's no use. Look."

The SS man in the nearest tower had his rifle aimed and was following the prisoner in his sights. We held our breath. The Jew was nearly at the fence, his arms extended toward it as if in greeting, when suddenly the shot rang out and he collapsed in the mud, still reaching out.

"We're going to get out of here," said Isaac, rain streaming down his dusky Mediterranean face. He and his brother both still showed signs of the health we had all enjoyed shortly before our arrival.

Several more days went by and we spent every moment together trying to plan an escape, but the more we talked the more obvious it was that there really was no way out. Then Schmuel, the kapo, came up to us one morning and whispered excitedly, his voice almost breaking, that he had heard that the Americans were in Ulm, to the west of us.

"Only a few more days!" he said, hope and fear both shining in his eyes.

"And will we still be alive when they get here?" asked Saul brutally.

Schmuel stared, then shook his head violently without a word, not wanting to think about it.

"Will we?" shouted Saul after him, but Schmuel sat down on a trunk and buried his face in his hands.

The next day there was furious activity in the SS compound outside the fence, numbers of military vehicles coming and going. At noon no food was brought out of the cookhouse, and hundreds of prisoners sat in the mud staring toward the door, hoping against hope that they would get their scraps of potatoes.

As dusk fell that evening two large trucks roared into the SS compound. In the distance the generators hummed to life and the searchlights lit up in the watchtowers. Then an eerie silence fell: the generators had stopped working! Quickly the three of us made our way to the door of the dugout and peered out. The searchlights were off, and in the SS compound there was no light except for the headlights of the trucks. Isaac squeezed my arm until I winced.

"It's now or never!" he whispered.

He no sooner spoke than the generators hummed to life again and the searchlights came on. Then the wire gates were being pushed open and SS men were running in, blowing whistles.

"Wait!" said Isaac urgently. "We're going last."

When all those who could do so had left the dugout we followed slowly, standing together in the last row. For the hundredth time since our arrival rain began to fall.

It was not a roll call. Without a word SS men began driving prisoners toward the two trucks that now rolled into the compound. They had not yet filled the first truck when again the lights went out and the whole camp disappeared in darkness. I took hold of Saul's sleeve and pulled him with me backward toward the dugout. Isaac followed, and together we ran, crouching, around to the back and squatted in the dark. The cookhouse and the watchtower to the right were faintly outlined against the overcast night sky. If there was a guard in the tower he could no more see us than we could see him. Once past the cookhouse we started crawling, praying that the lights would not come back on, and with them the current in the fence.

I reached the first fence ahead of the others, and when they came up beside me in the mud we were all three sobbing for breath.

"Let's go!" snarled Isaac in an undertone.

I raised my hand but could not bring myself to touch the barbed wire, sure that the power would return at any second. Then I took hold of it, nothing in my mind but the desperate desire to get out. The strands were not more than a foot from each other and so well fastened that it would have taken wire-cutters to separate them. I bit my lips as barbs tore my shoulders, but in a few seconds I was through. Turning, I helped Isaac, who, being considerably larger than I, almost did not get through. The barbs dug into his flesh but he uttered no sound, and finally he too made it and turned to pull Saul through the now enlarged opening.

The second fence was the same except that the bottom strands were buried in deep mud. I took my towel off my neck and placed it over the ground wire, sending Isaac and Saul through ahead of me. Obviously the Germans were counting on the voltage and the watchtowers to prevent escapes. By the time I pulled my feet out on the other side the brothers were already out of sight. Blindly I ran straight ahead into the wall of forest faintly visible before me.

"Here!" hissed Isaac as I blundered my way through the undergrowth. Then a hand grabbed my leg and sent me tumbling into a soft, cold mattress of soggy pine needles. We were out! We rested a few minutes, panting and hugging one another.

"All right, let's go," said Isaac suddenly, and obediently we followed him into the forest. All around us the thin black pines stood like sentinels, barely visible as we felt our way through the inky night. Gradually the ground rose and we were climbing, holding onto trees and to each other for support. Then we emerged into a small clearing and gasped. Directly below us, awash in light, was the camp. We heard the truck engines grinding and saw them pull out of the gate, driving north. Without a word we scrambled back into the forest. We had travelled in a semicircle and if it had not been for the lights and the noise would actually have returned unwittingly to Lager Turckheim!

Before dawn the blackbirds in the branches set up a raucous noise; then as the sun rose hungry sparrows hopped across the forest floor, pecking in the wet earth for worms. The cold had kept me awake much of the night, that and fear of capture, but as the air warmed up I slept heavily on the pine needles, my head wrapped in my towel. Finally I awoke to the sound of Saul saying his prayers nearby: "*Baruch ata adonai elohenu melech ha'olam....* Blessed art Thou Lord our God, King of the Universe...." In the undergrowth Isaac looked like a zebra in his striped uniform as he appeared and disappeared, rummaging for berries.

We were beside a small clearing, and as the sun grew warm we stripped off our prison rags and wallowed in the mud like pigs. When our bodies dried in the cold wind and bright sunlight we scraped each other clean, leaving dozens of lice embedded in the caked mud. Then we sat and ate the rose hips Isaac had gathered, nibbling at the delicious yellow part and throwing the insides away.

"We will not get typhus now," said Saul with what seemed to me unjustified conviction.

"What makes you think so?" I asked him.

"We're free, more or less. God would not be so cruel."

"If the Americans don't arrive very soon," added Isaac, "it won't make any difference. We'll starve to death."

We were in a small triangle with the camp, the village of Turckheim and the Augsburg autobahn as its points. After some discussion we put on our wet uniforms and headed back into the forest, walking toward the south. As we emerged into the next clearing even higher pine-covered hills appeared to our right, and on the left lay a deep valley in the centre of which was a picture-book farmhouse with smoke curling up from its chimney, several out-buildings and an expanse of muddy fields beyond. Hunger gnawed at all our bellies, and we looked longingly and helplessly at the house.

"One of the disadvantages of being a Jew," remarked Isaac gloomily, "is that one knows nothing about nature."

We had collected pocketsful of various berries and roots but had no idea which, aside from rose hips, were safe to eat. Grimacing, Saul popped the whole mass straight into his mouth, and we squatted, watching him with worried interest. The berries were obviously delicious, and when he was still alive a few minutes later we followed his example. It helped, but by the end of the day we were weaker than ever, having burnt up more calories looking for berries than we eventually derived from them.

When the sun came up on our second morning of freedom I decided to go down into the valley with the vague idea of spying out the farm for a raid. Slowly, keeping to the undergrowth, the three of us made our way down the steep slope. Suddenly we saw a man coming out of the farmhouse, now about five hundred yards away. We were only partly hidden and had the distinct impression that he was watching us, for he stood still in the middle of his garden. Quickly we slipped back into the trees and made a long, exhausting detour down the hillside, emerging at last at the autobahn. The farmhouse was opposite us, less than a hundred yards away, and there was no sign of life in it as we crouched in the bushes, watching. All afternoon we planned our raid on what was obviously the chicken coop, then fell into despair as a large dog was let out of the house at sundown. It ran to the edge of the road, barking at us, though we were out of sight. Then mercifully it lost interest; but raiding the farm was out of the question.

In the morning our hunger was so great that we decided to go to the farmhouse and beg, but just as we set foot on the paved expanse of the autobahn we heard the rumbling of distant traffic and quickly slipped back into the bushes. The inhabitants of the farm came out to listen as well, the old farmer, a younger woman and two children. Then they too withdrew, closing the shutters.

10

Liberation

WITH AGONIZING SLOWNESS the noise increased, coming from far beyond the bend in the autobahn a half mile away. Gradually the birds stopped singing in the trees and at the farmhouse even the smoke stopped coming out of the chimney. Then, just when I thought I could bear the anticipation no longer, a tank appeared around the bend, its great gun swinging from right to left. There was a star painted on the side. Isaac began to weep quietly; then the three of us stepped out of the bushes and walked to the centre of the highway where we stood waiting.

The first tank slowed down while we stood aside for it to pass. Then a truck passed, the two men in the cab staring at us wonderingly but not stopping. The next truck slowed down and out of the window flew chocolate, cigarettes and several tins of rations, closely followed as an afterthought by an odd-looking little instrument, which on inspection turned out to be a can opener. We were at once elated and depressed as the endless stream of American vehicles passed us. If it had not occurred to us before, it did now that the Americans had not come all the way to Europe just to liberate three Jews hiding in a forest. Obviously they had more pressing tasks.

Then a jeep pulled past the slower traffic and screeched to a halt at the sight of us. An officer wearing two silver bars jumped out and came up to us.

"Are you Jews?" he asked in bad German.

Somehow it seemed ominous that the first question our liberators should ask us reflected what I had thought was a European mania.

"Apart from being Jews," I replied, "these men are Greeks and I am a Hungarian."

The man blinked at the hostility in my tone; then his features softened and he introduced himself as Captain Bennett. His driver, a corporal, was second-generation Hungarian, and from then on our conversation was filtered through his sketchy memory of Magyar. They put us in the back of the jeep, and as we sped past the heavier military vehicles I was exhilarated by the breath-taking change in our circumstances. Also it was the first time I had ever been in an official vehicle without being under arrest.

At Bad Worishofen the Americans set up their headquarters with miraculous speed. Having heard all my life about German efficiency, I sat in a courtyard with Saul and Isaac open-mouthed, watching the transformation as several dozen Americans cheerfully and ruthlessly made the place their own. Most thrilling of all, oddly, was the way they dealt with *matter*—there was none of the almost cringing respect Europeans are apt to show toward valuable objects. These men tossed about typewriters and radios with a disregard that bespoke a vast and careless opulence. I was enchanted with them.

They disinfected us with spray guns, gave us hot showers, and while we ate our first mouthfuls of Spam, they began interrogating us, with infinite patience and gentleness, about the camp. At last Captain Bennett asked me if I were up to accompanying him, and a few minutes later his Hungarian-American driver, Corporal Nagy, spinning mud from the wheels, delivered us to the village of Turckheim.

There was not a German in sight in the village, and when we got to the camp the gates were hanging open. The watchtowers stood empty against the sky and there was not a prisoner in sight. My God, I thought, they've killed them all. But the mound of corpses outside the dugouts was no larger than when I had last seen it, except that now the bodies were bloated. I shuddered and looked at the ground. The truckload of soldiers that had followed us now jumped to the ground, tommy guns at the ready, and one by one they too turned aside at the sight and smell of the corpses, some vomiting.

Finally a soldier went over to the first dugout and kicked the door open. There was a pause, then a face appeared, followed by others, blinking in the light. Slowly men climbed out as the Americans opened the doors, then backed up in horror and pity as they came face to face with the ghastly matchstick creatures with their huge black eyes.

The prisoners gradually formed a semicircle around us, some of them reaching out, others standing still and weeping. Somebody had to do something, so I stepped forward in my striped uniform and said in what I hoped was Yiddish that they must come no closer. The Americans would bring them food immediately. They stared in silence but stopped approaching the horrified Americans.

Captain Bennett wanted to conscript the civilian population of Turckheim for the task of cleaning up the camp. But as there was no time to lose, I persuaded him to move the prisoners into the former SS barracks—the SS by now of course had blended into the rest of the population and become anti-Nazis of long standing. Fighting down their nausea, the Americans themselves helped the several hundred survivors to the compound, and within an hour trucks loaded with food and medical supplies rolled through the gates.

For my part, I wanted nothing more than to go to sleep in the SS barracks, but Captain Bennett insisted on taking me back to Bad Worishofen. There I fell asleep at supper and evidently was carried to bed, where I slept until late the next afternoon. I awoke to find a complete issue of underwear, socks, boots, fatigues and the rest on a chair beside my bed.

When we returned to Turckheim that night several prisoners had already died, some because the two overworked American medics had been unable to prevent them from swallowing more food than their shrunken stomachs could stand. Among the prisoners were three doctors, but they were too weak to be of any help and they pleaded in chorus that the whole camp be disinfected immediately—which it was, by midnight.

As we drove back we passed a long column of German civilians trudging along with handcarts, baby carriages, anything into which they could fit their possessions. I watched and thought about my own family, but again found it impossible to find a sense of revenge. The Germans cast frightened glances at us, but some of the children held out their hands, begging.

The good people of Turckheim village were not at all cowed by defeat. It was Sunday morning now and the streets were filled with well-dressed, missal-carrying Germans on their way to mass. Except for the fact that there were few males between sixteen and sixty, it was a normal Sunday crowd. I was suddenly sorry that I had dissuaded Captain Bennett from his original idea of dragging them to the camp and making them work there among their victims. But as I looked it seemed to me that it would take more than a few dead or dying Jews to wipe the smug self-righteousness off those faces.

We knocked at the door of the local physician, and his wife, trembling visibly, let us in. We sat in an ornate Bavarian parlour, and in a few minutes she reappeared, rattling in her fear the coffee cups and cream cakes she held on a tray. This time I thought not about the Jews but about the hungry refugees on the road.

Her husband, when he arrived, seemed even more frightened. He bowed stiffly; then without being asked, he began a long recital of his grudges against the Nazis, how he was apolitical anyway, and so on. Finally Captain Bennett raised his hand, shutting the man up. The American looked at the German with cold disdain and told him that he was coming with us to the camp, that he would work there, and that in return he would be fed and would receive medicine for his own patients. The doctor relaxed visibly and nodded.

As we drove into the camp a squad of soldiers was still spraying disinfectant. Lime had been thrown over the still-unburied corpses.

"Sweet God in heaven," said the doctor, staring at the ghastly pile, "to think that I am a German!"

I was impressed, in spite of myself, to see real tears roll down his cheeks. Still, I asked myself, how does a man contrive to live a stone's throw from such a place month after month without knowing of its existence?

Now I moved into the SS barracks near Saul and Isaac. Tons of food kept arriving in the mysterious way American things always appeared: out of nowhere and in monstrous quantities. The SS storerooms were soon overflowing and were named Canada, as warehouses were in every prisoner and refugee camp throughout Europe. We ate, we slept, and as the days warmed and lengthened we lay on blankets on the lawns of the SS compound, healing. Although I was, except for Saul and Isaac, probably the healthiest ex-prisoner in Turckheim, I was still so weak that climbing a flight of stairs left me gasping and dizzy. Many, however, were in really serious condition; not a day passed without someone dying, and the doctor from the village worked like a demon to save those he could. I helped him on his rounds from time to time and gradually came to admire the old man, whatever he had been during the war. His tenderness toward the dying sprang from the heart, and he bullied back to life more than one man whose will to live had deserted him at the moment of liberation.

The politics of liberation was rapidly making itself clear. Roosevelt and Churchill had given Stalin Europe east of Berlin and Vienna, though no one was yet prepared to believe that they had done so without reservations or strings attached—as turned out to be the case. The Russians were in Budapest, a new government—as yet non-Communist—had been formed and I began to be eager to return and work with the Social Democrats.

Captain Bennett got his hands on a Red Cross list of survivors of various camps. I pored over the pages concerning Auschwitz, then those for various other camps, but could find none of my relatives listed there. The chilling fact of absolute loneliness began to clamour for recognition, but I could not yet accept the truth: they were all dead. I told the Americans I wanted to return to Hungary and soon I was issued with a document certifying that I was a former concentration camp inmate, and thus exempt from orders directed at the German population. This entitled me to free transportation home as well, but I put off my return from week to week, unable to face home without my family to go with it.

One afternoon early in the summer I was cycling between the camp and the village—I had "liberated" a bicycle from the former SS supply depot—and as I reached the gates I saw a large group of former prisoners in a circle on the parade ground. I worked my way through the crowd and halted in astonishment before a shiny green Mercedes. Leaning against it, one foot resting in the door, stood a tall, fair-haired man in an elegant double-breasted suit, chatting and joking with the crowd of Jews, who for their part were openly admiring his dapper appearance. It was Ludwig.

I was still gaping when suddenly two men shoved their way past me and confronted Ludwig. Saul held a length of rope in his hands while Isaac grabbed the astonished German and twisted his arms behind his back. Sudden panic swept across Ludwig's face and the ex-prisoners, smiles vanished, stepped back slightly as they began to realize what was happening.

"What are you doing?" shouted Ludwig, terror in his voice. "You have no right to touch me! I did only what I was ordered to do!"

Isaac flung him to the ground and Ludwig stretched out a fistful of documents, proving that he too had been a prisoner.

"Who is this man?" asked a small, very frail Jew, frowning at Isaac.

"A murderer," said Saul, and as Ludwig lay in the dirt pleading for help, the two of them tied his arms and feet together, then fastened the rope around his neck. They began to run, dragging Ludwig behind them. His pleading ceased as the rope dug into his neck. I closed my eyes, remembering the death of Sergei, and when I opened them the brothers were coming back, walking now, exhausted and sobbing for air. Ludwig was dead. The group of emaciated Jews stood absolutely still. Dropping the rope, Isaac came up to me, a sick expression on his face. I could find nothing to say, so in silence I took his arm and led him to the barracks, where he collapsed on his bunk.

The only American to witness the execution of Ludwig had been Corporal Nagy, who was badly shaken by it but had not attempted to interfere. I took him aside and gave a lengthy explanation in simple Hungarian.

"There's no sense in telling anyone about it," I concluded. "It was justice and it's over now."

He nodded, and when I asked him to help cover the whole

thing up he arranged for Ludwig to be buried not far from the graveyard for prisoners who had died. They won't have to look far for him, I thought, on the Day of Judgment.

A few hours later the Mercedes too disappeared, and someone, I hoped, had at last got some profit out of Ludwig.

For a long time I had been wondering about my friends in Dachau but could get no information at all. Captain Bennett told me privately that on the day the camp was liberated the Americans had been so outraged that they had shot many of the SS out of hand, and when on the same day an SS division had counterattacked and been repulsed the American officers had found it difficult to persuade their troops to take prisoners. But no list of survivors was available, so when one day the captain asked me if I wanted to accompany him to Dachau I jumped at the chance.

The countryside between Augsburg and Munich was in full bloom, with nothing to remind one of the devastation of the cities. When we arrived at Dachau the vast camp, looking the same except for the absence of striped uniforms, seemed unreal, a nightmare that had occurred elsewhere, not in this Bavaria of pink-cheeked peasants and flourishing fields.

There were comparatively few people in the camp now. Captain Bennett went into the administration building and soon came back with the sad news that Uncle Eugene had died just after the Americans arrived. As for Father John, even though I did not know his surname, everyone knew him from my description. They told me I would find him in the hospital barracks.

He was sitting up in bed at the far end of the long ward, scribbling away at a writing board on his lap, his white beard almost reaching the paper. Someone had placed two flowers in a jar on his bedside table. Deeply moved, I looked at him from the foot of the bed. He was so immersed in his work that at first he did not notice me. His parchmentlike face was paler than ever, crisscrossed with tiny blue and red blood vessels like a road map of Europe. When at last he looked up his face broke into a joyful smile, and without a word he held out his arms and we embraced in silence.

"You know about your Uncle Eugene?" he asked at length. I nodded.

"It was his heart, an easy death. He spoke about you often, you know, right up to the end."

I looked away and swallowed as Father John continued regarding me gravely.

"Well, just look at you!" he went on more cheerfully. "You've become an American. I suppose you'll be going back to Hungary now?"

Again I nodded.

"I'm an old preacher, my boy, and I can't let you go without a little sermon. It's time you became a Jew. After everything that's happened even good Jews are going to start doubting the existence of God. Don't give in to that, my boy. What you've suffered you've suffered because you are a Jew. Don't render it meaningless by abandoning the faith of your fathers."

"But I wasn't here as a Jew," I felt constrained to object. "I was here for fighting the Germans, Father John."

"I suppose you will go home and get yourself involved in politics again," he said a little ruefully, though without condemnation. "Well, at least get yourself a good education in the meantime. God is patient. Read, study, think! If you are determined to change the world, at least realize that you must start with yourself. Remember that it is the silliest sort of sophistry to think that you can harvest goodness without first sowing and cultivating it!"

"And what will you do, Father John? When you're well, I mean?" He looked much older than when I had seen him several months before, and the pallor of his skin was tinged with grey.

"As you see, I'm not entirely well just now, though perhaps not so ill as the doctor here thinks." He looked down the long row of beds toward a young army doctor who was checking the pulse of a corpselike man. "I had cancer about ten years ago. It disappeared, and now it's back again. Perhaps it will go away once more, perhaps not." He chuckled, as if amused to find himself in possession of such an unpredictable carcass, then went on, "It doesn't do to speculate too much in these things. They're 'outside our control,' as your good Uncle Eugene would say. You know, sometimes I wondered if that man was really Jewish? A Jew storms against fate and argues with God, at least up to a point. He, never. He was, I think, the only true stoic I've ever met."

"What God did for you once, Father John, maybe he'll do again. And then where will you go?"

"Oh," he replied, waving his fountain pen airily, "back to Paris. Perhaps to Rome. Someplace where the Holy Office won't pester me and where the local bishop will feel obliged to take care of an old refugee priest. Someplace where I can finish my book, such as it is." He opened his palm toward the pile of papers in his lap, sheets filled with Hebrew, Greek and Latin. "But it really doesn't matter. Would you believe me if I told you that I'd be just as happy staying in Dachau under our charming new masters?"

I smiled and shook my head.

"Well, I would. When you've lived as long as I have—God keep you out of any more concentration camps—if you've kept your eyes open you'll have seen everything worth seeing. There's not all that much, you know. Look and listen, store everything away in your head for future reference, then learn to contemplate. I've seen and read too much, that's my trouble. I've absorbed too much material to organize in one lifetime. Your problem, my boy, is just the opposite." He paused and gave me a keen look. "My first advice was the best," he said.

"About being a Jew?"

"Yes. If you should after all decide to take that advice, I beg you to remember one thing. Look for God in men and in nature before you start looking for Him in the synagogue—or the church, for that matter. I'm not altogether sure just why, but it never works the other way around. Do you understand?"

I nodded vigorously, understanding nothing.

"You had better go now," he said gently. "It's very hard rewriting this from memory without reference books, and God alone knows what the Gestapo did with the original in Paris. Perhaps they thought it was in code," he chuckled into his beard. "Come, let me give you my blessing."

I bent my head over him as he muttered something in Latin and made the sign of the cross over me.

"George!" called Father John as I reached the door. He had stopped work again and was craning his neck to see me. "Remember! No more politics, for God's sake. It always ends like this!"

Saul and Isaac were going back home to Greece. Theirs was the only country in East Europe which the Allies had not given to Stalin as a gift. It was understood to be within the "British sphere." When they came to say good-bye we toasted one another with watery American beer, and I felt a greater wrench than I would have thought when the next morning I waved as they set out for Munich in the back of an army truck. Having no family made me feel totally lost in the universe, and the departure of friends filled me with desolation. I would have gone home as well now if I had not got myself involved with a certain Ursula. My heart was already home in Budapest; but my body, thanks to Ursula, refused to leave Bavaria.

I had met Uschi one afternoon in Bad Worishofen, where, having been more or less adopted by the Americans, I made myself useful and in return enjoyed an almost American standard of living. I was peddling home on my bicycle, holding a small bag of soap and cigarettes, when suddenly a tiny blonde stepped in front of me, almost sending me over the handle bars. She propositioned me in the middle of the street, and for a moment I was at a complete loss. She was not only extremely pretty but had a virginal convent-school look about her, all braids and dimples, as unlike the dumpling-fed girls of Bad Worishofen or the scrawny whores of Munich as one could imagine.

"You don't look the type," I finally managed to say.

"I'm not!" Uschi replied, pulling down the corners of her mouth in a wry grin. "But everyone else is doing it. You look nice. You've got soap, haven't you?" she added, as if that clinched the matter—which it did.

I headed toward Turckheim with Uschi on the back of the bike. Taking her in was of course forbidden, but I reasoned, correctly as it turned out, that if I could get out of Turckheim under the SS I could get back in with Uschi under the Americans.

"Don't you object to sleeping with a Jew?" I asked her later that night as we lay in our comfortable bed in the storeroom.

"Not at all," she replied archly. "You're the conquerors, aren't you?"

"Who?" I asked in amazement.

"The Judeo-Plutocrat Bolsheviks!" she replied simply.

"Are you a Nazi, Uschi?" I asked wonderingly.

"You bet your ass I'm a Nazi!" she shot back matter of factly in ripe American. No expert in these matters, I had suspected that Uschi was not a virgin; but now I could see that a long line of "conquerors" had been there before me.

"All my family are Nazis," she went on, combing her hair. "My father especially. My father says the Führer is alive and just waiting for the Allies to leave. He would kill me if he knew I was with you. Are you really a Jew?" Then, evidently remembering anatomical details, she pursed her lips and answered her own question.

It occurred to me that if Uschi's father was a professing Nazi, he must be the only one in all Bavaria. I had yet to meet anyone who would admit to having been anything except a staunch anti-Nazi since 1933. A certain dreamy vagueness crept into German eyes at the very mention of the word Nazi, a polite lack of comprehension, as if one had said something in Swahili by mistake and they were waiting for a translation. I was rather proud of Uschi's forthright fascism, and the idea of her no-doubt hulking blond giant of a father out for my Jewish blood for having ravished his little Brunhilde added a certain piquancy to our relationship.

Several days later, however, we ran into the man in the streets of Bad Worishofen. He was smoking a Camel, which he carefully butted before tipping his hat and shaking hands with me. The only Nazi he resembled was Heinrich Himmler, mousy and utterly nondescript, as bloodthirsty as a rabbit. I felt humiliated for Uschi, who observed a stony silence throughout our short conversation.

"Likes to smoke, does he, your father?" I asked Uschi as we went on our way. I now knew where all the cigarettes I gave her went. She raised her eyebrows but did not reply.

"Are you sure you want to go?" asked Corporal Nagy, whose memories of Hungary were all secondhand.

"I don't want to at all," I replied, "but I've got to."

We shook hands and I watched him drive off through the ruins of Munich. Two days earlier I had passed Uschi on to a sergeant, far better placed than I was to keep her in soap and cigarettes. Captain Bennett and the others had presented me with a large suitcase stuffed with more of the same, as well as other items that would be worth their weight in gold in Budapest. Corporal Nagy's jeep disappeared in the wasteland of rubble, and as I faced the great shattered railway station I almost turned back. Then, determined, I entered.

Inside the American authorities were trying to sort out mobs of people all clamouring to go somewhere on a limited number of trains. I stood at the back of the crowd, watching. The Americans were obviously at the end of their wits trying to feed a starving population, set up an administration, clear the rubble and send untold thousands of prisoners back to their homelands. Their expressions betrayed a mixture of contempt, impatience and pity for the Europeans milling around them. Well, why not? I thought. What else should they feel for a continent that had again attempted suicide and again bungled the job?

Captain Bennett had evidently provided me with a high priority, because when I showed my papers I was put on the first train toward Czechoslovakia, and before sundown I was gliding through the moonscape of Munich in what had once been a first-class carriage. Now the windows were boarded over broken glass. The train was jammed and the unwashed bodies pressing each other reeked of stale sweat and undernourishment. But we were moving, we were all going home, and the air of the carriage was supercharged with a kind of hysterical, frightened gaiety that kept people chattering to one another in six or seven languages until long after dark.

Sticky with sleep, I awoke at dawn to find the still obviously German landscape unrolling beyond the chinks in the window. Across from me was a new passenger, a tall, hawknosed Jew wearing a black overcoat in spite of the warmth. He was clutching a cardboard box to his chest.

"Are you Hungarian?" I asked.

"I'm from Pozsony," he replied, which meant that he was Hungarian, Slovak or Austrian, depending on which language I addressed him in.

"I've been in a monastery for four years, if you can imagine that!" he went on. "The Benedictines at Helmstedt. Beautiful place, nice people." He began chanting. "... *sicut erat in principio, et nunc....*" Those just waking around us stared in amazement.

"What will you do now?" I asked.

"Go into business. With this," he said, tapping the box, and a dreamy smile came over his face.

Shortly before noon the train jolted to a stop as we left the American zone of occupation and entered the Soviet. For the first time it came home to me that there were no more borders in Europe, only zones. Suddenly there was shouting in the corridor, both Czech and Russian, and the door opened to reveal a short Russian soldier in an incredibly filthy uniform. He demanded our papers. As everyone present was Jewish, all had papers issued by the Americans, which seemed to infuriate the soldier, who shouted and began waving his tommy gun around dangerously. Then another Russian came in, and the two of them began throwing our luggage out the window, the planks of which they simply kicked out with their boots.

The man across from me set up a loud lamentation as they snatched his box and sent it flying onto the platform, where other Russians now appeared to cart off the loot. The stubby Russian listened to his complaints for a moment, then reached down and took his papers, tearing them into small pieces, smiling all the while. I held my breath. Captain Bennett's suitcase was gone, but beneath the seat, well back, was my rucksack. They overlooked it.

Several hours later it was a glum company that climbed down onto the platform at Pozsony. Everyone was penniless, except for myself. My rucksack was filled with cigarettes, and with these I headed for a kiosk in the station and was flooded with nostalgia when I found the *Nepszava* and other Budapest papers on sale there. The vendor's eyes lit up in disbelief as I offered him two American cigarettes for the paper. He snatched them; then trying to return my generosity, he leaned over and whispered in Hungarian, "A word of advice, friend. Speak any language you like here, but better not Hungarian or German."

I sat on the floor of the waiting room and devoured the paper, memories welling up. Around me people spoke only Slovak, and suddenly I learned the reason for the vendor's warning. An elderly man, seeing my paper, asked me the time in Hungarian and immediately the people around us became agitated and began muttering.

"This is Slovakia!" snarled a woman. "If you want to speak Hungarian, go to Hungary!"

Sadly I pushed my way through the crowd in which I felt I could no longer breathe. But if I had doubted it before, I knew now that I was really close to home, east of the Danube. Nothing had changed here. The only thing that could rouse these people out of their lethargy was hatred—racial, religious or political.

When the Budapest train pulled in I elbowed my way on with such angry force that a fat Russian woman in uniform burst into laughter from the top of the steps.

"Davai! Davai!" she encouraged me as I barged through the mob, exposing a single tooth gaping in the centre of her mouth as she laughed, obviously approving of my present attitude toward Slovaks and Hungarians.

Like an animal I marked my territory in the corner of the

compartment and flung open the *Nepszava*, ready to dismember anyone who came too close. On the third page of the paper there was an article by Justus. It was the first indication I had of his survival, and as I read my head filled with plans for the future, turning over the wonderful choices that lay before me: studying with Justus again, entering the university, going home and rebuilding the family business. Now for the first time the tension I had maintained for nearly a year, never daring to let go of myself, burst suddenly. The paper blurred before my eyes and I turned away from the other passengers, resting my forehead on the cool window glass as tears rolled down my cheeks.

People shoved and elbowed their way off the jammed train into the glassless hulk of Budapest's Western Station. Now that my own fury had subsided, it seemed to me that defeat had made my compatriots more sour and rude than usual. Everyone seemed to be nursing a private grudge.

"Watch where you're going, you stinking. . . ." The man I had bumped into caught himself just in time, his face twitching in rage, as he saw my fist half raised, ready to smash into his face. The word "Jew" died on his lips and he slunk away. Sickened, I made my way out of the station and onto the street. So those of us who have survived are still "stinking Jews," I thought. Then as I looked at the shattered city before me, for a moment something in me almost rejoiced that scum like that had at least paid something for their crimes.

At a kiosk I exchanged two cigarettes for ten thousand *pengo*, a fortune before the war, tram fare now. As I headed toward Klausal Street the full extent of the war damage revealed itself. During the siege the Germans had blown up the beautiful bridges over the Danube; the centre of the city was a shambles, though not the graveyard that Germany's cities had become. At a crossing I sank ankle-deep into soft soil and realized that I was standing in a shallow grave: corpses were buried haphazardly everywhere, and suddenly I identified the sweetish smell of putrefaction that hung in the air.

Smiling, plump Russian soldiers, many with Asiatic faces, were coming and going on almost every street, weapons slung over their shoulders. The Hungarians, in contrast, wore worried looks. Everyone carried a stick (for protection, I wondered?) and a string bag or sack. The whole population had become scavengers, scurrying about in search of something to eat or sell. Along the streets people stood behind trays holding everything from cigarettes (at incredible prices) to chipped Sèvres teacups. The only thing not in sight was food: transactions of that magnitude were done in private. Among the passers-by I noticed several mumbling to themselves.

Unlike Munich, few houses in Budapest were in total ruin. Sometimes the top story would be missing, and nearly everywhere windows were glassless and boarded up. There was evidently a water shortage as well: wherever several people congregated the stench of body odour was appalling. Turning off toward Klausal, I confronted a wall covered with posters of Soviet marshalls and generals, a row of sinister little Asiatic heads placed comically on squat, bemedalled torsos. All the little shops on Klausal Street were boarded up. At the doorway of Aunt Lina's building I hesitated, took a deep breath and entered. Unbelievably, the elevator was working.

When Aunt Lina opened the door she stared uncomprehendingly a moment, then uttered a terrible cry and fell on my shoulders, sobbing. Her two daughters appeared then, and together we helped her back inside as she kept fondling my head and looking at me in almost demented joy.

Soon Aunt Lina had herself under control and gently I began teasing her for having grown so plump, as if World War II had been a feast! She shrugged and looked around the apartment, which was unchanged except for a lot of missing porcelain bric-a-brac sold for food. It turned out that someone from my trade union had told them that I was among the ten thousand the Arrow Cross had shot into the Danube. They had given me up.

"And what about the rest of the family?" I asked softly.

Aunt Lina opened her mouth and began to move her lips but no sound emerged. Finally she looked away, blinking.

"Your brother is alive," said Manci, the oldest daughter. "The others all died in Auschwitz."

I heard this in silence, then went into the bathroom and washed my face in cold water. When I came back they recited the list of all our relatives, friends and acquaintances who had been killed.

Gradually they told me everything that had happened during my absence. On the day of my arrest Szalasi had taken power. Horthy had wanted to arrest the Nazi leader, but the Germans had prevented it, forcing Horthy to resign by threatening the life of his son. Then the old admiral was taken to Germany as a prisoner. On the day of my arrest the leadership of the Social Democratic Party were rounded up. Few resisted, with the notable exception of Bajcsi-Zsilinszky, an independent MP who had awaited the Gestapo with a pistol and shot several of them down before they subdued him. Szalasi had him hanged.

In the meantime, by October 16 the Red Army was less than eighty miles east of Budapest, and Hitler decided to defend the city with two hundred thousand Germans and a great number of Hungarian troops under German officers. By Christmas Eve the Red Army had encircled the city. By then the Szalasi government and its hangers-on had already left for the Austrian border, insanely convinced that Hitler's new wonder weapons would mean victory at the last minute. But before they headed west they forced about two hundred and fifty thousand Jews out of their homes. These people were allowed to take along only a small amount of food and clothing and had to leave their doors unlocked so that their Hungarian neighbours could take what they liked.

Some ten thousand were shot still in Budapest; others were driven on foot toward Austria. Eichmann, who had had such success deporting Jews from the provinces, could not repeat his performance in Budapest: there were no trains, and anyway Auschwitz was in Soviet hands now. Many thousands went into hiding. Some were hidden by the Catholic and Protestant clergy, others by the Swiss, Swedish and Portuguese legations. Some were hidden by gentiles in exchange for vast amounts of money, and not a few were sheltered by right-wing Hungarians who hoped thereby to insure themselves against retribution when the Russians arrived. Many simply acquired false papers and joined the mass of army deserters.

Miraculously, Aunt Lina's flat had never been raided. Their closest call had been when an ex-priest named Kun entered Klausal Street one day with thirty Arrow Cross men and shot between thirty and forty of their neighbours.

The winter of 1944-45 was exceptionally severe, which caused great suffering but also kept down epidemics. As the Germans had commandeered all motor vehicles, food reached Budapest in horse-drawn carts. When the Russian bombardment began hundreds of horses were killed and the population hacked up the frozen carcasses for food.

But even as Aunt Lina was telling me this, her daughters brought in dinner for us. Some sort of underground economy was thriving in Budapest, because they piled the table with beef, various vegetables, bread and a pot of real coffee. At the end of dinner they produced pastry as well, the first I had seen in a year. Even the Americans could not provide anything to match Aunt Lina's puff pastry with—God help us!—whipped cream.

After dinner I looked out the windows, whose panes had been replaced with pigs' bladders. Aunt Lina was embarrassed by this and told me that the local rabbi had condoned this infringement of the law, pointing out that even after a thousand years in Hungary they were still, obviously, "travelling in a foreign land." It was six-thirty and the street was emptying as people quickened their step to be indoors before the seven-o'clock curfew.

The two girls went down to the courtyard with buckets for water. The water supply had failed during the siege and it was then that the inhabitants of the ghetto, the oldest part of Budapest, discovered that the old bricked-up Turkish wells in their courtyards were still full of sweet water. When the Russians arrived gentiles began coming into the ghetto to ask for water.

"They looked at us with fear," said Aunt Lina, "as if we were going to revenge ourselves on them! What a country," she sighed. "What a people."

There was an enormous din coming from below, and I leaned out to see a group of ten or twelve Russian soldiers banging at the gate of our building, shouting, *"Barishnya! Barishnya!"* They were after women. Aunt Lina groaned and grabbed my arm, telling me that more than once the porter had let the Russians in and half the women in Budapest had already been raped.

I was just wondering what I was going to do to keep a dozen Russians out of the flat, when suddenly an even louder din broke out. I peered through the broken branches of the half-blasted trees lining the street and saw windows opening everywhere. Women were leaning out hammering on pots and pans and shouting at the top of their voices: "Patrol! Patrol!" The Soviet military police no longer condoned rape, and the troops, even when drunk as they usually were, lived in fear of the NKVD. The noise became ear-splitting and at last, with a few final petulant kicks at the gate, the Russians staggered off down the street.

"Well, George Gabori," I said to myself a little later, trying to get to sleep on Aunt Lina's old sofa, "you wanted to come

back to this shit-house of a country, and here you are! What
next?"

11

Socialist Paradise

THE FIRST MORNING AFTER MY RETURN from Germany I visited the new headquarters of the Social Democratic Party. They had moved to a building that had formerly been the Palace Hotel. The offices, hastily furnished, still had hotel fittings. No one under fifty was supposed to use elevators in Hungary at that time, but this restriction was meaningless as they seldom worked anyway. I climbed the stairs, thinking the shabby hotel a suitable headquarters for a party that, though one out of eight Hungarians now belonged to it, was still dirt poor.

The youth organization had its offices on the top floor. To my delight, Esther was there, thinner now, but still loudly jolly one minute and silently hysterical the next. She led me into another room where George Egri sat, having escaped from his forced labour camp without a scratch. We chatted for a while and Esther told me that her husband, Bela, had died on the eastern front during the war.

Later I ventured to complain about the Russians and their penchant for rape. "None of us would be alive without them," Esther rebuked me sternly. "We have to forgive them a few rapes."

"From which I take it you were not raped?" I replied with more cruelty than necessary.

Then they gave me a tour of the building, and I met old friends in almost every office, at last running into an old man shuffling down the corridor.

"Uncle Szabo!" I shouted, recognizing at once the man with whom I had blown up fuel barges. He blinked and stared.

"He is not Uncle Szabo, but Andras Soskuti," explained Esther. "Andras, you remember George Gabori?" But he had never seen me without make-up and dyed hair.

"I know the name Gabori but not the face—and you know the face of Soskuti but not the name!" Then he threw his arms around me. "I hoped every day to see you come home safely from Germany," he said. "I knew the Gestapo had you, and there I was, escaping torture."

"Forever!" commented a man who happened to be passing by us.

"Don't count on it," muttered Soskuti to no one in particular.

It turned out that Paul Justus had become one of the three chief leaders of the party and was in charge of all cultural, educational and ideological affairs apart from heading the propaganda department. Alone I went to his office and he received me with great friendliness. As I had expected, he immediately delivered a short political lecture explaining how lucky we were for not having been liberated by the Americans, who would no doubt have kept the neo-Fascist Horthy government in power. Instead we had the Russians, who would of course help us construct a socialist and democratic Hungary.

"Are we to cooperate with the Communists then?" I asked, hardly believing my own ears.

"Dear boy, we must ally ourselves with them even though there are points of disagreement. But we have every reason to be optimistic about the future."

He talked on and on about politics, his luminous eyes radiating confidence, full lips shaping themselves precisely as he poured forth Hungarian sentences of rare beauty and literacy. I was almost hypnotized when at last he asked if I would like to work for the party, perhaps in the youth organization?

"It would be a first step in your political career," he added, "and I would be able to keep an eye on your progress."

I agreed, and Justus promised to put my name forward at the next meeting, adding that right-wingers like Soskuti might be opposed, however. I assured him that Soskuti would vote for me.

As I left his office I had to flatten myself against the corridor wall: young men were passing with hampers filled with bread, vegetables and fruit, which they distributed from room to room. At that time inflation was over five hundred percent a month, and as a result employees everywhere were paid only part of their salaries in cash, the rest in kind and on a daily basis. The fact was that while the government was a mess the economy was enjoying a mild boom; food production was soaring, and it was clear to everyone that the reason for this was untrammelled free enterprise. Justus's statements about the right wing of the Social Democratic Party had in fact dismayed me. Evidently remaining his follower would place me squarely in the left wing. But I was still twenty years old; I had placed myself under Justus's tutelage, and for the time being at least I would stay loyal. It was going to be some time before I realized that my master, for all his fame, culture, erudition and political experience, was in fact devoid of all wisdom and in his political judgments a catastrophically naïve dilettante.

The next night I took the train to Putnok to visit my brother. Jumping down on the familiar platform, I was flooded with emotion. Suddenly I felt enormous arms around my waist and I was lifted off my feet to stare eye to eye with Uncle Feri Gyuran, former cellarmaster in the family business. Tears were spilling down the old man's cheeks.

"Thank God they did not murder you," he said at last, putting me down. "But all the rest, son, will be resurrected in our Lord Jesus Christ."

Nothing had changed in Putnok. The buildings, the gardens, everything was still untouched under a light coat of dust in the clear morning air. The only difference was that the town seemed to be emptier and slightly vulgar-looking.

My brother, Andrew, saw me from far down the street and we ran toward each other, arms extended. A few minutes later we were sitting in the house, nearly empty now, and he told me everything he knew. All the Jews of Putnok, about five hundred souls, had been sent to Auschwitz in freight cars. Our cousin, known as the most beautiful girl for several counties around, had married a year earlier and had given birth to her child in the freight car. The baby died en route, and when they arrived at Auschwitz Dr. Mengele directed the whole family, including the hemorrhaging mother, to the gas chambers.

"Nine people came back," said Andrew, "five girls and four older people. In my labour battalion we were luckier: six of our thirteen are still alive. A Hungarian soldier shot me in the thigh, and evidently I'll limp a bit the rest of my life, but it's nothing," he finished, forcing a pathetic smile.

He showed me the house, the garden and the wine cellar. Most of the furniture was gone, though the neighbours gave him back two beds, a kitchen table and chairs. The wine cellars, which extended over a hundred yards into the rocky hillside, were nearly empty. Once they had been filled with racks of enormous barrels from end to end; now only two small casks sat beside the door. My brother was trying to restart the business and was going to convert these into hard liquor.

"Well," said Andrew, sitting on a cask, "they tell me that about three percent of the gentile population perished, as against sixty-five percent for us. We have to forget. What else can we do? You've come back from the dead. Stay here with me, George. We'll both marry, raise families and rebuild the business of our ancestors."

Though my brother was barely a year older than I, he was still head of the family now, such as we were, and I could not easily ignore his wishes. But I had to tell him the truth: that I was expecting a call from Justus at any moment telling me that permission had been given for the Social Democratic Party to hire me. What I could not tell him was that we had both changed. I preferred the life of the capital and would no longer know what to do with myself in Putnok.

"Forgive me," he said. "I ought to have asked first about your plans. Well, even if they give you the job in Budapest, I'll send you half my earnings. But, George, why on earth are you becoming a Communist?"

"But I'm not!" I protested. "I'm a Social Democrat!"

"Communists and Social Democrats agreed perfectly when they nationalized big business some weeks ago," he replied.

"And I agree as well. Profits should go to the workers and not to the capitalists."

"That's nonsense," he shot back. "The profits will go to the state, not to the workers. Or do you believe that the workers of the Soviet Union have become prosperous since the state nationalized everything right down to their shoe laces?"

"But this is Hungary," I protested lamely. "Even the Communists admit that we have to have a degree of private enterprise and democracy here."

"Have you lost your wits?" he asked. "Do you believe that they are going to say the same thing once they're firmly in power? At least your friend Paul Justus is less hypocritical about it. I read a booklet by him advocating the national-ization of every last boutique and fruit stand in the country!"

"Justus is a theoretician," I replied. "I can't see him trying to nationalize your two casks of liquor here!" But in fact I could see him doing just that.

Later in the afternoon we sat in the garden, surrounded by the buzzing of bees and the heavy scent of pollen. The Jewish youths returned from the labour battalions arrived, accompa-nied by four of the girls back from Auschwitz. Two of the young men, brothers, were wearing the insignia of the Communist Party in their lapels and at first sneered at me quite openly. One was the local party secretary, the other a police lieutenant. Gradually their sneering stopped, however, as my brother set out wine and cake. We were after all the survivors of the Great Flood, sitting alone on Mount Ararat.

"I have to praise your brother," said the party secretary with evident sincerity, "for taking part in the reconstruction of the economy. Still, I can't understand why he stays aloof from politics, and why you, for that matter, are a Social Democrat. There's only one party that's fighting the Fascists and their rearguard."

"Then tell me," said Louisa, a frail girl with bone-white arms and her five-digit Auschwitz number clearly visible on her wrist, "tell me how it happens that all the small-time Nazis of Putnok, those who stoned us when we were driven into the cattle cars, are all now members of your Communist Party?"

The party secretary pulled a face and stammered, so his brother came to the rescue, saying, "Simple people were misguided by Nazi demagogy. They are being reeducated, and our party, supported by the glorious Soviet Union, will see that it is done."

"I won't argue with you about the justice of all this," I broke in, "because it would be in vain. But let's suppose, for the sake of argument, that your superiors ordered you to expel all former Nazis and to jail them."

"I would follow orders, of course," said the police lieutenant.

"I know that. What I want to know is what would you think about it?"

"I would think: all right, we are getting rid of the scum of the earth, maintaining the purity of the party, as Comrade Stalin taught in his oration at Lenin's funeral."

We all laughed at this example of double-think, even his brother; but there was an air of menace hanging over us as we sat amidst the droning of the bees, sweating from the heat and the wine. Louise and I began to dance to a scratchy old gramophone record, and when we came back to the table the others were arguing about Zionism.

"I have no intention of remaining in this country," one of the girls declared.

"But most of the mass murderers are either in American custody or else have been hanged in Budapest. If you go to Palestine you will find Arab murderers, armed by the English." The lieutenant looked at her in frank astonishment, and added, "What is Zionism anyway, except Jewish racism, Jewish Nazism, if you like?"

"The Soviet Union, as far as I know, is supporting the movement for a Jewish state," I broke in, "on the grounds that it is against British imperialism. Now where do you stand?"

But the girl did not wait for him to answer. "Look, George," she said, "this is not a subject for idle political chatter. It's a question of feelings and instincts. You want to build a country here; we want to build one in Palestine. It's as simple as that. Do the Arabs reject us there? Well, what have the Hungarians done to us here?"

There was nothing to reply to that. Evening approached, and with it, a cool breeze. We danced as the sun went down and the bees went to their hives. We were surrounded now by fireflies. The old songs scratched away on the gramophone and gently we swayed around the garden, holding the sticklike girls, in their shabby frocks, in a ghostly dance.

I stayed with my brother a week and was ready to leave anyway when Justus's secretary phoned to tell me that I had been unanimously elected by the twenty-one-member presidium of the Social Democratic Party as secretary of the youth movement for Budapest. The other news that day was brought to me by my brother who learned from the radio that the Americans had dropped atomic bombs on the Japanese cities of Hiroshima and Nagasaki. We had no idea what atomic bombs were, except that the radio explained something of their power and that they worked on the energy of the sun. But it was obvious that World War II, finished for us, was now finished for the rest of the world as well.

On the train for Budapest I mused about this amazing bomb and what it might mean. The Soviet Union clearly intended to stay in all the territory it had occupied during the war, including even the Danish island of Bornholm. The United States was infinitely more powerful than the Soviet Union, and now its power was unlimited. It was reasonable to assume that now the Americans would use this power to force the Russians to get out of those areas they had no right to stay in. No sane man could imagine that the Americans, with the atomic bomb, would let the Russians dictate to them, let alone blackmail them as they were to do in Berlin in 1948. I arrived back in Budapest more optimistic than ever.

I took up my post at once, worked as hard as I could and spent all my free time, in the traditional Central European way, in coffeehouses with my friends, especially with Esther and with George Egri, who eventually became my chief in the youth movement.

Among those who joined us now was Janos Garamvolgyi, a seventeen-year-old boy with red hair, a perfectly round head, bespectacled blue eyes, freckles and marble-white skin. He was frighteningly precocious, and he outdid even me in impudence. On top of this he was cynical to a degree that was at once amusing and intolerable. He was completely unsentimental and enormously ambitious, and so, I thought at first, capable of treachery. But nothing was farther from Janos. With devastating wit, he could reduce a politician to stammers by a single question and, when he chose, cause any meeting to break up in disorder. Later, when the Communist onslaught began against us, he proved one of their most serious obstacles and earned the nickname the Disorganizer.

Another man who became a friend was George Balazs, who

had fought for de Gaulle in Africa and Europe and then hurried home to join our ranks. He brought with him a French wife, a charming girl who never quite overcame her melancholy at being stranded on what she obviously considered a Barbary Coast. Then there was the poet George Faludy, famous throughout Hungary since his early youth. He was about ten years older than most of us, having gone into exile in 1938 and then been invited to America during the war by President Roosevelt. After the war he returned home, not for political reasons but, as far as we could make out, simply out of curiosity. He worked for the Social Democratic Party not out of any profound political convictions but, as he told us, because it was the most decent group around. Usually he refused to enter into arguments even when he joined us, as he sometimes did, during our coffeehouse sessions. At first I thought him cynical for his attitude and was confused that a man who rivalled Justus in erudition could at the same time be so different. I was still far away from knowing the difference between a fanatic and a humanist.

I first met Faludy in Justus's office. I walked in to find Justus arguing with him about something or other, but I could pay no attention because I had never seen anyone dressed that way before: suntan-coloured trousers, a semi-transparent shirt I thought silk (but which turned out to be my first glimpse of nylon) and shoes of leather so soft they appeared to be made of cloth. A dandy, I thought, but then changed my mind as, for the first time, I heard someone reply to Justus in a Hungarian as precise as his own and, even more surprising, besting him in argument.

Before the war most Hungarians followed the unwritten law that a respectable man did not marry before the age of twenty-eight or thirty. Strangely, though the war had relaxed both the morals and the hypocrisy of most people, many of my friends were getting married—as if lovers were not as easily obtainable as dates in Baghdad. Perhaps it was the result of having had the transitoriness of things demonstrated to us so vividly: suddenly everyone wanted to acquire the most permanent possessions available, a piece of land and a spouse.

It was not long before I joined the rest of them. Addressing a meeting one day, I found myself speaking largely to a lovely girl in the first row. She had masses of dark hair piled high on her head and she was so beautiful I had trouble remembering my text. Within a month we were married. The party obtained a flat for us—unless one had thousands of US dollars, this was the only way to get one—and we moved in along with her mother and her younger sister. A year later Judith gave birth to our daughter, Susan, and it was she who for the time being held together a marriage that was fast becoming untenable.

In the meantime Hungary was reviving with amazing speed. Most of the livestock in the country had been driven into Germany during the last months of the war, and that which remained had been slaughtered by the hungry Red Army. But the peasants were performing miracles with the small plots allotted to them during land redistribution. The camels of the Budapest Zoo, long missing, were discovered harnessed to a peasant's plough—which surprised no one, as many peasants harnessed themselves and their families for the same purpose.

When I had first arrived home the bread, made of corn flour, was practically inedible. The only cigarettes available were on the black market for dollars. Trainloads of citizens travelled in cattle cars or on the roofs of trains (the carriages were reserved for Russian soldiers), carrying carpets, bed sheets, silverware, anything at all into the country to exchange for bread, butter and chickens.

But two years later, in 1947, the economy was booming. Shops had opened up everywhere. The peasants, believing that they would keep the land they had been given, worked like demons. Factories were producing at capacity, their workers happy at the implementation of the social democratic principle of thirteen months' pay a year. The Communists for their part never ceased to point out that they wanted nothing more than free peasants, free commerce and full democracy. At election time Communist posters appeared reading: The Communist Party Defends the Property of the People. This was not, however, to be their last word on the subject.

The attitude of the Red Army was somewhat different, however. When I had arrived home from visiting my brother in Putnok, the first thing I saw in the Eastern Station was a company of Russian soldiers painting a beautiful new engine and row of carriages olive green, slapping paint on it hastily until it looked ancient and shabby. Amazed, I asked one of the silent onlookers what was going on.

"A Swiss Red Cross train arrived about an hour ago," said the man, whispering: "It brought back some old people, refugees, and carloads of medicine. The Russians told the old people to go home and then they took the medicine away in trucks."

Even as he spoke the Russians were painting CCCP (USSR) on the side of the engine.

"For God's sake," I protested, "they have wide-gauge tracks in Russia. They can't even use it! Are they crazy?"

"Son," said the old man, "you can stand here until your beard is longer than mine and you still won't figure out the Russians."

The next day I mentioned the incident at Social Democratic Party headquarters and caused a bit of a row. My colleagues explained that the Red Army could do as it liked. Someone pointed out that a Swiss train was nothing: how about the Gamma factory, our chief manufacturer of precision instruments? The Russians had claimed it for war reparations, and when their troops destroyed the equipment by attempting to get it off its mountings with dynamite the Soviet government demanded that we pay for the damage.

"And what about the thousands of people they rounded up after the armistice and have carried off to Siberia?" I protested.

"They'll come home after a proper peace treaty has been signed," said one of Justus's followers.

"Certainly they will," sneered Garamvolgyi, "provided, of course, there is no more work for them to do in Siberia."

"Why don't you complain to the Allied Control Commission?" shot back the young man.

"Because I don't speak Russian," said Garamvolgyi, "and the Americans have allowed Marshal Voroshilov to be put in charge of it! All complaints go directly to him. Then, if he cares to, he passes them down to his British and American colleagues, who, the asses, think this a splendid system. Besides, anyone who goes in there with a complaint usually soon finds himself in Siberia."

The next time I was called on to make a speech I addressed myself to the behaviour of the Soviet Union, attacking not only its policy toward Hungary but also the tyranny they were imposing wherever they went. It was during this speech that I noticed for the first time how far things had gone. It was not that my audience disagreed with me, but they were squirming in their seats, terrified at being in the same building as a man who dared utter such sentiments. Egri, sensing the atmosphere, stood up and did his best to take the sharp edge off some of my remarks.

The following morning as I entered the building I received a message to go to the office of Arpad Szakasits, secretary general of the party. Szakasits was known as a benign man, full of goodwill, so I was unprepared for the scene that awaited me. Even before I closed the door, he began pounding his desk in fury. Beside him sat Justus, lips pressed tightly together and an expression of cold disdain on his face. To my surprise, the other man present, Antal Ban, known as a right-winger and therefore theoretically my opponent, was looking at me with sympathy and approval.

It turned out that they had learned about my speech from two sources. One was the Communist Party, the other the secretariat of Marshal Voroshilov. Both groups were demanding my immediate dismissal on the grounds that I was a slanderer of the Soviet Union and a rabble rouser. Justus began scolding and Szakasits began bellowing about my "loud-mouthed insanity" in saying such things openly. I asked them if they found what I had said untrue, which silenced them a moment.

"Nevertheless," said Szakasits, ignoring my question, "we are going to have to expel you."

I paled at this, knowing that it meant I would probably be interned by the Communist minister of the interior, Laszlo Rajk. Then Ban came to my rescue, pointing out that if we as a party wanted to commit suicide, the quickest way to do it would be to start obeying the orders of Voroshilov and the Hungarian Communists.

"Should that come to pass," he added, pointing his hand vaguely in the direction of Justus and Szakasits, "the Social Democratic Party would be reduced to two members—you two gentlemen."

Ban made me take an oath not to make further "inopportune statements" in public and finally wrenched an agreement out of the other two to let me remain on that basis.

Several days later Justus invited me to his flat and we had a long discussion, which consisted largely of a lecture. First I provoked him by telling him about the case of a woman I knew of who had exchanged a fur hat in a village for a ham and had then taken the train back to the capital. Russian soldiers demanded the ham on the way back, and when she refused they shot her. I told him about the twelve young Jews who after spending months in a hospital in the American zone of Austria had been dragged off the train at the Hungarian border on their way home and deported to the USSR, charged with being "Fascist partisans."

"I know about all that," said Justus, "and much more. But if you compare it with the behaviour of the Hungarian army in the Ukraine during the war, the Russians still look like gentlemen. The fact is this country deserves a Russian army of occupation and we have nothing to complain about. I have been attacking certain aspects of their policy myself lately, and look, has anything happened to me? Do you imagine I could do the same thing in the American zone of Germany? For the first time in the history of our country we are laying down the cornerstone of democracy. Only the presence of the Red Army enables us to do this, and in addition it defends us against any possible return of fascism. It is obvious that Stalin knows that it is in his interest to have friendly, independent democracies on his borders, not satellite states. Be patient, George! The Nazis are gone; we are alive and free. The Communists are tolerating us; let us tolerate them."

He spoke on for some time, and although I noticed contradictions in his arguments I was, as usual, overawed by his erudition. Anyway, it was far more pleasant to believe him than not to.

I had wanted a life centred on politics, and for two years that is what I got: hard work that seemed to be having an effect. Then things began to change. The Communists never ceased to repeat their strange catch phrase: "Quantitative changes become qualitative changes." And for once they were right. As they gradually took over power, life slowly became intolerable for everyone.

We had expected a lot from the first general elections in which our party got eighteen percent of the vote, the Communists a little less and the democratic Smallholders' Party about fifty-three percent. We were happy with the Smallholders' majority if only because it meant that they would control the more important ministries and the country would at last be rid of the bully Rajk. But the day after the elections it became known that Rajk would not lose his job:

the Russians insisted and, reluctantly, our party gave its consent.

"What kind of democracy is this?" I asked Justus, outraged. "The army and the police are in the hands of the Communists. The secret police are exclusively theirs, and now we do not even protest when they keep their hold on the Ministry of the Interior!"

"You don't understand, my boy," soothed Justus. "At least this way we are keeping the most important posts out of the hands of the Smallholders. And as a new group of war criminals will soon be brought to trial, it is advantageous for us that the Communists should be the ones to hang them, not us."

Then Hungary was offered an enormous amount of badly needed equipment by the Americans. The Marshal Plan was beginning, and when the offer was made the leadership of our party met in an all-night session to argue about it. Those we called the rightists were all for accepting the American aid; the others, including Justus, opposed this and won. The next morning a tired and pale Justus explained to me, "The Marshal Plan is more a propaganda move on the part of the Americans than real help. You wait and see. The Russians will give us far more help in the reconstruction of our heavy industry. Anyway, it's no secret that Moscow doesn't want us to accept the offer. If we opposed them, they might intervene with force."

"Well, we certainly don't want to give them any excuse to do that, do we?" I replied, but Justus failed to notice the irony in my voice.

In the meantime our party was gaining strength among the population, and largely because of this we still dared to hope that the Russians would let us develop into a real democracy. The population evidently considered us the only means to keep the Communists away from absolute power and we, unknowingly, indulged them in this daydream.

Hungary's peace treaty with the Allies, including the USSR, was signed in Paris, but after a year the Red Army was still in the country in violation of the agreement. Still, the economy was booming—suddenly everything was obtainable—and not even the systematic plundering by the Russians could stop it. Then one day a bill was proposed in parliament ordering the nationalization of all factories, workshops, pubs and shops. It was Paul Justus who presented the bill, and when it was passed he was beaming with pride and happiness. Twenty-four hours later most merchandise had disappeared from the shops and meat suddenly became a rarity.

Now the Communists made their move against us. Using their usual tactics, they first attacked our right wing. The left wing stood by in silence while the best of our leaders were forced out. Needless to say, Justus took part in all this and was ready with ever shabbier excuses when I questioned his actions. By now even the rigidly doctrinaire training I had received since my youth, largely under his eye, could no longer prevent me from rebelling against the insanity going on around me. The respect I felt for Justus, which at one time had bordered on worship, still kept me from an open break, but I began avoiding him.

Finally the Social Democratic Party was merged with the Communists. I lost my job, of course, and after much effort finally found another with the National Wine Export Enterprises, where, as an ex-Social Democrat, I was sneered at and bullied by a wholly incompetent staff who owed their jobs to their status in the Communist Party. My brother's now-thriving wine business was of course taken over immediately, and the first action of the Communist manager was to mix the vintage wines my brother stocked together with inferior stuff from all over the district. This swill was now labelled "general wine."

Justus was made a deputy director of the Hungarian State Radio, where he received a high salary but was given no power. He was still optimistic, however, and when I visited him he explained carefully that since the Communists had relieved us of all responsibility we would now have time to think and to prepare for the future. I remembered my father's books and suddenly said to Justus that he reminded me of Pangloss in Voltaire's *Candide*. "In any situation you find yourself in," I told him, "even on the gallows, you will rejoice at living in the best of all possible worlds!"

"Yes," he replied to my astonishment and horror, "that's not a bad philosophy."

One morning in May 1949 I was stupefied to read in the Communist Party press (the only press left now) that Minister of the Interior Rajk and seven "accomplices" had been arrested and charged with a conspiracy to overthrow the people's republic and create a Fascist state; they were further charged with spying for England, Switzerland and the United States. One of those accused with Rajk was Paul Justus—who, as I well knew, hated Rajk so much he would not have given him the time of day, let alone conspired with him.

Four months later after an embarrassingly faked show trial Rajk was hanged and Justus was sentenced to life imprisonment. I had never liked Justus's wife much but felt it my duty to visit her. When I got to their disordered flat she was still numb with shock and repeated over and over that she had had no news from Paul. A few days later she was arrested herself, for "talking too much," and ended up sleeping on the concrete floor of the Kistarcsa Internment Centre.

Things had become intolerable, and Esther, Balazs and his wife, and Janos Garamvolgyi met secretly with me and we decided to try to get out of the country. By 1949 this was no easy task: the borders were death traps. But we had one thing in our favour. My brother still lived in Putnok, a few miles from the Czech border, and once inside Czechoslovakia it was far easier to get across into Austria. Balazs and his wife were to go first. They would go to Paris, where they could prepare for our arrival, Mrs. Balazs being French and a former member of de Gaulle's staff. For my part, I would have preferred going to England, but through the grapevine we learned of the experience of Antal Ban, who had escaped to the British zone of Austria about a year earlier. The officials of the British Labour Government then in power refused him entry to Great Britain, one of them even calling him a Fascist.

My brother came to Budapest and picked up Balazs and his wife. A week later he returned and told me that he had accompanied them to the likeliest border crossing, where he left them. The next day he saw them in the main street of Putnok in handcuffs, being led by two border guards. My brother was expecting to be arrested at any minute, as it was widely accepted that no one could hold his tongue under the tortures of the secret police. But the Balazses did not betray him.

So I too gave up all hope of escaping and, resigned to my fate, awaited my own arrest. I did not have to wait long. I was being followed by detectives everywhere I went. Then one day it was announced that Arpad Szakasits, president of the republic and former secretary general of the Social Democratic Party, had been arrested along with Anna Kethly, leader of the so-called right wing—that is, those who would not give in to the Communists—the minister of justice, several university professors and the poet George Faludy. Then it was my turn.

12

A Prisoner of the AVO

IT WAS JUNE 2, 1950. Like the rest of the overworked, undernourished and terrorized population, I was trying to get a good night's sleep before starting another dreary day. But someone was pounding on the door. I looked at my watch and was instantly awake. It was two in the morning, and all Hungary knew who knocked on the door at that hour.

My wife and baby daughter awoke, and then my mother-in-law rushed in, clutching her nightgown about her, pale with terror. I peered through the Judas hole and saw four men, obviously detectives. One of them I recognized: he had been shadowing me for days already. Now, however, he held a pistol in his hand while one of his companions flashed an ID card at the Judas hole.

"Are you George Gabori?" he asked.

"No," I shouted sarcastically at the door. "You've got the wrong address."

The AVO, Hungary's state security, were not famous for their sense of humour. When I unbolted the door they stuck a warrant under my nose. Two of them shoved me out of their way and began rummaging through the bedroom, while the women huddled in a corner and my daughter, Susan, began to cry.

"Get dressed," ordered my former shadow.

Now my wife, Judith, burst into tears and the detective turned toward her.

"It's just a formality," he said. "He'll be back in a week or two. It's just for a hearing."

"Can I give him his toothbrush and a towel?" asked my wife.

"He can bring along as much as he likes!" said the detective in a voice dripping with benevolence.

"Gentlemen," I said furiously, "the Arrow Cross arrested me in 1944 and gave me to the Gestapo. I doubt very much that you and your masters have learned any new tricks for robbing your victims. Kindly refrain from your little jokes with my wife!"

Their faces registered disbelief, and I knew that, not for the first time in my life, I had said something I was going to regret. Still stunned that a citizen had dared compare them with the Gestapo, the chief detective told me to take leave of my family. My daughter had already fallen asleep again. I leaned over her crib and looked a long time at her smiling face framed in silky red hair. Then I said good-bye to my wife and her mother and was led out by two detectives. Two others stayed behind to search the flat.

The second the door closed behind us I was doubled up by a blow to the abdomen. Then a pistol was produced and held to my head. There was not a sound in the building, although I knew that behind every door men and women cowered, thanking God that it was not their turn.

"You filthy traitor!" hissed the man with the pistol. "You dare mention us in the same breath with the Nazis? The mailed fist of the proletariat and the defenders of socialism?" His voice registered not only fury but real puzzlement. Another blow landed on my abdomen and they had to drag me the rest of the way down the stairs.

As they shoved me into the back of their car I experienced a sense of *déja-vu* almost amounting to nostalgia. When I recovered my breath I could not resist goading them some more.

"Why shouldn't I compare you with the Nazis?" I asked. "Six years ago men who looked and spoke exactly like you punched me around and put me in a similar car—German, not Soviet, manufacture. They called me a filthy Communist. Really, gentlemen, it's beginning to get boring."

Then I closed my eyes and waited for the pain, but there was only a flash of lightning as they hit me with the pistol butt. The next thing I knew I was being dragged into an office, obviously inside 60 Andrassy Street, once headquarters of the Arrow Cross Party, now the centre of the secret police apparatus. I faced an officer about my own age, with blond, slicked-down hair and baggy, watery eyes. He was picking his nose, examining the contents with interest. Then he looked at me with disgust and turned the desk lamp full into my eyes.

"George Gabori," he said in a strangely effeminate voice, "I am in charge of your case. We will begin with your personal data."

Then he switched on the overhead lights and I saw that there was a secretary sitting in the corner, pencil poised to take down my particulars. It was Eva Foldes, whose penchant for uniforms had now led her to the AVO. She looked smart, even smarter than in the Arrow Cross uniform I had last seen her in. She stared at me in confusion.

"This is your file," said the officer, stabbing a stack of papers with his forefinger. "The paper on top is your confession. You'll save us all a lot of trouble if you sign now."

He handed me a fountain pen and a cigarette, then shoved the paper toward me. It was blank except for a signature line on the bottom.

"Do you take me for an idiot?" I said. "Do you really think I'm fouling my trousers with fear and ready to sign a blank paper?"

"You'll sign eventually. You know that. You'll sign your grandmother's ass away before we're through with you!"

"My grandmother died in Auschwitz," I replied softly. "I survived other camps. You see," I added still more softly and with a smile, "I'm quite familiar with all *this*."

"You lousy Fascist!" he shouted. "I hope for your sake that you're not comparing me with the Nazis!"

"By no means, sir," I replied.

"I know your race and your type, Gabori. I'm looking forward to our next session."

"Just for the record, sir, my race is Hungarian."

He pressed a buzzer, guards came in and I was taken through the labyrinthine corridors to a cell. The guards shoved me inside the tiny cell. There was a slop bucket, three bare planks for a bed, a bulb burning in a wire cage overhead, and nothing else. Then, suddenly, the nervous tension I had built up during months of fear broke inside me, and I began to laugh in relief that it was over. The guards stared a moment, then locked me in. From time to time a warder would peer in through the Judas hole, but for the time being it seemed they were going to leave me in peace.

I began pacing back and forth, two and a half steps in one direction to the wall, about-face and back again. I did this carefully, like a child playing a game, and gradually my mind began to function in the same manner, thinking coherently and analytically, something that had become increasingly difficult to do in Hungary.

The twelve months before they arrested me had been an uninterrupted nightmare, with conditions growing visibly worse from week to week. There had been waves of suicides, and one gradually lost the habit of thought: to do anything except cultivate small pleasures behind closed doors was an invitation to despair and self-destruction. But now all that was over for me, and I felt enormous relief. There was nothing I could do to help my family, and for that matter they were probably better off without my presence. Now, at last, I could think in peace.

"Get up, bandit!" The guard's voice was loud but bored.

As he led me down the corridor I could hear sounds coming from the neighbouring cells, men muttering to themselves, some lamenting, others arguing with imaginary companions. There was a system of stop lights in the passageways. We waited until the light turned green, then continued. They wanted at all costs to prevent prisoners from catching a glimpse of one another.

"Put your nose to the wall. Keep it there and take two paces backward," said another guard as I was led into an office.

I obeyed, and though it became more and more painful as the minutes passed, I noted with pleasure that the extreme fear and anxiety I had experienced when the Gestapo arrested me were missing now. My feet were not shaking and a strange sort of indifference, mingled with contempt, was dominant in my mind. After about twenty minutes they took me into another office, where I was immediately blinded by bright lamps.

A fist lashed out and hit me in the stomach, striking again at the base of my neck as I doubled over. Then I was lying on my back looking up at a man with bloated lips, a greasy-looking face and an obviously Semitic nose. Behind him, smiling, stood the blond investigator who had interrogated me earlier.

"Awake?" asked the Jew benevolently, and only then did I realize that I had passed out.

"Let's cut the comedy," said the blond. "Sign now!"

Clutching my stomach, I dragged myself painfully into the chair before the desk. He shoved my confession—filled out this time—and a pen across to me.

"May I ask a question?" I said, addressing the Jew, who nodded almost eagerly.

"What does it feel like to beat up a fellow Jew?"

Even before I finished speaking, the blond jumped up, ran around and hit me with such force that the chair accompanied me to the floor. Leaning over, he continued slapping me back and forth, stopping only when blood began splattering the sleeves of his uniform. I got up, oddly feeling little pain, wiped blood off my face and smeared it all over the confession.

"I feel much better being beaten up by a gentile," I mumbled through split lips to the Jew. "After all, it's in keeping with the national tradition."

At this the Jew grabbed my shirt front and screamed in my face, "I'm not a Jew, you son of a bitch; I'm a Communist!"

He flung me to the floor, then placed one well-polished boot on my chest.

"Bring up that crap again," he said, "or compare state security with the Arrow Cross, and I'll personally break you on the wheel!"

"Listen, Gabori," said the blond, "be reasonable. I am going to get a confession out of you, but I also intend to demonstrate to you the difference between us and the Arrow Cross. Imagine," he added, bemused, "comparing us with them!"

I licked the blood away from my upper lip and faced him: "I can't say that I've noticed the slightest difference so far."

"It depends on you. Tell us the truth about your crimes, and you'll see our attitude change as well. You are a spy and a bandit, and our job is to protect the people's republic from people like you."

"First," I replied, "tell me if you're serious or indulging in a particularly crude joke."

"Your idol Justus has already confessed to his crimes. Now it's your turn."

"Justus was my friend long ago," I replied. "I don't know what you forced him to confess, but I have nothing to do with it. I am neither a spy nor, to use your quaint jargon, a bandit."

"You're even more insolent than your reputation, Gabori," said the blond, then he yawned. "We'll break you, however."

A guard was summoned and I was taken to a corridor of cells, where at a green door, number fifty-eight, we stopped and I thought they were putting me back in my former cell. But then the guard suddenly pushed me farther, stopping again at a steel door with no number on it, and shoved me inside.

The cell was about three yards long and two wide. Above the bare plank bed ran a sewage pipe that dripped watery filth onto the planks in a steady trickle. Keeping to the edge of the planks, I sat down, buried my face in my hands against the harsh overhead light and immediately fell asleep sitting up. A few minutes later I jumped to my feet as a guard, peering in through the Judas hole, banged on the door.

"No sleeping permitted!" he shouted.

Sitting up again, I reflected on my fate. It did not bother me so much that they charged me with trying to overthrow their rotten state: that was almost flattering. The spying annoyed me, however. As the hours passed I had to find something more constructive to occupy my mind with, so I began repeating all the poems I had memorized from childhood on, setting myself the task of reconstructing all the passages that were hazy in my memory. I was so engrossed in this that sweat broke out on my forehead and I scarcely noticed when a warder came in with a mess kit with the slops that passed for supper.

"After you've eaten," he said, "you can sleep. Lie on your back, cross your arms on your chest and keep your face toward the light. No other position is allowed."

A little later I wiped the puddles of filth off the planks and stretched myself out along the edge, but no matter how I lay the sewage dripped on me. Sleep was impossible, so I got up and paced back and forth; then, suddenly furious, I kicked at the steel door until an astonished warder appeared.

"Are you out of your mind?" he shouted.

"No," I said. "Give me a blanket!"

"Go fuck yourself, Fascist," he said, with more amusement than anger in his voice.

Sitting at one end of the planks, I tucked my knees up under my chin and at last fatigue overcame me and I slept. Sometime later I awoke as something tugged at my shoes. Two plump rats jumped off the plank and scurried into the corner, where they turned to face me, tiny red eyes glittering in the light. I sat absolutely still, and after a while they approached again, cautiously.

"Go to sleep!" said a guard through the Judas hole, "or I'll put you to sleep!"

"Get rid of these rats!" I shouted back, but no reply came.

For the rest of the night I slept fitfully a few moments then was awakened by the rats nibbling at me. By morning I was shaking with exhaustion. At breakfast I saved a bit of my bread to bribe the rats with; the stench of the sewage was so nauseating that I could not eat all of the little bit they gave me anyway. Then I paced up and down while the rats stayed out of sight beneath the planks, and recited the poems of Mihaly Babits, beginning with:

> The Lord said: Rise and go to Nineveh
> And shout against the city wherein evil
> Flows like filth across My feet!
> Vileness rises there and overflows its banks!
> Jonah rose to run, but not to Nineveh. . . .

At that point my memory failed and it took me the next two hours to recall the following lines. I was so engrossed in this game—it had been years since I had had the leisure and the peace of mind to indulge in it—that I scarcely noticed when the warder came in with a mess kit of greasy beans for dinner. I left about a third of the revolting mush for the rats this time, but it did not help: they kept me awake that night as well.

Each morning I scratched a mark on the sewage pipe. After ten days I began to hope that they had forgotten all about me. I was giving the rats almost half my rations some days, and at last they left me alone at night. I had not had a chance to wash since my arrest, and now I began to be disgusted by my own stench. My face was covered with stubble and my eyes were inflamed and gummed up. I tried to tell myself that the death camp at Turckheim had been worse, but it was no use. Death was closer there, but we had known the war was nearly over and the Americans would soon arrive. Now there was nothing to fall back on except poetry, and I spent all my waking hours remembering lines until I had recalled enough for a two-hour recitation at least.

On the morning of the fifteenth day they came for me at last. I was taken to the first floor, where the corridors were covered with a luxurious red carpet, and the doorways, of carved wood, reached to the ceiling. The office I was led into was even more impressive. The desk and tables were of mahogany, some with gilt legs. There were leather chairs here and there, and on an Empire table in the centre was a silver coffeepot and cups. The smell of fresh coffee made me dizzy as I stood alone, left by the guard, and blinked at the garish socialist-realist paintings on the walls, the mandatory portraits of Stalin and Rakosi, the Hungarian premier, and of course Lenin, asking the advice of an old workman.

Behind the desk, framed against the background of heavily brocaded curtains, sat a man in an elegant grey suit. He was puffing on a cigarette, exhaling smoke through the nostrils of a nose once badly broken, and watching me through narrowed eyes. I was certain I had seen him before but had no idea where.

"Do you smoke, Gabori?" he asked, motioning me to take a seat. "Have you had a look at yourself lately? You look like dog shit. My officers are complaining about you, you know."

"I've been complaining about them as well, sir," I replied. "May I ask you a question?"

He smiled slightly and raised his palms in a gesture of supreme indifference.

"I thought I recognized you, and now it occurs to me that I saw you before the war, at the trade union resort at Göd. Weren't you a glovemaker then?"

"Correct. I was at Göd before the war. Now, since I am indulging you, what is it you think you have to complain about?"

"The rats in my cell," I said. "It's very unsanitary. I noted in my previous prisons, Dachau and some other German institutions, that it was the rats who spread typhus. As for the beatings, of course I'm quite used to that, though more from anti-Semites than . . . ."

I stopped as someone knocked on the door and the man raised his little finger for silence.

"Comrade general!" an officer said. "I've brought the dossier!"

As he put the folder on the desk I saw his face and felt my blood turn to ice at the double revelation: the "comrade general" was Peter Gabor himself, the head of the secret police; and the officer speaking to him, a lieutenant colonel now, was Hugo Nemeth, who had once expelled me from the trade union and then turned Gestapo informer. For a few seconds fear of the consequences held my fury in check; then I jumped to my feet.

"Well, Nemeth! You've risen quite high in our people's democracy—considering you were a Gestapo informer the last time I saw you! Seeing you here really ought not to surprise me, though, since there are two other rats in . . . ."

Nemeth, purple with rage and with panic in his eyes, smashed his fist into my mouth. I did my best to laugh as I hit the floor, delighted at this corroboration of my claims, but he followed up the blow with a furious kick to the back of my head and I passed out.

I woke up in a clean, whitewashed cell, lying on a real mattress and covered with a blanket. There was a young guard, a peasant boy of no more than twenty, sitting beside the bed. The second thing I noticed was that there was a handle on the door: I was no longer in a cell.

"Can I wash?" I asked him. "I haven't washed in two weeks."

"Where have you been for two weeks?" he replied.

"In the cellar with the rats."

"You must be joking! We don't have any rats here."

But when I asked again, he led me down a corridor to a shower room, where I luxuriated under the hot water until the boy lost patience and led me off, wrapped in my bed sheet, to another room where my hair was trimmed. There was no question of shaving me, as my face was a mass of bruises and scabs. Then I was put in a cell with a table, a bunk and, of all things, an armchair! Except for the Judas hole, it looked like a provincial hotel room. What next? I wondered, stretching out on the bunk.

A few minutes later the blond investigator arrived, clutching a pile of paper.

"The comrade general orders you to write a full account of that period of your life when you knew Colonel Nemeth. I shall return every hour to check on your progress."

The blond stared and compressed his lips in anger as a

smile of delight broke out on my face. I had been right! An ex-Gestapo informer was too much even for these scum! He made no move to strike me, however, so I concluded that for the time being the general had ordered them to lay off me. When the blond left I sat down and, beginning with my trade union days, wrote down everything I could remember that had the slightest connection with Nemeth. If I could get the son of a bitch downstairs with the rats it would be worth my own arrest. I scribbled away, my tongue exploring the sweetish gap where Nemeth's boot had cost me yet another tooth.

Soon the young guard appeared with my clothes, freshly laundered and pressed, and lunch, which now was of noticeably better quality. From time to time the blond came in and carried off what I had written, complaining loudly that my writing was illegible. This went on for a week, and my delight began to pall when they forced me to continue. Finally I was inventing new villainies for Nemeth, just to have something to write. When the stack of paper was used up, the blond came in again.

"The comrade general orders you to begin all over again, from the beginning!" he said and left.

For the next two weeks I wrote until my arm was half paralyzed, repeating the section about the Hotel Majestic at least twenty times, but they were never satisfied. Only gradually did I realize my predicament: Nemeth was one of their comrades; if they could demonstrate that I was lying about him, I would be lucky to get off with a quick bullet in the neck. At the end of the eleventh day they would not let me go to sleep but kept me up writing all night and so through the next day and night.

Trembling and barely able to sit on the chair, I was ready to beg them to take me back to the cellars. Then, suddenly, when I rebelled and stretched out on the bunk, no one came in to wake me up. I must have slept sixteen hours when a new guard came in with black bread and coffee.

"Come with me, bandit!" shouted the blond as I was finishing the coffee. He had a gleeful expression on his face, which made me extremely nervous. A few minutes later I was again facing General Gabor, the second most powerful man in the country.

"Here is a synopsis of your statements about Mr. Nemeth," said the general. "Read it and sign it."

So it was *Mister* Nemeth now! Carefully controlling my expression, I took the papers and began reading.

"As for you, Gabori," he continued, "I suggest you don't make a habit of informing on the officers of state security."

Suddenly I realized that if he had not had some reason of his own for wanting to be rid of Nemeth my outburst two weeks before would have cost me my life. Reading the last page of the document, from which it was clear that Nemeth had already been arrested, I signed quickly.

"Follow the example of your Trotskyite friend Justus," said the general. "It will save your life. I assure you, if you confess, you will get off with a life term."

"With your permission, sir, a life term seems rather long to someone my age."

"Not half as long as eternity," he said, and he nodded toward the guard.

As I was led down the corridor someone made a mistake handling the traffic lights. We went past a green light, around a corner, and straight into another guard and prisoner. The other guard flung his prisoner toward the wall, but too late: I had seen the bruised and battered face of Istvan Riesz, former minister of justice.

I was put back into cell fifty-eight. There were no rats in sight and I almost rejoiced at the familiar filth of the place. At least there was no writing table. This time I did not continue reciting poetry to myself but invented a new game. Justus had made me memorize long passages of the excruciating works of Marx, and I began reciting these now and matching them up with the various decrees of Stalin and Rakosi, gradually building up a mass of *prima facie* evidence that the latter gentlemen were deadly opponents of Marxism.

Four or five days later they came for me in the middle of the night and took me to the blond.

"Have a seat, Gabori," he began amiably enough. "Your confession has been prepared. Sign here. The rest is up to the judges."

Quickly I glanced over the pages in which I confessed to conspiring to overthrow the people's republic and to *having imported chocolate bars containing orders from the French Deuxième Bureau for my fellow spy, Paul Justus*!

"Let's make a deal," I sighed at last. "We both know there's not a word of truth in all this. At least leave out the part about spying. It means a death sentence and I won't sign it."

Without replying, the blond pushed the buzzer on his desk,

then sat on the edge, swinging his leg lightly so that it kicked my knee.

"You'll regret this. In a short time you'll be begging me to permit you to sign," he said as two stocky guards came in and rolled up their sleeves.

I was taken to a room lined entirely with rubber. There were two tables in the centre, a powerful reflecting lamp above each. The blond followed us in.

"For the last time, will you sign or not?"

"Not the spying part," I said.

"Take off your shirt, shoes and socks," said one of the guards.

I was expecting a repetition of the Gestapo's foot-beating, but instead they made me sit on one of the tables with my knees drawn up and my arms around them. Then they tied my ankles and wrists together, put a pole under my knees and suspended me between the tables. Immediately I rolled over, so that my head was toward the floor. Then the blond grabbed my hair and began spinning me around like a ferris wheel, and as I revolved the other two beat me full force from both sides. Each time I lost consciousness they revived me with cold water. At last they put me back on the table. My body felt as if I were lying in a bed of hot coals.

"Ready to sign now?" smiled the blond. "Or shall we begin again?"

I said nothing, and they helped me back to my cell where I swayed on the edge of the planks, trying to shake off the sickening sensation of spinning. I stretched out and immediately began hallucinating: the ceiling was filled with rats trying to climb down to me.

"Sign the confession!" insisted a voice in my head. "They're going to kill you anyway, so why not choose the quicker death?" Then, my head clearing, I remembered the former minister of justice, Riesz. They were hauling in the big fish now and no doubt would hang them. When that happened it usually meant life terms for the smaller fry. I sat up, more determined than ever not to sign.

Soon a guard came in screaming for me to get up. He took me upstairs to the blond's office.

"Do have a cigarette, Gabori," he said.

"Why not?" I said, and lit up as he handed me the text of my confession. Nothing had been changed.

"Really, sir," I began, "I'd like to make your job easier, but I have one reservation still."

"Yes?" he said with almost childlike eagerness. Obviously he was being pressured to get my case out of the way.

"That bit about the chocolate bars. It's much too precise."

"Why?" he asked, sincerely puzzled.

"It sounds true. Take that out, leaving the whole spying part vaguely worded, and I'll sign it. Then even if you hang me no one will doubt my innocence."

"Do you think I'm one of your flea-market Jews, Gabori, that you can bargain with me?"

"General Peter is a Jew," I replied. "Comrade Rakosi, the secretary general of the party, is a Jew; Minister of Defense Farkas is a Jew; half the Politburo are Jews; and finally I'm a Jew. It seems to me, sir, that you're in a flea market—as you call it—whether you like it or not."

I waited for the blows to fall, but he did not move a muscle.

"Will you sign or not?" he said at last.

"Not as it stands now."

As he buzzed for the guards I puffed furiously on the cigarette, as if nicotine would give me courage. Five minutes later I was on the floor of yet another room, being rolled up—it was almost nostalgic—in a wet blanket, then strapped into a chair.

"Is this all you've learned from the Gestapo?" I muttered to them. "I'll scream awhile, then be unable to talk even if I want to. If you were professionals you'd know rubber truncheons are far more effective!"

This was not really the degree of cockiness it sounded. Oddly, all sense of fear had left me and I was almost indifferent to what was coming. One of them held my head and stuffed a rag into my mouth.

"Sign!" shouted the blond.

I began to shake my head when suddenly it flew back to hit the chair as the current convulsed me. The old hammmering began in my brain and my arteries felt as if they were bursting. Thrusting my feet against the floor with all my strength, I toppled the chair over backward and landed with a crash.

"He's passed out," said a guard. "The Fascists trained the bastard too well."

"Wake him up," said the blond wearily.

Unstrapping me, they began massaging my heart and one pulled the rag out of my mouth. Unable to fake it any longer, I finally opened my eyes.

"Is it worth it, Gabori?" asked the blond, peering down at

me. "Why make trouble? You are an enemy of the new order. Even if you were not a spy, it was only because you had no opportunity. You're guilty in any case. Don't you see? So sign!"

"I won't sign my life away on the basis of that dubious logic," I sighed. "Obviously, if you break me I'll sign. In the meantime, you have not broken me."

"I'm a tolerant man," he said. "Again I'm going to give you time to think it over. But I warn you, if I have to bring you back to this room again you'll leave it crippled for life—or not at all."

A little later I sat on my plank bed thinking over what he had said and knowing that he had meant it. Then suddenly there was shouting from somewhere down the corridor: "Comrades," someone pleaded, "give me a hearing! I am a Communist!" As if in reply another voice echoed, "I must speak to Comrade Rakosi! He promised he would set me free if I signed the confession. Comrades, I have signed!" Then the first voice began singing the "International" in so pitiful a manner that I put my hands over my ears to shut it out.

At last I heard guards running down the corridor; then all was silent again, and my pity gave way to disgust. There had been no one, either in the Gestapo prison of Budapest nor in the camps of Germany, who would have made a scene of that sort, pleading that he was a loyal Nazi! That's how far we had come under our new socialist order: now the victims, betrayed and deluded fanatics, still pleaded love for their tormentors.

A few hours later they took me upstairs again, this time to the Jewish officer I had not seen for some weeks.

"You have a very bad opinion of us, Gabori," he began, after offering me a chair, cigarettes and coffee.

"On the contrary, sir. I am beginning to be impressed with your efficiency. Do you remember how after the burning of the Reichstag Goering was unable to prove that Dimitrov was guilty? Well, compare that with your spectacular success in the Rajk-Justus trial, to name just one example."

"Are you enjoying your cigarette?" he asked with interest, as if it were a matter of some consequence.

"Yes, I am. I think you have a bad conscience for having beaten up a fellow Jew, and now you are trying to bribe you way back into favour with the Almighty with small favours. Yes, I enjoy the cigarette, and the coffee is excellent. Perhaps for dessert you will suggest a way in which I can escape the gallows for a crime I did not commit?"

"I am not in charge of your case," he replied softly. "I need you as a witness in the cases of Vajda, the humourist, and the actress Ladomerszki. I believe you know them?"

"Another cigarette, please, and more coffee. To help my memory."

Hastily he gave me both, then said, "I've been speaking with the officer in charge of your case, by the way. It's possible that certain details may be dropped from your confession. But first of all, give up the insane idea that you are here to give us advice! You've caused enough trouble already, and I don't think you appreciate how lucky you are after what you've done. A lot of our men are itching to torture you to death because of their comrade!"

"Nemeth?" I asked. "Gestapo informers get what they deserve!"

He watched me in tight-lipped silence as I lit another cigarette and began thinking furiously: if Vajda and Ladomerszki were already in prison it was unlikely that a statement would be asked from me. I respected both of them and had no intention of saying a word about either.

"I will make no statement," I said simply.

"No? Well, what about Thomas Racz?" he asked.

This was unexpected. Racz had been a police informer, put into the youth movement of the Social Democratic Party by the AVO themselves. If they had turned against the scum I would be happy to help them.

"Racz?" I began, in mock astonishment. "Well, I don't think I can say anything about him that you don't already know. I don't like the man, but I have always respected him for his Trotskyite principles."

"Indeed!" said the Jew happily, and he began scribbling hastily as I went on to give the most damaging account I could think of concerning my dealings with Racz.

After I signed the statement in triplicate I was taken back to the cellar. Beginning that night, I was taken every night for three weeks to the rubber-lined room and each time tortured in a different way. First they played what they called the ball game, which consisted in shoving me violently from man to man until I fainted. Then I was made to stand on tiptoe far back from the wall, against which I had to lean supported only by my finger tips. When I collapsed from this I had to do push-ups and was truncheoned each time I collapsed from that. On other days they spun me on the pole again, beating me as I revolved between the tables. And finally, after various other tortures in which they outdid even the ingenuity of their Russian instructors, they tried electric shock again. They kept this up so long that in the end I could neither speak nor move, and they deposited me in my cell and left me alone for many days.

I was beginning to get some of my strength back when, one day, they came again and took me back to the blond.

"You've had all the time to think that we intend to give you," he began. "I hope you've come to the right decision. You could have saved yourself all this by signing in the first place!"

He looked at me with marked distaste, and no doubt I was a shocking sight. He handed me the confession and I slumped over in the chair and looked at it. It was the same; they had changed nothing.

"As you say, you've given me time to learn my lesson," I muttered, "and I've learned it. Now I'm going to give you all the time you need to learn your lesson. Take your confession and forget about it. I won't sign it as it is."

He threw me a murderous look, then, drumming his fingers on the desk top, finally picked up another document and handed it to me.

"Read it!" he snarled.

As I had long hoped and expected, they had drafted a second version. This one said vaguely that I was a dangerous conspirator against the state and had in all probability spied for an unnamed foreign country. Without a word I picked up the pen and signed.

"You don't deserve this leniency, Gabori," he said, "after the trouble you've caused, not only to me but to the general."

"People have been arresting me all my life," I replied. "If on occasion I give in to the temptation of pointing out certain home truths, well, sir, you have the choice of beating me to death or else facing those truths. But really, don't you think it a bit thick, your complaining about *my* behaviour?"

"Do you want to know what Justus said about you? He was a tougher nut to crack than you were, by the way."

He handed me a paper in which Justus had evidently stated that I was a Trotskyite capable of leading the Trotskyite faction and a man who, given the chance, would fight actively against the existing order. He also praised my political knowledge and organizational ability.

"I'm flattered," I replied truthfully. "But there's hardly a case against me here—not that you people require one, of course."

"Hasn't it yet penetrated your thick skull, Gabori, that you're under preventive arrest? We're not under Roman law here, you ass. The workers' and peasants' state has demanded your detention because of the crimes you intended to commit."

"Seriously," I replied, "what have you people to do with the workers and peasants? You've never once consulted any of them, not regarding their wages, the collectivization of their land, their working conditions, not about anything. That you evidently really believe that, having no connections at all with the people, you nevertheless somehow express their will— well, talk about thick skulls. . . ."

The least I expected as a result of this conversation was a bad beating, but he continued to look at me quite calmly, even indulgently, like a psychiatrist with a patient.

"I won't argue with you about it," he said. "If you really can't see that the party, under the leadership of Comrade Rakosi, is working for and with the people, I must assume that you are either insane or mentally retarded."

"Possibly," I shot back, "but considering that the prisons of this country are overflowing with prisoners, one suspects then that there is some genetic fault at work in the nation. So many insane, so many mentally retarded. Except, of course, for those who are really your enemies—those of your own comrades whom you have arrested and tortured to death!"

"That's enough!" he shouted, but still did not hit me. "If we need you again, we'll send for you. Otherwise, Gabori, prepare yourself for at least twenty years in prison."

They left me alone for about three weeks, during which time I sat alone in my cell. My constitution seemed to thrive on the bean mush they gave me every day, and my cuts and bruises healed rapidly. As for my mind, the constant repetition of my growing repertoire of poems kept it active as did imaginary philosophical dialogues I constructed, conversations between Voltaire and Marx, Plato and Stalin, Hitler and Rakosi. Then I was summoned for my last visit with the blond investigator.

The curtains in his office were open and I stared at the leaves of the trees on Andrassy Street shaking yellow in the autumn wind.

"You lucky swine, Gabori!" he began. "Some angel is looking over you. Come, sign this."

It was a document stating that I was to be interned "for an indefinite period of time."

"Charming!" I said, handing back the pen and blowing on the ink. "Instead of twenty years in a cell I'm being sent to a camp. Well, I don't suppose it will be any worse than life is out there." I nodded my head toward the street.

"You son of a bitch; you Fascist bastard!" he screamed. "Get him out of here," he bellowed as the guards came in.

13

A Humanistic Education

THE GUARDS TOOK ME DOWN to a small courtyard where a large number of people were lined up facing the brick walls. Walking down the line, I saw the poet Faludy, black hair hanging almost to his shoulders now. My heart leaped at the knowledge that I would be going with him, and as I passed he smiled slightly, glancing sideways, and I was filled with joy.

Beside Faludy was George Egri, which made me still happier. Wherever they were sending me, I could not complain about the company. I slowed my pace, knowing the guard would kick me, which he promptly did. Stumbling, I caught myself against the wall just between Egri and Garamvolgyi, and as I had hoped, the guard left me there. Garamvolgyi's glasses were shattered and the cuts they had made around his eyes were still fresh. It was like a reunion.

Obviously everyone who had had any connection with the Social Democratic Party had been rounded up at the same time.

Soon they herded us into black marias and, though the guards cursed us, we huddled together in the dark and whispered furiously. Three-quarters of an hour later we arrived at the Kistarcsa Internment Camp, a prison left over from the old regime. Faludy, Egri, Garamvolgyi and I were pushed into the same cell and immediately fell on one another in glee.

For the first two nights we scarcely slept at all but sat on the two-tiered bunks and talked endlessly, whispering even at night until our voices gave out, exchanging stories. Faludy's was the most fantastic. Hoping that he was going to be given a public trial, he had confessed to the AVO that while in America in 1942 he had regularly met with two CIA agents at a drugstore at the corner of Broadway and Forty-second Street. One was Major Edgar Allen Poe, the other Colonel Walt Whitman. When pressed for details by the delighted AVO, Faludy added that sometimes they were joined by another CIA man, a club-footed agent known as Z.E. Belbub. He also confessed that more than once they had taken him to CIA headquarters, where they all got drunk to the gills on Coca-Cola.

Egri, who had been the general manager of the National Paprika Export Enterprises, had "confessed" to mixing the powder of crushed red bricks into the paprika so as to sabotage the national economy and bring the Hungarian people into disrepute.

As for Garamvolgyi, he had not the slightest idea why he had been arrested, but after the first beating he took the pen and, with total indifference, signed his confession without even reading what they had written.

"Well," he said raising his eyebrows, "we are not all idiots like you, Gabori, letting ourselves be beaten half to death just for the pleasure of telling the AVO how much they resemble the Gestapo!"

"How did you know that?" I asked, astonished.

"We had the same investigator, that blond bastard. He divided his time between beating me up and complaining about you."

When pressed, Faludy told us that he had spent his weeks in solitary confinement composing poems in his head, the first word of each poem beginning with the next letter of the alphabet to keep them in order. Being somewhat older than the rest of us, he was afraid his chances of surviving our imprisonment were slimmer than our own and asked us if we would memorize some of the poems. Needless to say, we were all delighted at this opportunity to become part of the literary history of the nation, as it were, and we began at once. So we spent much of the third night whispering over and over some of the most beautiful lines any of us had ever heard, at last falling asleep with the words still echoing in our minds.

We did the same thing the next day. Egri's almost photographic memory outstripped the rest of us: he remembered everything so exactly that years later, when the poems were printed in the West, he was able to correct passages the poet himself had forgotten. Perhaps the most beautiful of all, and certainly one of the most astonishing lyrics in a literature overflowing with lyrical poetry, was Faludy's poem to his wife: "To Zsuzsa, From My Tomb." I was so taken with it, and so pleased to be chosen to memorize it, that I begged the poet to repeat it over and over to me; then I paced back and forth for hours, repeating it silently until by nightfall it was locked away forever in my mind. In this way, without even trying, Faludy kept our spirits up by the sheer loveliness of his art. The AVO continued to leave us more or less in peace, and for the better part of a week we almost forgot where we were.

When our minds were exhausted from the effort of memorizing, Faludy would entertain us with stories from his travels all over the world. He had lived in Paris, had roamed the deserts of North Africa with Berber nomads, had been a tail gunner in air raids on Japan and had fought with the US Army from New Guinea to the Aleutians. In the midst of all this he had found time to acquire a vast and thorough store of erudition, to memorize the better part of the *Iliad* in Greek, to translate medieval Latin hymns and to haunt most of the galleries of Europe until he had seen nearly every great painting left on the continent. From this mass of knowledge he gave us capsule lectures on history, art, philosophy and literature, but never politics—for unlike Justus, the poet's erudition was wholly at the service of mankind, not ideology.

It was the third time I had met someone of this sort, the others being Uncle Eugene and Father John in Dachau, and finally it began to sink into my mind that this adamant refusal to pay attention to politics was not, as I had suspected, an escapist tactic of dissident intellectuals. Listening to Faludy talk one evening, I looked past him, his words blurring in my ears, and realized that the most decent, the sanest and evidently the happiest men I had met so far had shared this trait. It made an impression, but at twenty-seven I was still not ready to take the lesson to heart. Once I drew the poet aside and tried to get him to discuss politics with me. He listened patiently awhile, then smiled. "Let me give you a quotation from Erasmus of Rotterdam," he said. " 'When faced with a choice of evils the wise man does not choose.' "

"But," I protested, "the Social Democratic Party is not an evil!"

"Of course it's not," he replied evenly. "But it seems to me that if you spend your life thinking only about politics, even Social Democratic politics, you are unlikely to find the wisdom Erasmus was talking about. The only choices we ever have in this country are between evils. We need wisdom, not politics."

We had been in Kistarcsa about ten days when they came for us and led us to a huge room where mountains of old army uniforms and boots were heaped all over the floor. We spent the next two days sorting these out and making them up into prisoner's kits. A wide red stripe was painted on each outer garment. We knew that we would be wearing these ourselves soon. The only question was whether it would be in a Hungarian camp or in Siberia.

Then on the third morning we were taken to a courtyard where hundreds of prisoners were already standing in formation. An AVO man bellowed the order for us to strip. Shivering in the cold wind, we piled everything—underwear, watches, toothbrushes, all we had—at our feet.

"Our socialist order," shouted the AVO man from a stool, "is permitting you to work and earn your own liberation. We are issuing you new uniforms now, and you will wear them until the day of your enlightenment!"

"*Arbeit macht frei*," I whispered out of the corner of my mouth, glancing at Faludy beside me; but he did not respond and I saw with astonishment that, even now, he was busy thinking about something else, probably a poem.

We stayed in formation until around mid-afternoon, when some six hundred prisoners had been issued uniforms. The trousers that came to the knees on some men and over the boots of others would have been comical had it not been for the fact that if we ended up in Siberia inadequate clothing, especially boots, might well mean death.

We were sagging from exhaustion when at last the first of twelve trucks pulled up to the gates. With kicks and blows we were driven fifty at a time into them. Egri and I flanked Faludy to protect him. Confronted with an AVO man, he was like a small child facing a rabid dog: unafraid, and because of it in deadly danger. Within a few minutes we were driven to the Kistarcsa railway station and herded into freight cars. It was exactly like the trip to Dachau, except this time we were given no food or water.

All we knew was that we were travelling eastward, and throughout the cold night we were chilled further by the fear that we were heading for the USSR. The next morning the train stopped, and through the planks we could read the name of the tiny station, a name some of us had never heard of before: Recsk. We were high up in the mountains of northern Hungary, and after a moment someone remembered that Recsk had once been the largest gold mine in the country.

Some time later military commands were shouted on the platform, the doors were opened and we were ordered out. Flanking Faludy, Egri and I formed up as hundreds poured out of the freight cars and AVO guards strode up and down before us, looking so much like SS men that I had to blink to bring myself back to the present. The view before us was breath-takingly beautiful. In the distance the tallest mountains of Hungary rose in a blue mist, hovering in the cold air.

"Anyone who tries to escape or falls out of line will be shot on the spot," bellowed a short, fat AVO officer. "When I give the command, march! And you will sing military songs until I tell you to stop."

The AVO man ordered Kalman Kery out of the ranks. Formerly chief of staff of the First Hungarian Army, Kery had flown to Moscow in 1944 to plead for an armistice with Stalin. For this crime the Communists had later arrested him. A small, energetic old man, Kery stepped forward and told us politely that if we did not object to obeying his orders we might begin to march: "Forward, march, if you please!"

Singing the inane songs ordered by the AVO, we climbed steadily upward for the better part of three hours until at last we were halted and left to stare at a double fence of barbed wire surmounted by watchtowers and machine-gun nests. It looked just like Turckheim, except that here there were only four barracks.

From the moment we entered the gates the brutality of the guards was such that, instead of *Arbeit Macht Frei*, a more appropriate motto for this camp would have been Abandon all hope, ye who enter here. We were formed up for roll call, and dark clouds rolled over the mountains and began to pour cold rain on us. The AVO were even less talented with numbers than the SS, and the sergeant did not get the count right until the sixth attempt. This cretin immediately became known to us as the professor of mathematics.

When he was satisfied he ordered one hundred and twenty of us into the first barracks. We tried to run through the mud in our ill-fitting boots, and finally, panting and straining to keep ahead of the guards' kicks, we stumbled into the wooden structure. There were about forty prisoners already there, those who had built these barracks and were now constructing others. The first I saw was Uncle Szabo, with whom I had blown up the Danube barges during the war. After the war he had become manager of the national gas works and now, being an honest man, he was, as he pointed out to me, in the largest group of honest men ever assembled in our country.

The next acquaintance I met was Paul Arkos, a manager of the country's nitrogen works. His plant had been rebuilt after the war by a British firm so, according to the inscrutable logic of our overlords, the Russian advisers of the secret police, he had been charged with selling the plans of the factory to British intelligence. His attempted defence, that MI5 could more easily have got the plans from Manchester than from him, brought sneers to the faces of his interrogators.

Among the others I found Peter Csaplar, former president of the Social Democratic Trade Union Council. A bus driver in his younger days, he was a man of great humour, equanimity and gentleness. Some I knew only by sight, anti-Nazis from the war years or pacifists. There was not one man among them who had not worked, one way or another, for justice and workers' rights—which, of course, was enough to get them a life term in our workers' paradise.

The earthen floor was ankle deep in mud now because the roof had not yet been finished. The bunks were tree trunks with smaller branches placed crosswise for "mattresses." We were told that soon we would be issued straw sacks. The only solace in this stable, which no peasant would have put his animals in, was a brick stove—well-stoked and radiating heat. We draped our sodden greatcoats around it and immediately the air filled with the acrid stench of hot wool.

"Don't be a hero here, boy," said Uncle Szabo, taking me to one side, "not even with your mouth. The camp is crawling with informers. And remember this, the AVO are not required to account for those of us they kill."

He was interrupted by an AVO man who had appeared in the doorway shouting for us to get outside. First he made us run in the mud, then ordered us to crawl through it on our bellies. We did so and other AVO men came up and amused themselves by walking across our backs and pressing our faces into the deep mud. At last they let us return to the barracks.

Left in peace for the rest of the day, Faludy, Egri, Garamvolgyi and I took bunks near the ceiling. Word had of course spread that the most popular poet in the country was among us, and immediately men came over to shake hands with Faludy, asking his opinion on everything from the Communists to our probable fate. With the forthright openness he always displayed, Faludy began answering their questions. Remembering Uncle Szabo's advice, however, I interrupted him.

"Gentlemen," I announced to the group around us, sounding hopelessly pompous even to myself, "we have years ahead of us in which to discuss these matters. Don't be offended, but I must tell you—this is far from being my first concentration camp—that the first rule in a place like this is *never talk politics with someone you don't know.*"

Faludy gave me a look of mild reproach, and I saw that the question of informers had not even occurred to him.

Gradually the crowd broke up and as evening fell we were given boiled potatoes and water for dinner; then the AVO, leaving the light bulb burning, locked us in. There was no question of sleeping, tired as we were, and as we whispered to one another a middle-aged man near Egri came over and introduced himself as Dr. Berzsenyi, a Budapest lawyer.

Dr. Berzsenyi had been held prisoner a long time by the Russian NKVD, who were under the misapprehension that he was a Gestapo agent named Schultz. For this he had spent uncounted months in the central jail of Moscow, the Lyubyanka, where he discovered that at least a dozen other supposed Schultzes were also interrogated daily. When at last he was released and sent home, the AVO arrested him on no less ludicrous charges.

Lying on the branches around us were also Paul Jonas, a leader of the university students, and Istvan B. Racz, the son of peasants who had educated himself and become not only one of the country's best economists but also its youngest member of parliament. Then there was Zoltan Nyeste, scion of a line of Calvinist preachers that extended back to the Reformation. Like the others and myself, Nyeste had been arrested during the war by the Gestapo.

That same evening Faludy, at our repeated insistence, gave us the first of a series of lectures that would continue—except for the months he would spend in solitary confinement because of informers—over the next three years. Each night he would either tell us in detail of historical events, recount passages from world literature or give us straightforward academic précis of the method of Plato or the system of Hegel. His words, as he spoke softly in his low voice and beautiful Hungarian, were so imbued with the gently persuasive reason of the humanistic tradition that all of us found at once strength to hold out as well as a temporary escape from our horrible situation.

When Faludy finished his lecture that first night, Uncle Szabo cleared his throat and said, "My friends, I don't want to depress you, but as I've been here awhile I think I ought to tell you about this camp. We were sent here last summer to build the place. 'The country is yours; you are constructing it for yourselves!' as the Communist slogan has it. Well, when we got here, in the middle of the oldest forest in the country, we slept in a sheep pen. First we put up the fences, stringing up the barbed wire even while the AVO beat us. I am told that one of your first jobs will be to cut down this forest of sixteen hundred acres. After that, or so I hear, we are going to hack out a stone quarry. As for living conditions: they are as you see. There is one water tap. It trickles out barely enough to drink, so there is no question of washing. When they send you out to work tomorrow, learn quickly how to fake it. Otherwise on this diet you will soon die. The only way to survive this place is sabotage," he finished, glaring around in defiance at any informers who might be listening.

"Tell me," I asked him, "do they really want to get work out of us, or is it like with the Germans: we contribute to the economy until we oblige them by dying?"

"It's like with the Germans," he replied.

A little later we were called out into the dark for another roll call, then left in peace to sleep. One hundred and seventy-four men lay practically on top of each other, trying to find space to sleep on the tiers of tree trunks.

Awakened long before dawn, we received black coffee and some bread. After roll call they issued us saws, axes, shovels and spades, and then, divided into brigades of from thirty to forty prisoners, we were marched into the dark forest to cut down trees.

Each brigade was in the immediate charge of a *nachalnik*, a Russian word meaning kapo or overseer. Just as in the German camps, the *nachalniki* in Recsk were favoured by the authorities either because they were common criminals or else former Communists fallen from grace. They had been told that they would be liberated only after the rest of us had died of exhaustion or malnutrition, and believing this, they outdid even the AVO in brutality.

Each six-man team within the brigades had to cut down two trees a day, saw them into sections and stack these in a pyramid. Faludy, Egri, Garamvolgyi and I were given two men in their early twenties as helpers. One was a peasant boy named Istvan Kovacs, who when he came up to Budapest in 1945 joined the Social Democrats and entered university, only to find himself thrown out with the other non-Communist students a year or so later. He had tried to escape to Austria but was caught at the border. The other boy was Elemer Foldvary, son of an upper-class family whose wealth had been confiscated after the war. Foldvary's family had hidden some twenty Jews in their flat during the final months of the war by building a false wall. He himself had studied philosophy at the university until he got himself mixed up with a group of students opposed to the new regime. The AVO got wind of it and here he was. Foldvary looked like a Greek statue, so perfectly and classically proportioned was his face with its nose joining his forehead in a straight line, like Hermes chiselled by Praxiteles.

None of us had the slightest idea how to go about cutting down trees except for Kovacs, who saved us all. Garamvolgyi was too frail to be of any real use, so we posted him as a lookout; and Faludy, scarcely less weak after his months in the cells, we asked to sit in the undergrowth and cheer us by telling stories while we worked. After only an hour of hacking away at the huge trees our palms were blistered, our backs ached and we were shaking from weakness. It was obvious we could not last six months at this rate. Something had to be done. Then an idea hit me.

"Listen," I said to the others, panting as they leaned on their tools, "look at those woodpiles over there! Every day, with Garamvolgyi looking out for the *nachalniki*, we can extract logs from those and make a new pile of our own. That way we'll have to cut down only one tree."

"George," said Egri in the near ecstasy he always fell into when we were outwitting the AVO, "who would have thought it? You're a genius."

From that point on we worked much more slowly, our minds concentrating on the things the poet told us. In the afternoon the rain returned and, soaked and miserable, we wielded the axes, which struck the wood almost silently in the roar of the forest downpour. Finally we were given some potato soup, and then, Garamvolgyi signalling the all-clear, we began picking out logs from other woodstacks and adding them to our own.

It was almost nightfall when the AVO showed up and were visibly astonished at the amount of work we had done. As the brigades assembled I saw that the soles of many boots had already come off in the mud and men were trying desperately to find anything they could use to tie them back on. It was totally dark when we arrived back inside the compound. The searchlights came on and played back and forth upon us as we stood in the rain. The other work teams, it turned out, had not had our idea, and so, having failed to fulfill the norm, they now were forced to lie in the mud and do calisthenics. Our pleasure at outwitting the AVO turned to shame.

The barracks were filled with steam and the smell of wet wool as men rushed to dry their greatcoats around the stove. Some, too exhausted to remain standing, collapsed on the bunks still covered with mud. The rest of us stood under the eves of the barracks and washed in the downpour.

We had not been in Recsk twenty-four hours, yet some men were already showing the first signs of animalization, fighting to be first in line when the cauldron was brought in for supper, scarcely retreating as the AVO guards and *nachalniki* kicked and slapped them back. After dinner three cigarettes were given to each of us, which filled me with astonishment until I remembered that this piece of liberality was also in effect in some Soviet camps. As Egri and Garamvolgyi did not smoke, they gave their cigarettes to Faludy and myself. Straw mattresses had been given to us now, and wallowing in the luxury of it all, we lay on our backs puffing away while Faludy recited a poem he had heretofore withheld from us: "To a Byzantine Theologian." Egri whistled in admiration as Faludy finished the beautiful yet deadly poem in which Marxist theoreticians and party hacks were held up to crushing ridicule, and he began at once to memorize it. As Faludy began again, other prisoners came up to listen, first knocking softly on the bunks for permission—a custom throughout the camps of both the Third Reich and the Soviet empire—and as news spread of the recital men began to arrive from other barracks as well.

Thus it happened that on our second night in Recsk Faludy's bunk became, in effect, the spiritual headquarters of the prisoners. Wet, cold, permanently hungry and exhausted, members of every social class arrived to listen, barons and counts side by side with peasants and workers, all the same rank now. Even later, when we began to resemble the skeletons of the Nazi death camps, men would use their last strength to sit alert in the night, listening to the poet's soft voice. And among them were many who for the first time learned a lesson they would not easily forget: when it comes to survival, spiritual food can be the most important kind.

That first night, when he had finished with his own poems, Faludy recited Byron and Keats in Hungarian translation and told us about the England of their time. Then he asked for others to speak. One man recited several of Shakespeare's sonnets, and another, a youth called Tony Rainprecht, acted out the whole first act of *Hamlet*, playing each role in a different voice. He finished long after lights-out and, while the most exhausted were already sleeping here and there, promised the rest of the play for the following night.

The next morning it was obvious that Garamvolgyi was ill. His pale, lightly freckled face was drawn and flushed with fever and he swayed on his feet. We reported this to the *nachalnik* and at roll call an AVO man strode over and lifted Garamvolgyi's chin, demanding to know what was wrong with him.

"I beg to report that I have a fever, sir," said Garamvolgyi in a scarcely audible voice.

"Listen, all of you!" shouted the AVO man. "Broken legs are to be reported as illnesses here, not fevers! We have a cure for fever here," he concluded, and still holding Garamvolgyi's chin, he struck him with his free hand, sending him sprawling into the mud, where he lay still. "Any other fevers? No? Well then, off to work."

We lifted Garamvolgyi, unconscious now, and Istvan Kovacs put him across his broad shoulders and strode up the mountainside with him. At our workplace we put Garamvolgyi in a shallow ditch, covered him with our coats and then scattered leaves and twigs over him to keep him out of sight of the *nachalniki*.

By now the incessant rain was beginning to get on the guards' nerves, and from all over the forest we heard the shouts of the AVO and the cries of prisoners being beaten. Once, not very far away, we heard the voice of a man, half desperate, half defiant, telling his guard to go ahead and beat him to death, to put him out of his misery. This was followed by raucous laughter punctuated by screams.

Darkness was descending that evening when, just before we stopped work, I caught a glimpse of an AVO man among the trees. He lowered his trousers to relieve himself and I saw that he extracted a piece of newspaper from his pocket to use as toilet paper. When the man was gone, I dashed over, gingerly extracted the precious paper and, cleaning it on the wet leaves, hid it in my pocket. A little later I gave it to Egri, who hid in the bushes and read it, then returned looking crestfallen.

"The news it contains," he said, "is about as valuable as the shit on it. It's all about kulaks sabotaging the wheat harvest— that sort of garbage. If it means anything at all, we'll probably have an influx of peasants before long."

By the end of the day Garamvolgyi could walk but his fever was higher than ever, so after roll call I sought out Count Hoyos, who before becoming an unperson had been a noted physician. He examined Garamvolgyi, then shrugged helplessly, saying that he had no medicine.

"The Nazis at least kept up a pretence of medical treatment for us in Dachau," I said bitterly.

"You don't know me, Gabori," said Count Hoyos, looking up sharply. "How do you know I'm not an informer?"

"My dear count," I replied gravely, "I have an inner sense, perhaps inherited from my ancestors, that tells me who's kosher and who is not. You are."

At this he nodded and took me outside the barracks, where we shook hands in the darkness. As he left I found that he had left four aspirins in my palm. They acted on Garamvolgyi like penicillin, and the next morning he was on his feet again.

There was bean soup for supper, and with our stomachs almost full we waited for lights-out, when Tony Rainprecht would begin the second act of *Hamlet*. Then, just as Tony began, Egri, who was posted by the window as lookout, gave the danger signal.

Men scattered, diving into the nearest bunks as the lights went back on and the guard we called Ivan the Terrible appeared in the doorway, gaping at us.

"Reveille, Fascists!" he shouted.

Men sat up in the bunks, and then he shouted again. "You, Gabori, get dressed and follow me!"

Trembling, I slipped out of bed and stepped into my boots, then followed the AVO man up the hillside to the administration building.

Inside the brightly lit, overheated office sat the political officer, a first lieutenant, and two detectives. One of these was the man we called the Skier because he was never without a ski cap; the other looked like a Zulu, his hair sticking out in all directions. As for the lieutenant, a tall, thin man we had already dubbed Macaroni, he had been a grocer's apprentice in a town not far from Putnok, and he was a Jew.

"Listen, Gabori," began Macaroni, "we are not interested in your past experiences among the Germans. If you want to stay alive here you'll stop talking about all that with the other prisoners. Do you understand?"

"Yes, sir," I replied, at attention. "I don't say those things to make you angry, sir, but whenever I close my eyes out of fear I always see my past, I always remember the German camps."

"In that case, Gabori, I advise you to stop closing your eyes. What do you think of this camp?"

"It's too soon for me to have formed an opinion. . . ."

I did not have a chance to finish because the detective closest to me stood up and landed a kick squarely in my stomach. In the same voice Macaroni repeated his question, but, doubled up, I could not answer.

"My opinion?" I finally managed to gasp. "My opinion is that this is a death camp. When you've seen one you've seen them all."

"You see," continued Macaroni, "there's nothing you say that's not reported back to us. But I wanted to hear it from your own mouth, you son of a bitch. Personally I find it sad that you, a Social Democrat who, according to your files, took a rather heroic part in our national struggle against the Nazis and went to Dachau for it, that you of all people should still side with the Fascists! I find that very painful, Gabori."

"I assure you, sir, that my belly hurts me more."

"Look," he went on ignoring me, "in a year or two we may well suggest to higher authorities that you ought to be paroled. But in the meantime I want you to sign this agreement, as a sign of good faith. I want you to agree to inform us concerning what your fellow prisoners are saying."

"May I ask a question, sir? Do you think I am the sort of person who would do that? I did not do it for the Nazis and I will not do it now. And I don't think I could buy my freedom that way even if I were willing to, which I'm not. Do you take me for a fool?"

I closed my eyes, waiting for the blows to fall, but nothing happened.

"Very well, then," said Macaroni evenly. "I can assure you that you will never leave here alive."

Ivan the Terrible was in the room now, and Macaroni turned me over to him, saying that I was "all his." He led me out through the mud and to the potato cellar, which in those early days of the camp was all the AVO had in the way of a punishment cell. He made me open the trap door, then kicked me down the nine or ten steps to the bottom where I landed in knee-deep water. I was just beginning to ponder this turn of events when Ivan the Terrible ordered me to come out, so I climbed up the steep steps where he awaited me, but when I reached the top he slammed the door against me, knocking me all the way to the bottom again.

"Sing, Gabori," he shouted, laughing. "Sing love songs for me!"

When I remained silent he ordered me out and set me to doing push-ups in the mud. Tiring of this, he began kicking me. It dawned on me that Ivan the Terrible was either mentally retarded or, like many secret policemen, suffering from some particularly unsavoury form of sexual maladjustment. For the rest of the night he followed me around, kicking me sometimes, other times ordering me into the cellar, screaming at me to sing. Finally dawn arrived and he handed me over to the *nachalnik*. I went out with the others to work and got through the day only because they hid me in the bushes and covered for me.

That evening as they helped me to my bunk I told them, in

a loud voice so that the whole barracks could hear it, that obviously there was an informer among us. And we agreed that, whoever it was, he would wish he were dead if we ever discovered his identity. Depressed by the fact of a traitor in our midst, we worked harder than ever to forget for a while where we were. Zoltan Nyeste, though an engineer by profession, knew more poems by heart than any of us except Faludy, and that night he gave us a long, beautiful recital of Goethe and Heine. He was just beginning Schiller when guards burst in the doorway shouting, "Air raid!"

This was one of the games the old Hungarian army had used to break in recruits. Immediately we threw ourselves onto our stomachs in the mud beneath the bunks. Then they ordered us to bring our straw sacks to the centre of the barracks, and there they ripped them open, looking for the pitiful possessions prisoners always collect. This was followed by a body search. Within the space of an hour the barracks was transformed from a slum into a bomb site.

By now there were some eight hundred prisoners in Recsk, working from dawn to dusk seven days a week, and though most of us did as little work as we could manage, little by little the tree-covered mountain surrounded by barbed-wire fences took on the look of a well-organized concentration camp, a corpse factory, where first the spirit was destroyed, then the body. We were building our own cemetery, rows of barracks, as well as those proofs of the superiority of socialism, a bathhouse and an infirmary. But our main job remained clearing the mountain of trees so that a stone quarry could be dug. The only task that had a higher priority was a long building of tiny cells where selected prisoners could receive special treatment, a prison within a prison as it were.

Now the tempo of work was accelerated by threats and beatings. Whereas men had until now usually collapsed from the effects of hunger, now those lying face down in the freezing mud had usually been beaten unconscious. Finally the administration gave several of the physicians imprisoned with us the right to assign the weakest men to several days' barracks duty in order to recover. Evidently they noticed that they were killing us off too quickly, for about the same time the food improved somewhat—the larger part of the rations allotted to us was sold on the black market by the AVO, who padded the figures to get more. But none of this could get more work out of men who were sinking into despair. Prisoners walked about in an almost comatose state. Even those of us who sat next to Faludy each night had the utmost difficulty in maintaining the will to live: it was simply becoming too painful.

It was in fact the exact opposite of what I had witnessed among the prisoners of German camps. There the all-pervasive atmosphere of terror had seldom overcome the dogged determination of the prisoners to survive; some, it is true, had given up hope, but most of those who died had wanted desperately to live. Here it was different. The AVO inspired fear, though not usually the paralyzing terror caused by the SS in their victims. In its place we suffered a will-sapping despair mixed with a hatred that frequently gave way to indifference and then death.

One night in the middle of December the guards burst in and took away our peasant boy, Istvan Kovacs. We were all disturbed and puzzled by this. There was not the slightest possibility that Kovacs was an informer. Nor could we think of anything he had done to provoke the AVO. We stayed awake late, waiting, but they did not bring him back that night.

Just before dawn the door was opened and two guards threw Kovacs in. The second they left we all raced to where he lay face down in the mud, picked up his battered body and laid him gently on a bunk. I lit a cigarette and held it to his lips for him, and saw that his face was a mass of green and blue bruises.

"I was an idiot not to have listened to you, George," he said through split lips. "To think that there was ever a time when I believed the shit they tell us!"

"Sleep," I urged him, for we still had a half hour or so before roll call.

"No!" he said. "I won't sleep. You know, when I was arrested I listened to those around me, other young peasants. When we got to Recsk we decided to submit a petition protesting that our reeducation was against the spirit of socialism and that this camp was a betrayal of Marxist principles! You didn't know we did that, did you? We got some paper from a cement bag, the other peasant boys and I, and we made a petition. What idiots we were! The worst was that after the detectives beat me, Macaroni called me into his office and asked me if I was hungry. He pointed to two eggs on his desk and gave me a document to sign. My God, how long has it been since I've seen an egg! I picked one of them up and cracked it on the edge of the desk, but it wasn't boiled. Macaroni grabbed my hand and smashed the egg in my face. That made me so angry that I wiped my face with the document—I suppose it was an agreement to become an informer. Then he kicked me in the balls and gave me to the others. So here I am."

14

The Punishment Brigade

ONE DAY AS I STOOD IN THE BUSHES stealing a few minutes' rest a voice shouted behind me, "You there, red-headed bandit!" and I spun around expecting an AVO man to fall on me. But it was Zoltan Benko, a cheerful fellow with great protruding eyes, one of those who, like Faludy, did his best to keep up the spirits of his fellow prisoners. Lately they had had the added task of combatting rumours, some spread by the AVO: stories that the Americans had landed in Albania, or the British in Poland. Those who believed these encouraging reports frequently began working furiously in the hope of early liberation, and not a few of them collapsed and died. Benko, among others, took upon himself the thankless task of persuading the credulous that none of the rumours were true.

"Have a look!" said Benko, holding out a piece of

newspaper.

It was a rare treasure, that scrap of toilet paper. There was part of a report saying that the United Nations was going to debate the situation of those countries occupied by the USSR. Then there was a section of Rakosi's speech saying that we all had to tighten our belts for the sake of our comrades fighting US imperialism in Korea.

From this we deduced that rations were going to be reduced still further and that the Americans were beating the hell out of our "Socialist allies" in the Far East. We passed this news along, and a day later the rumour mill had it that the UN had ordered the USSR to retreat from Hungary and that the Americans had driven the North Koreans deep into China.

After supper one night around Christmas the cattle bells they now used to summon us began ringing and we were ordered to form up before the administration building up on the hillside. Even the dying had to be carried from their bunks and up the steep hill. It had rained at least once every day for the past fifty days, a national record, and the whole denuded area was a vast sea of deep mud in which men slipped and fell head over heels into those climbing behind them. We formed up and finally the camp commander appeared, an incredibly stupid man who could scarcely put together a coherent sentence in his native language, closely followed by Macaroni and several other AVO men. Heaving his paunchy form onto a woodpile, the commandant turned to address us, Caesar to the troops.

"You criminals!" he began, "you rotten Fascists, spreading false rumours about the Americans! You will be punished, those of you who are rehabilitating—that is enticing—those who are rehabilitating themselves for our Socialist order. From now on we will have a punishment brigade and I shall now read the names of its first members. If you hear your name, fall out! Pallfy, Dalnoki, Gabori, Benko. . . ."

He went on, reading a hundred or so names, but apart from my own, the name of Dalnoki continued to ring in my ears. Quickly I stepped forward with the others, astonished that my former comrade in Dachau should have been here all the time without my knowing it. I picked him out of the new formation and, ignoring the AVO, shook hands with him.

"What are you two bandits up to over there?" shouted the commandant.

"I beg to report, sir," I replied, "that I have just met a man I have not seen since we were together in another camp, when we were prisoners of the Gestapo in Dachau."

In his stupidity the man found no irony in my statement and went on reading names from his list. When he finished, Macaroni told us that we were forbidden to communicate with the other prisoners and any disobedience would be punished with ferocity. Then, as the rain dwindled into a light drizzle, we were dismissed by barracks.

The eyes of most of the hundreds of prisoners expressed open relief that their names had not been read out, but when George Egri passed me he was evidently infuriated at having been excluded. And at this another difference between Communist and Nazi camps occurred to me: in Dachau, with few exceptions, there had usually been a certain distance and reserve between prisoners. Here, on the other hand, we were almost all of the same nationality and almost all of us had been imprisoned on charges that even our tormenters knew to be sheer nonsense. There was a degree of comradeship among us that would have been almost impossible in a German camp, and we owed our survival to that more, perhaps, than to anything else.

Finally we were alone on the windswept hillside, a young guard whom we called Vipla ("Cap-tooth") standing before us.

"Crouch!" he bellowed. "You will march to your barracks like ducks!"

Obeying, we waddled through the mud until, reaching the steepest slope, all fell forward and slid the rest of the way down. A newly completed barracks had been reserved for us, exactly like the others except that the stove was never lit. As the roof was unfinished the floor here too was awash in mud, and now Vipla ordered us onto our bellies in it as he strode on us, from back to back, keeping his boots clean, as he explained.

We slept three men to each straw sack. Pallfy, Dalnoki and I stayed together, but since Pallfy was a big man, well over six feet, we had difficulty staying on the sack. The rain stopped and the moon showed through the open roof, shining on Pallfy's bald head. My own spirits were at low ebb, but Pallfy amazed me by his cheerful acceptance of our situation. He was a religious man, it turned out, and as he whispered to me in the dark I was reminded of Uncle Eugene in Dachau— though Pallfy's serenity came from a simple, inherited religious belief, while Uncle Eugene's had derived from a humanistic and stoic philosophy he had with great effort worked out for himself. I asked Pallfy to tell me about himself.

"I was chief of staff of an armoured division," he began. "We were stationed not far from Budapest in 1944, when Baki, the undersecretary of state, tried to deport the Jews from the Budapest ghetto. Admiral Horthy ordered me to use my armoured division to stop Baki's plan. I was delighted, of course, and did so. It's not often a soldier has an opportunity to save civilian lives, you can imagine! Well, later I asked to be pensioned off rather than join the so-called People's Army. So they arrested me, of course. I hope you don't think I acted wrongly in that."

"On the contrary," I replied.

"My God," whispered Dalnoki, lying on the other side of me. "Whoever would have thought, back there in block twenty-three at Dachau, that you and I would meet again, and in a Communist camp!"

"We may survive this just as we did Dachau," I replied. "On the other hand, that animal in the Kremlin may live another hundred years and we'll be buried here in the mud—unless, of course, the Americans decide finally to stand up to the Russians."

"Do you think they will?" asked Dalnoki.

"No," I said. "Pray to God that He removes Stalin from this world. Things might get better then, but it won't be thanks to the Americans. The Americans just can't believe that the Russians really are like petty officials everywhere in Central Asia: cringe before them and they'll bully you; slap them when you first meet them and they'll bow before you. It's sad, but true."

Pallfy said, "I think you underestimate the Americans. You do them an injustice if you think they are not willing to fight for human liberty."

"Maybe," I replied, "but just recently they were the sole possessors of the atomic bomb and they could have brought Stalin down by sheer bluff. Now their chance is gone. If they were afraid to stand up to the Russians in Berlin in 1948, do you think they will do it now? Of course they are lovers of liberty and I'm sure their hearts go out to us—provided, of course, that they even know of the existence of camps like this. Our captors have one great advantage over the West: they are united in their insane ideology, while the West mouths liberal platitudes and has an ideology as wide open as the legs of a whore."

Dalnoki began to protest, but just then guards came in and made us do calisthenics in the mud, tore our straw sacks apart and singled several men out for a beating.

The construction of the punishment block was completed on Christmas Eve, and to inaugurate it a formation was called by Macaroni. "The following men will receive two weeks' solitary confinement," he began, "with one meal a day and two hours' binding every night." Binding was what they called trussing us up like market animals, hands and feet together, so tightly that men fainted from the pain and the cut-off circulation. "Benko," continued Macaroni, "B. Racz, Nyeste, Gabori, Pallfy, Dalnoki, Jonas, Faludy. . . ." and so on down the list, an honour roll of those who resisted the AVO most strenuously. "Those I have named," shouted Macaroni when he had finished, "are the Fascists who are destroying the spirit of this camp! If conditions are less than ideal here, men, it is because of these counterrevolutionaries!" Now his voice rose in pitch and he pointed a shaking finger in my direction. "As for the rest of you, if you meet the work quotas you will again receive three cigarettes a day and you will even be allowed to write a letter home!"

The searchlights clicked on as darkness fell and just at that moment the first snowflakes of the winter began to float down on us. Macaroni roared on and on, but eight hundred prisoners, glancing upward, both nostalgic and afraid of the coming hard frost, ignored him completely. The snow fell more thickly now, flakes melting on my cheeks and eyelids, and I remembered my grandmother telling me how, when I was born on Christmas Eve in 1924, snow had fallen and my mother's groans had mingled with the crunching footsteps of those on their way to midnight mass, then her cries and finally my wailing had competed with the pealing of the bells announcing the birth of the Christians' Messiah. A kick brought me back to reality, and I stumbled after the others to the punishment block.

The guards assigned to us, Kulak and Vipla, were two of the worst in the camp. At one end of the building was a kind of office where the two AVO men sat, with a desk and chairs. Beyond this was a corridor of boxlike cells. The one I was put into that first night was smaller than a telephone booth; one could only stand or slump in it but not sit down. There was a Judas hole in the door, and Vipla watched me for a while, then laughed and walked away. A little later we were all taken out of our cells and trussed up on the floor of the office, cords cutting into ankles and wrists and broomsticks thrust beneath our knees.

"If anyone dares to talk he'll get an extra hour of this," said Vipla.

"Tell us stories," said Kulak, a squat, ugly young peasant who had swallowed all the propaganda the regime had carefully fed him and who was convinced that the wretched creatures at his feet were the great landowners and exploiters of Hungary's past. "Tell us stories, Fascists!" he ordered.

Faludy, lying beside me, told them how when he was in the American army and they landed in the Philippines the first partisan group they ran into had been led by a Hungarian named Katona ("Soldier"). Kulak was delighted with this story and ordered Nyeste to speak next. Nyeste recited a Babits poem with the lines "Brother persecutes brother, and the Lord of heaven is blasphemed thereby . . . ," whereupon Kulak darted over and kicked him into silence. Then B. Racz, who like Kulak was of peasant stock, told the story of his childhood, how he and his three brothers shared one pair of shoes, taking turns going to school because of it, and how nevertheless he educated himself and refused to become the lackey of any regime. This earned him an even more savage kick, followed by a gob of phlegm spat in his face.

When it was my turn I told Kulak about the day the Americans liberated the camp at Turckheim. Not wanting to be outdone by the others, I told him that we former prisoners, armed by the Americans, had gone around looking for ex-SS guards and when we found them we hanged them on the spot. Kulak, very interested, asked me who these SS were, and I explained to him that they were the AVO of the Nazis.

"You deserve hanging," said Kulak, his bushy eyebrows knitted as he tried to come to terms with this information. "We are reeducating you for the new order and you do not even appreciate it!"

"Please tell me, sir, why it is more important in the new order to build a punishment block than an infirmary. The slogan of the new order is 'The highest value is mankind itself.' Will we have an infirmary soon or a gas chamber?"

Kulak looked down at me stupidly but did nothing. Perhaps he did not know what I was talking about. When the

two hours were up our group was untied, including two men
who had passed out, and as we were returned to the telephone
booths the next group was brought out. I could scarcely stand
and slumped down until my knees jammed against the wall
and I instantly fell asleep. Then, sometime later, I fell into the
corridor, landing at Kulak's feet as he opened the door.

"Stand up, bandit!" he shouted. Then he led me to another
cell, much larger but equally cold, where I found B. Racz.

"On your belly!" Kulak ordered B. Racz. "You, Gabori,
pick up that bucket of water and throw it over your cellmate."

I stared at the slop bucket in the corner and turned to stare
at Kulak as he repeated the order more loudly.

"Do you seriously think I'm going to do that?" I asked.
"You can't frighten me into doing something like that," I
added, disgusted to the point of not caring about the
consequences, "and if you try I'll go on a hunger strike!"

Fascinated at the idea of a hunger strike, Kulak's eyes
bulged out at me; then he turned to B. Racz and told him to
throw the water on me.

"If my friend won't do it, why should I?" he asked softly.

At this Kulak picked up the bucket and soaked us both
even as we dived under the bunk for shelter. Then he turned
and walked out, leaving us shivering in the subzero air.

That first time around they left us in the punishment block
for two weeks, and the results were hardly what the AVO had
planned. Instead of breaking our spirits, they moulded us into
a group of lifelong friends, men who knew they could trust
and count on one another under any circumstances in spite of
widely varying backgrounds and opinions. Our rations were
reduced to less than Dachau levels, we froze day and night, we
were beaten whenever the guards felt like it and constantly
tormented in other ways. But spiritually we were in great
shape, trusting one another perfectly and united in an almost
physical loathing of our guards and the system they
represented.

The morning they let us out of the punishment block we
were marched through the snow to the mountain top, where
on the other side a sharp precipice fell straight into a deep
valley. Stakes were driven into the snow to mark out each
day's work assignment, for now we were cutting away the
frozen earth and stone to begin the quarry. The AVO had set
an impossibly high quota, too much even for fit men, let alone
skeletons like us. To see that we met it, however, they gave us
the worst *nachalniki*, men who lived in a comfortable

barracks and were well fed. Their leader was a man called Dezso Tamas, and his chief assistants were Sandor Jeges and a certain Pellach, both of whom were AVO officers who had fallen from favour. Hoping to regain their reputations, they outdid in brutality anything the AVO had ever thought up.

That first morning I stood between Foldvary and Dalnoki, appalled. We had to break twelve cubic metres of stone by nightfall. The *nachalniki* disappeared and we began work. An idea had already occurred to me and I told it to Foldvary, who slapped his forehead and laughed silently. We waited until the *nachalniki* had come around again to kick us into greater activity, and then when they left I quickly pulled the stakes out of the snow and moved them closer to the precipice, while Foldvary, behind me, filled the post holes with snow.

"Wonderful!" chortled Foldvary. "Half a day's work done in thirty seconds. If they discover it, they'll kill us, you know," he added more gloomily.

"They won't," I said firmly. "Do you remember how they defined socialism as maximum productivity for the maximum benefit of the maximum number? Not even the ass who thought that up ever believed it. Socialism has nothing to do with productivity; it's the brainstorm of a nineteenth-century sociologist who had never so much as seen a shovel or a pick—not to mention a hammer or a sickle. It works best on paper. In fact that's the only place it works. When they see our work they will note our 'productivity' on paper and be delighted with it. The paper will prove to Budapest that we are producing. Then other papers, newspapers, will announce the further triumphs of socialism."

We were soon given a new *nachalnik*, a sloe-eyed, Gypsy-looking man called Golubovits, who was in Recsk for having run a refugee-smuggling business across the border into Yugoslavia. Golubovits's sadism had been known to shock even the AVO. When he came to inspect our work at the end of the day he made each of us pick up a heavy rock, squat and then, holding the stone overhead, waddle down the steep slope to the barracks. After a few feet men began to fall and roll downward in the snow. Finally dozens of prisoners were sliding and rolling out of control and the AVO, afraid of an escape in the confusion as darkness fell, screamed at Golubovits to stop it.

Each day a prisoner was chosen to stay in the barracks to keep the stove going, and one day to everyone's surprise Golubovits selected me for that much-prized duty. When the others had left, I began carrying in firewood and generally tried to make myself invisible as Golubovits and Ivan the Terrible sat beside the glowing stove. Finally they called me over and demanded that I tell them stories, in return for which I would get a double ration at lunch.

I thought desperately for a moment, then began telling them tales from the *Decameron*. To judge from the effect, Boccaccio might have had Hungarian peasants in mind when he wrote those stories. Both men listened wide-eyed, roaring with laughter at the dénouements, and at lunchtime they piled my mess kit high with food. After lunch Ivan the Terrible had to go on duty, and I was left alone with Golubovits. Suddenly I broke off in the middle of a story.

"Listen, Golubovits, I have a better story, one that is also instructive. Once, when I was in a German concentration camp, very much like this one, we had a certain kapo."

"What is a kapo?" asked Golubovits.

"A *nachalnik*. Now this kapo used to carry a club about with him and whenever he was in the mood he clubbed prisoners to death with it."

I said this in a cheerful storyteller's voice, smiling the while as Golubovits listened eagerly, only the tiniest doubts beginning to furrow his brow.

"Well, one day this kapo nearly broke my head with his club, but you know I really didn't mind it much."

"Why the hell not?" demanded Golubovits.

"Because, you see, I knew the Americans were going to liberate us very soon. Sooner or later the Americans, or someone, always arrive in these cases, you know. Well, just as I thought, the Americans arrived shortly afterward. Pretty soon we found the kapo, my friends and I."

"What happened?" asked Golubovits uneasily.

"We tied a rope around his neck and dragged him until he was dead. Of course, when this camp is liberated, as it certainly will be, nothing like that will happen. Take you, for instance. You don't carry a club! And here we are sitting beside the stove, talking! No, I can't imagine that anything like that will happen here when the day arrives."

Golubovits's face began, but abandoned, several tentative expressions, and finally he walked off, still silent, explaining that he was going to inspect the quarry workers, and I did not see him again that day.

From then on, to everyone's astonishment, not least of all mine, Golubovits not only ceased to torment us but actually went out of his way to do prisoners a good turn. After some two months of this the AVO relieved him of his rank as a *nachalnik* on the grounds that discipline was slack in the punishment brigade.

Early in the spring there was a further influx of four hundred prisoners from Kistarcsa. From them we learned that new and worse waves of terror were sweeping the country. The prisons were overflowing and Rakosi's absolute grip on the country was so effective that the only emotion anyone felt besides terror was despair. Those of us in camps were actually envied: at least we had the initial tortures of Andrassy Street behind us.

One day when I slipped away from the punishment brigade to use the forest latrine, Foldvary walked by and out of the corner of his mouth whispered that Egri, who still had not made the punishment brigade, was waiting for me in the undergrowth not far away. I stumbled through the brush until at last I heard Egri's soft whistle.

"Listen, George," he said, "Faludy sends you the message to cut out the heroics. Stop talking back to them or they're going to beat you to death. By the way," he went on, more loudly for the cold wind had risen to gale force and was howling through the forest, "Garamvolgyi has been made a swine herd. He's stealing food from the pigs—the AVO can't figure out why they're so skinny—and he sends you this little present."

He handed me half a mess tin filled with pig slops.

"Are you serious?" I asked, shocked. It was hard for me to remember that my own metabolism, through some happy malfunction, enabled me to survive on far less than the others.

"Don't be stupid," said Egri, offended. "This is straight from the garbage cans of the AVO! There are hundreds of calories here!"

"Dear Egri," I replied, softened, "we all have to survive this place in our own way. I'd be happy to have some cigarettes, if you can get some. Otherwise, tell the others that I'm getting my extra nourishment from the fact that I'm in the punishment brigade. It's great food for the spirit!"

Egri nodded, and then he told me that during my last two-week stay in the punishment cells four men had committed suicide. The infirmary had opened at last and there were twelve men there in the last stages of exhaustion and malnutrition.

"And I have another gift for you," he went on.

He took a packet from the pocket of his greatcoat and, as I stared in disbelief, he explained that they had stolen paper from cement bags over a long period and at great risk, and when they had enough they wrote, in tiny script with a stolen pencil, the best of the poetry from the nightly recitals. Then they bound the pages together and were giving it to me for the use of the punishment brigade. "This is only the first project," said Egri, beaming. "Nyeste is publishing his own book: *An Outline of the History of Physics*. We'll give it to you as well as soon as it's finished."

I agreed to meet him in the same place a week later. Then I returned to the punishment brigade, where that same night we posted lookouts and began a public reading of the anthology, moved beyond words not only by the poems but also by the loyalty of those we were segregated from.

After a few springlike days winter came howling back with renewed strength. The scarred and pitted mountain was buried again in snow and our hands froze to the crowbars as we tried to pry the rocks out of the iron-hard earth. By now our reflexes had slowed down, and not a week passed without at least one serious injury, as men could not—or sometimes would not—jump out of the way during rockfalls.

One morning, sensing that I was not going to make it through the day, I begged Foldvary, with whom I was at work breaking stones, to smash my finger with the eleven-pound hammer. If the nail had to be removed in the infirmary with luck it would get me several days' barracks duty. Horrified, Foldvary protested, but when I pleaded he at last gave in. I put my finger on a flat stone and looked away. The pain was far worse than I had expected, and in spite of myself I screamed as the hammer struck and blood spurted all over the snow. Guards and prisoners came toward us and then I was led to the infirmary.

Count Hoyos took one look at my finger and extracted the nail without a word. He had been given iodine and bandages and a few other things by now, as well as the power to assign sick prisoners temporarily to barracks duty. He gave me a document permitting me to stay indoors for three days.

The next morning I was just beginning my three days' rest

when Macaroni made a tour of inspection, heading straight for me the moment he entered the barracks.

"What's the matter with this one?" he asked Count Hoyos, who accompanied him, and at the same time jabbed his finger in my chest.

"I beg to report, sir," said Hoyos, "that his finger is smashed."

"He goes back to work tomorrow. This isn't a sanatorium, you know."

So the following day I was back outside trying to break stones with one hand, this time under the eyes of a *nachalnik* ready to fall on me at the slightest provocation.

"Do you know why Macaroni hates you so much?" muttered Benko, working beside me.

I shook my head; the pain in my hand throbbed through my entire body and I was beyond speech.

"He hates you because you are a Jew, like him. Probably he was in a forced labour batallion during the war. Now he's joined the Communists and he knows that he's taken sides with his former persecutors. He loathes himself for it, and he loathes you for not having done it. What other attitude could he have toward a man who was a resistance fighter, who survived Dachau and then came home to be a youth leader in the Social Democratic Party? Macaroni the Nazi-Jew every day betrays his ancestors all the way back to Jacob, and you, Gabori, by your very existence remind him of it. Here, man, take a rest!"

Benko caught me as I stumbled and would have fallen had he not eased me down behind some rocks. The *nachalnik* had disappeared for the time being and the others kept watch for me.

After six months we estimated the average prisoner had lost one-third of his original weight. Hunger was now our worst torment, followed by endless cold and the brutality of the guards and *nachalniki*. Nevertheless, by the end of spring we had at last finished the camp. There was a bathhouse, a laundry, warehouses, workshops and a slipway for the tip cars that carried stone from the quarry. And now that the camp was finished, Budapest was evidently expecting production to rise sharply, for the guards suddenly took a much keener interest in our work, and not just on paper. They began promising us that the harder we worked the sooner we would be freed. Few believed this, but some persuaded themselves that it was true and began working like animals.

It was in the middle of this "productivity drive" that Macaroni formed us up one day and announced that from now on anyone who consistently fulfilled his daily quota of stone-breaking would be allowed to write a letter to his family. Hundreds of men broke into cheering, accepting this cynical lie as the truth. Macaroni beamed and asked if we had any requests. Without hesitation, Dalnoki raised his hand.

"Just one detail, sir," said Dalnoki politely. "I would like to know how many rocks my wife has to break in the kitchen before she is permitted to reply to my letter—to prove that she ever got it."

An amazed silence fell over the huge formation. Macaroni, not believing his own ears, gaped; and Dalnoki, without waiting for the order, stepped forward to await his punishment.

"Four weeks in the punishment block," said Macaroni at last in a low voice. "Four hours' binding each night." Then, recovering his self-possession, he added, "And while we're about it, we might as well send your Dachau friend along with you. Gabori, forward!"

My heart sank at the thought of four weeks in the telephone booth, and for a moment I hated Dalnoki more than I did Macaroni.

"Any other requests?" shouted Macaroni to the formation in a voice heavy with sarcasm. Then he gaped still more as Foldvary spoke up.

"Lieutenant," he said, a smile illuminating that face that had been known to soften even AVO hearts, "my mother has just been exiled from Budapest by the government. How can I write to her without knowing her new address?"

"How the hell do you know your mother has been exiled?" said Macaroni, his voice rising with nervousness and irritation.

"I read it in the papers, sir," replied Foldvary simply.

This was more than the prisoners could stand, and snorts of laughter here and there quickly spread until hundreds of men were laughing uncontrollably.

"And if you don't mind my asking," shrilled Macaroni, instantly restoring silence, "what paper do you read?"

"Why, the official paper of the Communist Party, sir. The one your men use to wipe their asses with," said Foldvary sweetly.

There was no laughter now. Rows of men stood in silence, wishing the earth would open to swallow us before Macaroni took revenge. But all he did was silently to beckon Foldvary to join Dalnoki and me, and a little later the three of us were bound tightly on the floor of the punishment block, so tightly that after a while I passed out.

The next four weeks were probably the worst for me of my entire imprisonment in Recsk, and it was not until they let us out that I realized how unjust I had been in my anger against Dalnoki and Foldvary. As it turned out, their sudden burst of defiance had had an enormous impact on the whole camp. Men who had felt nothing toward the AVO except terror now began to despise them and to realize that everything they told us was a lie. They suddenly began to appear ridiculous in their stupidity and brutality, and those who saw them so gained strength from it.

When we were let out it was May. I was dazzled by the sunshine as they took me up to the quarry and suddenly became so dizzy that I would have fallen had Foldvary not grabbed me. We were so weak we could scarcely climb the mountain. At the top the new *nachalnik*, Kerekes, handed us twenty-pound hammers and ordered us to begin splitting the seams of some enormous blue-grey boulders. I managed to get the hammer above my head, but the weight of it pulled me over backward and I fell onto the rocks. When I stood up my hands and knees were bleeding. Realizing he was not going to get much out of us this way, Kerekes put us to work loading the tip cars with cut stone. The quota was twelve tip cars a day. After filling the deep car, we had to shove it to the edge of the precipice and send the load down the mountainside. Before we reached the precipice a guard stationed along the way would hand us a token; twelve tokens had to be shown at nightfall. We worked as hard as possible, but by midday we had filled only four carloads.

At lunch time I wandered in the direction of the latrine, and suddenly Faludy, whom I had seldom seen since joining the punishment brigade, appeared and whispered as he passed me that there was some bread and some cigarettes for me just behind me in the bushes. I squatted in the bushes and puffed furiously on a cigarette, and then the solution hit me. The *nachalniki* almost never came into the stone dump where we loaded the tip cars. The AVO guard never left his post where he handed us the tokens. We were saved!

When we went back to work I told Foldvary my idea, and quickly he measured the length of the car where the sides tapered toward the bottom, then dashed into the forest and reappeared with saplings broken to the right length. After making sure no one was in sight, we jammed these lengthwise in the tip car, until at last we had made a strong false bottom. Then we began filling the car and soon discovered that one-third of a normal load now filled it completely.

Dalnoki stood beside me watching as Foldvary pushed the car down the gentle grade past the AVO man, who handed him a token. We held our breath as he emptied the car at the tip and then we groaned with pleasure as he returned, his mouth twitching with withheld laughter. We decided then to be cautious. We would not fulfill the norm by more than one hundred and forty percent, even though we might easily double it if we wished. For the extra forty percent we would be rewarded with cigarettes.

At the end of the month the few men who overfulfilled the quotas queued up before Macaroni, who handed out tobacco, marmalade, cigarette papers and lumps of starch sugar. Macaroni's face twitched with annoyance as he handed the three of us our rewards, far more than anyone else got.

"I hope you men are demonstrating with this work that you have changed your attitudes and have decided to get into step with history," Macaroni said coldly to us. "Well?" he prompted.

"I can't say that I've changed, sir," I replied. "I'm very fond of tobacco though."

"If you ever learn to answer with a yes or a no, Gabori, then there might be hope that you'd get out of here one day. Though I doubt that," he added with a smile of pure malice.

On Sunday, 20 May, 1951, we were driven out to work not in the quarries, but to "tidy up the camp," as the commandant called it. The weather was beautiful and we took off our shirts as we transferred a woodpile from one point to another for no apparent reason. In the afternoon, the guards having exhausted their limited imaginations in inventing tasks for us, we were sent back to the barracks and locked in. Then it was time for roll call, which went fairly quickly, and we were sent inside again.

After about fifteen minutes guards burst into the barracks and began counting us all over again, ordering us to remain at attention even when they left. Then other guards ran in and counted us several more times, checking names against lists. As yet another roll call began, a thrill went through the masses of men. Someone had escaped!

Once every hour for the rest of the day and throughout the night we were counted all over again, and the following morning we could see hundreds of soldiers and many military vehicles, even a tank, near the administration building. We were kept inside all day Monday, AVO men periodically rushing in to line us up and stride down the line, slapping and kicking as they went. Tuesday passed the same way and it was not until Wednesday that we went out to work and learned from those better informed that eight men working in one of the tool shops had escaped. Everyone prayed silently that at least some of them might make it across the border to Austria and inform the West what was going on here. It never occurred to us that the Americans might already know all about Recsk and that the West might care as little about our fate as it did about the fate of the Jews during the war.

Late the following Sunday a black maria roared up to the administration building and we watched as prisoners were pushed out, stumbling between two rows of guards. We counted in whispers as they emerged. There were seven of them. One had not been caught! The seven men were led to a sprawling oak tree on the mountainside where the AVO bound them and left them hanging upside down by their feet.

A formation was called and Macaroni faced us, pointing up the hillside toward the dangling prisoners. "Those bandits are responsible for the rather harsh treatment you have received lately. Now I want each *nachalnik* to choose three men to go up there to take revenge for you on those seven Fascists!"

Within a few minutes the *nachalniki* had selected about thirty men, marched them up the hill and handed them clubs. Then, to our horror, we saw that they were obeying, they were beating the helpless men. But several, we could see even at that distance, were refusing to obey, and at this the AVO fell on them with the clubs. When it was all over the seven hanging men were still alive, but of those who had refused to beat them one prisoner was dead, clubbed to death by the AVO.

Soon after this the ground between the double fences was

raked smooth and trip mines were implanted in the soft earth. Finally we learned that the prisoner they had not recaptured was a man called Julius Michnay. What we did not know was that he had made it across the border into Austria and there undergone a fate I could scarcely believe even when, several years later, I learned all about it.

Michnay had gone without food for eight days, travelling cross country at night, avoiding villages and farms. When he got close to the border he was saved by a thick fog that descended over the countryside. Crawling on his belly, he found himself between two watchtowers outlined in the fog. Then he took off his shirt and inched forward until he felt trip wires against his flesh. These he cut with his teeth and then proceeded crawling like a worm until, after two hours or so, he was sure he was in Austria.

Free, he made his way to Frankfurt and immediately got in touch with the CIA, whom he told that he had memorized the names of over a thousand prisoners in Recsk. He begged to be allowed to broadcast these over Radio Free Europe so that their relatives would at least know they were still alive. The American officials expressed delight at the prospect and asked him to return the following day. When he did so, German civil police were waiting for him at the entrance to Radio Free Europe and they promptly arrested him and kept him in prison for a year on unspecified charges. And these were the people we in Recsk hoped would liberate us!

In many ways the summer of 1951 was the low point in the lives of many of us in Recsk. To add to our miseries, acute vitamin deficiency was causing boils and pustules to break out on our bodies. They had literally to kick us to work in the morning, and as the weeks went by an increasing number of men failed to make it through the day, collapsing where they stood and dying either on the spot or shortly afterward in the infirmary.

One day late in the summer three automobiles arrived in the camp and parked before the administration building. Within a few minutes we were ordered to the barracks, and then Macaroni came in obsequiously dancing attendance on four high-ranking officers, one of whom was a lieutenant colonel. They had first gone through the other barracks, and as they entered ours, the punishment brigade's, I noted that something resembling horror crossed their faces before they got them under control. We must have been a ghastly sight to an outsider, even an AVO officer.

"Men," said the lieutenant colonel, "we are an inspection team and our job is to examine conditions in your reeducation camp. If you have any complaints we are here to listen to them. You can approach us one by one. The officer beside me is a military physician who will examine you physically."

Absolute silence greeted his words, and the same conflicting emotions were at work in each member of the brigade. First, how wonderful it would have been if the "inspection team" were really that, men who would listen to our complaints and then cause conditions to be improved. But even as we stared at them that tiny hope flickered out. Obviously everything was perfect in the reeducation camps of the perfect society—and anyone who did not think so would be slandering the people's democracy.

"Well?" said the colonel to relieve the silence.

"Sir!" I said, raising my hand. If nothing else, I was determined to find out what they were up to.

A smile lit up the colonel's face and he beckoned me to approach. As I did so Macaroni, rubbing his hands together like a waiter, leaned over and whispered something into the colonel's ear. All right I thought, Macaroni: you're telling him I've got a big mouth and am a trouble-maker; I'll try to live up to your expectations.

"Sir," I began, keeping one eye on Macaroni, who was squinting at me in fury, "I just want to tell you, for the record, that we work fourteen hours a day here on a starvation diet. Those who are too weak to work are beaten and tortured. The suicide rate is higher here than in Dachau—"

"Dachau?" The colonel interrupted me in a shocked voice.

"Yes, sir. I'm not the only man here who was in Dachau, and I must tell you that conditions here are far worse than they were there. At least a third of the prisoners here no longer have the strength to lift a shovel, let alone use one. That's all, sir."

Of course nothing I said was news to the officer, but as he dismissed me he was clearly still taken aback by the comparison with Dachau. Then others came forward, some to the colonel, others to the physician who "diagnosed" the sick by the method he had learned from the Russians: peering into their eyes and pinching their buttocks.

Finally it was over and the colonel spoke again. "I promise

you, on my honour as an officer, that you will soon notice an improvement in your conditions."

With that they all left, and with them went any lingering hopes we might have entertained. There was no one among us who at one time or another had not been promised our liberation, or a reduced sentence, by an AVO officer swearing "on his honour" that if only we would sign the confession. . . .

After midnight that evening the doors were unlocked and a guard called my name. Friends clasped my hand in the dark to give me courage and then I followed the guard up the hill, cursing my big mouth all the way. I only hoped I would survive the beating Macaroni was going to give me. However, it was not Macaroni who was waiting for me up the hill but a young man in civilian clothes. He sat in Macaroni's office, smiled broadly beneath his mop of bushy hair and offered me a seat and a cigarette. Still on guard, I accepted.

"I've come here to get a statement from you, Gabori. And apart from that I'd like to ask you for a favour as well. Does that strike you as odd?" he added, seeing my no doubt astonished look.

"I've been a prisoner for over a year," I replied, "and this is the first time anyone's asked me for a favour. Of course I find it odd."

"Are you hungry?" he asked.

"Of course I'm hungry. Except for a few informers, there are about a thousand hungry men here. But I don't accept bribes."

Instead of the slap I expected, he widened his eyes and said, "I did not drive all the way here from Budapest to bribe you. I'm here to ask you for a favour."

"What favour?" I asked coldly.

"I would like you to sit down at the typewriter over there and type out for me Faludy's poem 'To Zsuzsa, From My Tomb.' "

"That is a different matter. For that I'll accept food. Also cigarettes—for my work and as royalties for the author himself. Twelve packets."

"Do you think I can get that many without arousing suspicion?" he asked in a low voice, and I nearly laughed aloud at the grotesque comedy of bargaining with an AVO man over cigarettes, both of us afraid of the authorities.

"How many have you got on you?" I asked.

"Three packets."

"All right," I said, "get four more. They won't find that suspicious."

"Too many!" he almost whined.

"Then I don't remember the poem."

At this he flushed and called for the guard outside the door.

"Bring in a cold supper," he ordered, "and three—no, four—packets of cigarettes. I didn't have time for supper in Budapest and forgot my cigarettes as well."

The guard left and the AVO man, belatedly feeling his humiliation, looked away in embarrassment. I sat down at the typewriter and began to pick out the beautiful poem, not finding it odd that in our poetry-loving country the very men who jailed the poet should be this eager to have a copy of the lyric in which he describes his imprisonment. When the food arrived I ate with one hand and typed with the other, then, when he was not looking I tucked some of the cold cuts into my bloused trousers just above my boots—more royalties for the author. When I was finished he produced a statement which he asked me to sign. For once it was a perfectly innocuous document that could not possibly get anyone into trouble, so I signed straight away. Then, like two businessmen concluding a deal, we shook hands and the guard led me back down the hill.

15

A Gradual Thaw

BY AUTUMN WE HAD FORGOTTEN ALL ABOUT the promises of the investigating team, and when in some ways life became a little easier it was certainly not due to any orders issued in Budapest. By now guards and prisoners knew each other thoroughly. The AVO were very seldom replaced, and a few of them seemed to lose their taste for tormenting men whom they saw day after day; others seemed to grow bored with the effort of beating us and now preferred to lie all day behind the rocks sunning themselves. On the other hand, there was no improvement in the diet, more and more men died of malnutrition and exhaustion and the rest of us were so weak that finally even Macaroni had to accept the fact that it now took three of us to do the work of one.

Then near the end of the long, mild autumn a column of trucks arrived one morning and about a hundred of us were sent up the hill to unload them. There were ten trucks, each loaded with cartons containing jars of goulash and other meat dishes. It transpired that they had been exported to the West but the spoilage rate was so high they had all been shipped back to Hungary. The expiration dates on the jars were for the previous year, so the government was distributing the jars to the prisons and concentration camps: spoiled meat might be dangerous to the health of delicate Westerners, but it was quite good enough for those undergoing Socialist reeducation.

For our part, we rejoiced. Each day now we were given a jar, and each jar contained more calories than our normal day's diet. The curious thing was that no one became sick from eating putrid meat: it seems a starving stomach can accept almost anything. But many of us were violently ill at first because we could not resist eating a whole jar at one sitting. One sad side effect was that a few of the less intelligent prisoners, swallowing a rumour that the inspectors had sent the meat to fatten us up before releasing us, began to try to impress the AVO by fulfilling our impossible work quotas. Ignoring the warnings of the rest of us, they worked like demons and several died of heart failure.

Then it was Christmas again, and as the snow fell the last of the spoiled meat was consumed and men went back to stealing slops from the pigs. Work on the quarry fell farther and farther behind schedule and Macaroni again read a list of names for the punishment cells, only this time those of us chosen were to be bound two hours each night, sleep in the telephone-booth cells and work in the quarry fourteen hours on top of that!

The chief guard of the punishment block at this point was a man we called the Slovak because of his strange way of speaking Hungarian. Seeing that we were numb when he unbound us each night around eleven o'clock, he would send us out into the snow and make us crawl through it. The first night when we could not crawl fast enough to suit him he fetched several of the guard dogs and set them on us. Then the Slovak slapped his thighs and hooted with laughter as the dogs sank their teeth into our legs and shoulders and ripped our uniforms to shreds.

The next morning several of us were struggling with a tip car when Macaroni arrived and flew into a rage. "What the hell have you been doing with your uniforms?" he shouted. "Do you know the penalty for sabotage, Gabori?"

"Your guards set the dogs on us," I replied with an

indifference born of despair.

That night the Slovak bound us as tightly as ever but did not send us into the snow afterward, and a few days later he was replaced by Kulak.

The first night Kulak was on duty he bound us in a semicircle around the stove, which he kept red hot. Among us was a prisoner called Daniel Kiss, whom Kulak had bound so tightly that he was weeping from pain and finally must have fainted where he lay behind the stove, because after a few minutes Zoltan Benko, beside me, shouted to the Kulak, "Sir! I smell flesh burning!"

"You smell nothing, you son of a bitch," snarled Kulak and turned away.

But then he too noticed the sickening stench and, going around the stove, grabbed Kiss and dragged him away. Unconscious, Kiss had fallen against the stove and his arm was burned to the bone from shoulder to wrist. The other guard went to fetch Dr. Acs from the infirmary, and in a few minutes the prisoner-doctor ran in and immediately loosened the cords cutting off Kiss's circulation. He regained consciousness at this and began screaming horribly. Kulak allowed Acs to carry him to the infirmary, where he treated him as best he could. Kiss rejoined us some weeks later, his right arm paralyzed for life.

The winter of 1951-52 was so bitterly cold that the AVO issued us with gloves and even allowed us to build fires during our fifteen-minute lunch breaks. From time to time now there would be the spectacle of a man suddenly dropping his tools in the snow and beginning to run in the direction of the forest. Those who went mad this way did not actually run in the deep snow but rather stumbled through it in slow motion until, as invariably happened, they fell in their tracks and died either there or else in the infirmary. There was a suicide or attempted suicide almost every day now. Those who tried to hang themselves in a tree and were cut down from the branch in time were taken to the punishment cells and beaten.

By the time winter began to turn into spring we were reduced to digging roots out of the frozen earth, trying to gnaw some nourishment out of them. It was at this time that I was put once more in the punishment block. For a week I received some beans and a bowl of cabbage soup once a day but did not have to go out to work. At the end of the first week the beans were replaced with lentils. I was of course starving; but if there is any food I have particularly loathed all my life it is lentils, and even now I could not force myself to eat them. I might chew on a root dug out of the earth, but I would not eat pig slops or lentils, not even to save my life. I left them in the mess kit.

For three days I shoved the mess kit back still full when the guard came to get it, and finally it was reported. On the night of the third day Macaroni suddenly flung open the door of my cell and stood facing me with folded arms. By now I did not have the strength to stand at attention but just looked up at him from the bunk.

"What the hell is this, Gabori? A hunger strike?"

"No, sir. I happen to dislike lentils."

He stepped in—I was in a larger cell now, no longer the telephone booth—and I dodged as he struck, his fist just grazing my chin.

"I'm serious, sir!" I shouted. "Give me anything else and you'll see that I'll eat it!"

At this he dropped his fist poised for another blow, and a look of amused skepticism crossed his face. In the corridor he told the guard to bring a loaf of bread, and when this arrived he handed it to me.

"Eat that," he said, "all of it. Now."

Very slowly and with enormous pleasure I began consuming the delicious bread as Macaroni stood watching. I was so engrossed in my task that I did not even notice when he left. Finally, my stomach distended from the unwonted fullness, I fell asleep sitting on the bunk, slumped over the remains of the bread.

I have no idea how long I had slept when suddenly the door was opened and two guards shoved someone in, a tall man whose body collapsed as soon as they let go of him and he fell on top of me in a heap. As the guards departed I eased the man onto the bunk. His breath came in rapid bursts of animallike panting and he was trembling violently from head to foot. Whoever he was, they had beaten him half to death: one eye was swollen shut and blood blisters covered much of his face. I began wiping the blood off his face with my shirt tail and, as he began breathing more easily, I gave him some of my bread.

"Where did you get bread? This is the punishment block." His first words were filled with suspicion.

"I'm not an informer, if that's what you're thinking," I replied and then went on to tell him the history of my loaf of bread.

"I've heard about you," he said, swallowing the last of the bread as I finished my story. "I'm Joe Dudas. They arrested me back in forty-eight, when I was a member of the Smallholders' Party. Since then I've toured the whole goddamned prison system."

"What did they charge you with?"

"Spying, of course. From 1944 on I was the official delegate of the Communist Party of Transylvania to the USSR. I was on my way to Moscow, and the NKVD arrested me as soon as I crossed the border. I escaped from the Soviet camp in 1945, came home and joined the Smallholders."

"That's a rather right-wing sort of group for an ex-Marxist," I said. The Smallholders was a middle-class conservative party.

"Of course it's right-wing!" muttered Dudas through split lips. "Who the hell else was trying to stand up to these animals when they were swallowing us all up? Certainly not you so-called left-wingers with all your mouthing about the workers and the rest."

Dudas and I, as wretched as we were, began that first night an argument that went on with only brief interruptions for a week. I think we were both trying to figure out not only what had happened to us and to Hungary but just what our response ought to be—assuming that we lived long enough to have a response. We argued about land redistribution as if we were the cabinet ministers responsible, about the sort of government we would form if we were in power—day dreams in which the Russians were happy and Hungary was democratic: an impossible combination.

At the end of a week Dudas had largely recovered from the beating they had given him and we had become lifelong friends. There was hardly a point we agreed on, but from the first each respected the integrity of the other. Finally, in the midst of an argument, Dudas looked at me and said, "It occurs to me that there is one sure sign by which we'll know that liberty has arrived in this country—if it ever does. No one will engage in arguments of *this* sort."

I had to agree. Even for me seven straight days of political argument, however entertaining, were a bit much. So I began telling him the Faludy poems, recruiting Dudas into the ranks of those who would preserve the poems in their heads. We had been at work about an hour on this when suddenly they came for him. I was not to see him again for months.

When they let me out of the punishment block I was overjoyed to discover that the punishment brigade had been disbanded. I was sent back to my old barracks to rejoin Faludy, Egri and my other friends.

A system of cable cars was operating in the quarry now, carrying the rocks we broke down to the railway station at Recsk. To inaugurate this Macaroni formed up the whole camp and gave a great speech in which he informed us that the quarry had been taken over by a state enterprise. From now on we would be paid for our work, with deductions from our salaries for our food, housing and the cost of keeping our two hundred guards. There was a moment of silence as he announced this, then, here and there, low laughter broke out, and this soon became a roar as nearly a thousand men stood in their rags before Macaroni and the pompous clown was completely nonplussed. I am not even sure he realized what we found so funny. At last he shrieked at us to lie down in the snow, and for nearly two hours he made us do calisthenics in the slush and ice until the ground was covered with the bodies of those who collapsed from exhaustion.

Faludy was too weak to lecture us that night. He had failed visibly since I had last seen him and now we had to help him up to his bunk. The next morning it was announced that the work quota had been raised by twenty percent and we were to have three new chief *nachalniki*: Pellach, Jeges and Dezso Tamas, who outdid in brutality anything we had previously seen. From that day on the death rate rose spectacularly and the guards increasingly cut down would-be suicides and threw them in the punishment cells. By now all of us preferred the telephone booths and the nightly binding to working in the quarries.

As we got weaker the *nachalniki*, defeating their own purpose, terrorized us all the more. Finally the first civilian arrived, a quarry master sent by the national mining enterprise. This man, whom we immediately dubbed the Quarry Ghost for the way he hovered over us all the time like an angel of death, was even more cruel than the *nachalniki*, if that were possible. The only thing that saved us was the fact that he was a chronic alcoholic and usually too drunk to go on beating or kicking a man for long.

One Sunday late in February, Faludy, Foldvary, Benko and I were struggling through the snow with a large tree trunk, far too heavy for our combined strength. Unable to go farther, we dropped the tree and sat on it, gasping for air. Just then the Quarry Ghost appeared on the slope. A short, spindly-legged man with a bulbous, pimply nose, he was weaving his way down toward us, leaning on the stick he always carried. He stopped before us and the stench of state-produced rotgut reached our nostrils in the frozen air.

"You filth, you bandits!" he gasped, blinking at us. "Holding back the progress of socialism, you scum!" Then he seemed to lose the thread of his little speech, because he turned and looked up at the mountains in the distance. "Do you see that new tower on top of Mount Kekes, Gabori?" he suddenly asked.

"I see it, quarry master," I replied.

"Do you know the purpose of that tower, Gabori?" he went on.

"Yes, sir. That is the tower from which the secret police watch over the entire country."

Faludy's face clouded over and he stared at me as if I had gone insane.

"You are an animal, Gabori," said the Quarry Ghost indulgently. "That is a meteorological institute, you idiot."

"It's just disguised to look like that, sir," I went on. "Actually the AVO are up there watching us all through telescopes."

At this he lunged at me with his stick, which I grabbed, pulling him face down into the snow where we rolled over and over as he tried to hit at me. Finally Foldvary came over and pulled us apart, and the Quarry Ghost, regaining his feet unsteadily, staggered off down the slope shouting threats at me.

"You've lost your mind!" shouted the others, clustering about me as the Quarry Ghost disappeared, but they all fell silent as I produced from inside my greatcoat an entire newspaper as well as two packets of cigarettes.

"I would have taken his rum bottle as well," I boasted happily, "except that I know you gentlemen do not drink."

Unfortunately the newspaper was a technical publication for miners, but the cigarettes were compensation. That night, as I had expected, I was taken off to the punishment cells, where I sat for two weeks.

On the fifteenth or sixteenth day Kulak came into my cell and ordered me out. The snow had melted into a sea of mud, and as we started up the hill Kulak kicked me to the ground and made me climb up to the administration building on all fours.

Awaiting me, to my surprise, was not Macaroni but the Jewish AVO man who had been my first interrogator on Andrassy Street. He gave me a curious look from behind Macaroni's desk. I noted that his black hair, for all his evident youth, was turning grey and his lean *shtetl*-bred face had become bloated and pasty. He had become incredibly fat and looked ill.

"How are things going, Gabori?" he asked. "It's been about three years, hasn't it?"

"I am sure, sir, that things are going as they are meant to...."

I stopped in midsentence and gaped. The portrait of Stalin hanging above the desk was draped in black ribbon. I heard a low moan and realized that it was coming from my own throat, the sound of inarticulate pleasure. I tried to control my expression as happiness flooded my mind. The animal was dead! That Mongol skull collector, the greatest mass murderer since Batu Khan, had gone to his eternal reward. Dear God, I thought, swaying on my feet, let him roast in hell! Then, losing control, I burst into laughter, slapped my thigh and performed what must have looked like a very grotesque Hassidic dance around the chair beside me.

"What's this, Gabori?" asked the AVO man. "I hope you're not going mad just now when I have a document for you to sign. Calm down, man! You are quite wrong, you know, if you think the death of the great Stalin is going to change your personal fate."

"He really is dead?" I asked, wiping the tears out of my eyes and adding with a straight face, "The leader of toiling humanity? The Friend of the Struggling Masses?"

"The death of Stalin changes nothing!" he shouted at me. "The death of the greatest statesman of our times, the founder of our Socialist order, is neither here nor there— as far as you are concerned," he amended quickly. "If you want to get out of here, I suggest you listen to me."

"You've come at the right time, sir," I replied. "This is the happiest moment of my life. I'll sign anything cheerfully now, even my own death warrant."

Then he offered me a cigarette and made the strangest

request anyone, I think, ever received from the AVO. He wanted me to write down what cha.. ges I thought the death of Stalin would bring in our society.

"I promise you it's not a trap," he said when I raised my eyebrows. "But if you don't want to write it, then say it to me. I assure you it won't go beyond these walls."

"I've been locked up for three years," I replied, "so you can't expect me to be *au courant* with what's going on outside. But, since you ask my opinion, I'll tell you. Throughout history whenever a tyrant has died his system has died with him. But let's suppose that this system is so solidly built that it survives. What then? The heirs, for all their undoubted talents, will never match the special genius of the Saviour of Downtrodden Humanity." I paused and smiled sweetly at the portrait with its cockroachlike moustache. "I suppose that they'll fall all over themselves proving that they had nothing to do with the genocide, the mass deportations, the thirty-five years of unrelieved terror. If the West had any sense they would have marched as far as Moscow already. Obviously they have not. As for our own beloved leaders, they'll continue to dance to whatever record the men in Moscow put on the gramophone."

Any one of my remarks was worth a twenty-five-year stretch of hard labour, and taken altogether they added up to a certain death sentence. But the AVO man was looking at the desk and tapping his fingers lightly on the blotter.

"Tell me," he said at last. "Assuming changes did occur in our society, what would your reaction to me be if we met one day, both in civilian clothes?"

"I would pretend not to recognize you. The alternative would be to spit in your face, just to prove to myself that I am a man."

"Are you hungry, Gabori?" he asked wearily.

A few minutes later a large meal of smoked bacon, sausages, onions and bread was brought in. More astonishingly, the two of us ate from the same dish. Then I signed two documents without even bothering to read them, and as an afterthought he handed me a full packet of cigarettes.

"I'm not allowed to smoke in the cells, sir," I told him. "Besides, I don't have any matches."

Again he summoned the guard, told him to give me matches and that I was permitted to smoke.

"As you order, comrade major," barked the guard.

Back in the punishment block, in a larger cell this time, I

lay on my bunk and immediately fell into a deep sleep—the first sleep I had enjoyed for some time without nightmares of Turckheim and gas chambers.

The next morning I was put back in the barracks with the others. I went up to Faludy, embraced him and quietly told him the news: the unspoken desire of countless millions had finally come true. The news spread like wildfire, the noise becoming so great that I was afraid the guards would burst in. For the first time in three years we dragged our skeletal frames up to the quarry with joy in our hearts.

All that day we argued in whispers about what would happen. Some were sure the Americans would arrive. A few thought that things would get even worse now, that Beria or one of Stalin's chief henchmen would grab power and start new waves of terror to maintain it. Others thought there might be a revolt or a civil war in Russia.

I was less optimistic and said, "The best we can hope for from that direction is that one of those who hated Stalin most will grab power and crush the others."

"Who, for instance?" asked Faludy.

"We can take for granted that Beria, Suslov, Molotov and the Kaganovitch will try to carry on the tradition of their chief. In my opinion that leaves only Khrushchev, who, if what Paul Justus used to tell me is true, was Stalin's favourite whipping boy. Anyway, he's a Ukrainian and, according to Justus, he hates the Russians—unlike Stalin, who as a Georgian had an inferiority complex regarding the Russians."

"Who the hell is Khrushchev?" asked Faludy. "A nobody! But if your guess is right I owe you a bottle of brandy if we ever get out of here."

One day in March Macaroni arrived at roll call with another of his lists of names. This time a new punishment brigade was to be formed to make a soccer field for the guards' recreation. I had the honour of being at the head of the list, and Faludy's name followed close after. We had to have it finished by the fourth of April, the holiday celebrating Hungary's "liberation" by the Soviet Union.

One of our guards now was a peasant of really exceptional brutality. We called him Ducsko after the way he pronounced the word tusko, meaning "log." He was stupid to a degree unusual even for the dregs of society recruited by the AVO, the vacant look in his eyes lightening only when he was beating someone up.

Ducsko soon singled me out for special treatment, and on the second or third day of work he began following me as I struggled to push a wheelbarrow.

"It's only half filled, bandit!" he shouted, shoving me into the barrow. "That's sabotage!"

"It's fuller than my mess kit," I replied, then came to attention and added the mandatory "sir."

"You stay there at attention," said Ducsko in a low, ominous voice. "Stay there until I come back."

I stood at attention while the others went on with their work, looking uneasy. A few minutes later Ducsko came back carrying a club.

"Bend over," he said. "I'm going to teach you to stop your sabotage."

"If you use that club on me," I replied, infuriated to the point that I did not care what happened, "I'm going to smash your face to pulp."

Now this was so far from what the AVO were used to hearing that I do not think Ducsko believed his ears.

"Bend over!" he screamed, and as I did so the other prisoners, keeping up a pretence of work, gradually formed a circle around us. I touched the ground with my finger tips, according to the rule, and then felt the numbing pain as the club landed on my buttocks. Without thinking, I picked myself up, spun around and smashed my fist into the guard's face with such force that blood spurted simultaneously from his mouth and nose. Groaning, Ducsko managed to put his whistle to his lips and emit a few feeble squeaks. Within a few seconds other guards arrived, dragged me to the punishment cells and threw me in head first. Shortly after that Macaroni arrived. I backed into a corner of the cell to have some defence, determined now not to be beaten to death without some retaliation. My fist was covered with Ducsko's blood and I rejoiced in it.

"You're not setting much of an example, are you Gabori?" asked Macaroni in a strangely mild voice.

"Part of being human," I replied, still in the corner, "is to defend oneself against the attack of wild animals. Now that Stalin is dead I've suddenly remembered that I'm a human being."

"Do you think that Comrade Stalin's death is going to change your fate, Gabori?" asked Macaroni.

"Yes, sir, I do."

Macaroni narrowed his eyes and remained silent for a long time, looking past me. His expression could be read like a book: he was no longer trying to decide whether or not to beat me to death; he was speculating about his own future.

"You'll go back to work tomorrow," he said at last and left.

That night I was neither beaten nor bound—another first in the history of the camp—and in the days that followed we all noticed the change that was coming over the guards. Some, like Macaroni, were filled with anxiety and began to behave in an almost human manner. Others became even more brutal.

As the weeks passed our initial optimism at Stalin's death faded, and more than ever men began to sink into despair. It seemed incredible to us that the West, and the Americans in particular, could not grasp the fact, childishly simple to everyone in Eastern Europe, that the Russians were in a panic, lost without Stalin to bully them around. For the second time since the war the West could have toppled the Soviet empire by using the Russians' own favourite method: bluff. But nothing happened, and we began now to lose hope.

"Be patient, George," said Faludy to me one evening when I was complaining about the Americans. "It's true that the world is not at all interested in our wretched country, and even less in us. But look: they didn't touch you in the cells even when you hit a guard. Two months ago they would have killed you for it. Believe me, things are changing outside. The guards are opportunists, just like their masters in Budapest and Moscow. They're waiting to see what will happen, and that's what we have to do as well."

It might seem that there was not much encouragement in Faludy's words, but after three years the poet's moral authority was so high among us that all of us, listening to the man, himself an emaciated wreck by now and hardly able to stand, felt his strength and borrowed some of it.

And he was right. Early in May the first signs of the thaw going on throughout the Soviet empire began to appear in Recsk. First the punishment brigade was disbanded again. Then from day to day other improvements were made. We began to receive more food, and of better quality. The worst brutalities of the guards became sporadic and then halted altogether except when one of them forgot himself and his orders. Even the *nachalniki* were forbidden to beat us at work. For a few days we were treated to the spectacle of *nachalniki* asking a guard's permission to beat someone who could not work hard enough and seeing the guard shake his head and walk away.

One day in June Benko came up to me in the barracks, towering over me with his huge frame from which the flesh now hung in folds.

"Do you know, you Fascist bandit, that you're going to be free in three months?" he asked, beaming.

"You're fantasizing, Benko," I replied.

"Imre Nagy is the new prime minister!" he announced, his always protruding eyes fairly popping out of his head now in triumph.

I was skeptical. Of all the Marxist leaders who had come back from Russian exile after the war, Nagy was the least likely to come to power now. In fact it was something of a miracle that he had survived Stalin, for among that whole crowd he was the only indisputably decent man: a Marxist who put humanity before theories, a Communist who did not act as if the end justified the means. In other words, Benko was telling me that an honest man had become prime minister of Hungary. It was too much to believe, but there it was before my eyes, for Benko had pulled a piece of newspaper out of his pocket and I now stared at it. Imre Nagy was not only prime minister; he had even announced that the cases of political prisoners were to be reinvestigated and that an amnesty would be forthcoming. We both ran to Faludy with the paper, and in a few minutes the whole camp knew. There was wild happiness everywhere. In some corners men were pounding each other on the back and embracing; in others some sat quietly and wept.

In July an "investigating commission" arrived from Budapest, and one by one our cases were examined and discovered—to nobody's surprise, least of all the commission's—to be pure fabrication. Little work was required of us now, and we spent the summer days leaning over our shovels in the quarry, occasionally lifting a load of dirt just to keep up appearances.

It was toward the end of the month when the guards suddenly summoned Egri, Garamvolgyi and myself and took us to the punishment block. It was unrecognizable now: the bunks had straw mattresses and blankets. In a few minutes we came to attention as a tall, good-looking AVO man came into our cell, immaculate in white shirt and gleaming blue uniform. He was smiling.

"And how is the notorious Gabori?" he asked.

"Rather better than my reputation, apparently," I replied.

"I have brought you paper and pencils," he went on, still smiling. "I would like the three of you to write a history of the Social Democratic Party from 1945 until the time of your arrests. Please feel free to say anything you like, about yourselves and the rest of the party's leadership. When you've finished, call the guard and give him your work. All right?"

"No, sir," I replied. He was still smiling, but the muscles at the corners of his eyes were twitching.

"And why not?" he asked.

"My handwriting is quite illegible. We need a typewriter, and since what you're asking for will require quite a lot of thought, we'll need about three packets of cigarettes a day. Each."

"I always thought your reputation for insolence was exaggerated by my colleagues," the officer replied, "but I see that it was not."

"What do you want us to write?" I asked. "The history of a now-defunct party or how, in our opinion, it ought to be reorganized now that things—have changed?"

He laughed at this. "There is going to be no Social Democratic revival in our country, Gabori. You can forget all about that."

"May I ask another question, sir? Who is the new secretary of the central committee of the Communist Party in the Soviet Union?"

"Really, you gentlemen have been cut off from events here, haven't you! It's Comrade Malenkov, of course."

None of us knew who Malenkov was, Egri having some vague memory of a poster of a tiny head upon a bulging bemedalled torso—a Central Asiatic face exactly like that of the other malign ogres who made up the Soviet leadership. My only emotion was chagrin that I would have to give Faludy a bottle of brandy when we got out. I had no way of knowing that by the time I acquired the brandy my original prediction would have come true: in less than a year that genial fat Ukrainian peasant Nikita Sergeievitch Khrushchev would be sitting firmly on the necks of a population who once again (if Montesquieu was right) got exactly the government it deserved.

We were given a typewriter and more food than we had

seen in years. Even the cigarettes arrived. We took turns dictating and typing, blowing smoke rings at the guards when they looked in from time to time. Garamvolgyi, being the best typist among us, worked far too fast, so in order to keep the food and cigarettes coming as long as possible we slowed him down and spent many hours typing out our mental store of Faludy poems.

By the end of August no work was demanded of us, and by now the population of the camp was thinning visibly as more and more men were released.

"Perhaps they will give us financial compensation for our years of false imprisonment," suggested Egri hopefully.

"Not a chance," laughed Faludy. "If they did that for everyone unjustly imprisoned the country would go bankrupt. Don't forget, we will still have criminal records. We'll be lucky to find jobs when we're out."

On the third day of September the guards came into our barracks, called attention—we were no longer in the habit of jumping up unless ordered —and read out the latest list of those to be freed. When I heard my name read I was overcome with dizziness and had to clutch the wooden post beside me to keep from falling. Tearfully I embraced Faludy, Egri and Garamvolgyi, who were not to be freed until later, and then I was marched to the administration building where I exchanged my uniform for civilian trousers, a shirt and a pair of oversized shoes. An AVO man gave me a paper with my name on it and a stamp reading "Internment Hereby Ended." The signature was illegible. Then they handed each of us being released a ten-forint note, wages for three years' labour: the price of half a carton of cigarettes for three years of our lives.

As I stood in the queue with the others waiting to be released it was not bitterness or even irony that I felt but a sudden sense of loss, for I was being separated from my friends, who were quite probably the most decent group of men still alive in Hungary. It was by them that the great gaps in my education had been at least partially filled, and most of all, I learned by living with them what society could be when people refused even in the face of hunger and torture to sacrifice their human dignity. I ought to have given the AVO sadists their ten-forint note back. I owed far more than that to Recsk.

16

Freedom of a Sort

MY FRIEND ISTVAN B. RACZ AND I walked slowly down the dirt road out of the camp. The railway station of Recsk was about five miles away, and some of those with us began running toward it. Some sang as they walked; others stopped and wept openly. Soon all were out of sight, leaving Istvan and me treading through the dust. The shoes they had given me were too large and had no laces, so the third time they slipped off my feet I picked them up and continued barefoot.

"You know," said Istvan, "I've always wondered why you didn't empty the slop bucket over me when the guard ordered you to."

"You know why," I replied. "All of our group made the same decision when we came here. We decided to live with

233

dignity even if it meant dying with it."

"And what will you do now?"

"Are you serious?" I asked. "What should we do but tell everybody we meet what they've done to us. I know we've signed statements promising to say nothing, but to hell with that. We have only one duty: to tell everything to everybody, to rub their faces in it. Imre Nagy is prime minister and he's already made changes. If he stays in power, we will be the yeast of still more change."

When we finally reached the station of Recsk I saw Istvan off on the daily train to Budapest. The AVO had given each of us a ticket to his home town. Then I went into the station and placed a call to my brother, who was working in the national wine industry in Gyongyos. Standing in the one-room station, holding up my trousers and wearing shoes big enough for a clown, I began to attract the notice of a few peasants. Finally an old woman came up and asked me if I was from *there*. I nodded, and within a few minutes both men and women approached and handed me bread and smoked bacon from their bundles.

"The Lord be praised that the young man is out of that place!" said the old woman, and the others nodded, gnarled, weather-beaten faces looking at me as if I had done a great thing. I was so moved by all this that it was a relief when the clerk called me over. My call to Gyongyos had gone through.

I heard a woman's voice at the other end, almost drowned by the noise of another train coming in. I heard only that my brother would meet me at the station in Hatvan. The train was pulling out and, leaving the receiver dangling, I dashed for it and succeeded in jumping onto the last platform, losing one shoe as I did so. A peasant picked it up and stared after me, so I tossed him the other shoe as well.

An hour later I stepped out onto the platform of Hatvan and fell into the arms of my brother, Andrew. The crowd of passengers swept around us with curious glances at the tall, sun-tanned man embracing an emaciated, barefoot scarecrow. Then we went into the waiting room and ate the food Andrew had brought for me.

"The AVO came to me," he said. "They told me that for three thousand forints they'd give me information about you. I paid it of course; then they just laughed when I asked for the information. Believe me, George, it hasn't been any picnic out here either in our so-called freedom. They kicked me out of my job after your arrest."

"And my family?" I asked.

Andrew looked uneasy at this but said they were well. He had given them money whenever he could. Finally the Budapest train pulled in and Andrew put his hands on my shoulders.

"You're going to need this, little brother," he said, reaching into his pocket and extracting a roll of bills. Then the train began moving and I clung to the steps, barefoot on the hot steel, and watched my brother disappear in the distance, black hair gleaming beneath the summer sun.

Standing in the great cavern of Budapest's Eastern Station, I reflected that all the turning points of my life seemed to occur in this place. I was still barefoot, and the passers-by, as shabby as most of them were, stared and instinctively moved out of my way. At last I found a taxi in the street and a few minutes later I was ringing the buzzer of our flat on Bokreta Street, panting for breath after the climb of three flights.

My daughter, Susan, opened the door and stood almost hanging from the door handle; tiny with flaming red hair, her blue-grey eyes wide with wonder, she smiled at the tramp in the doorway. Then I knelt down, told her who I was and kissed her.

"Uncle Andrew said you would come!" she shouted and threw her arms around my neck.

Then Judith appeared, and for a moment I had the feeling that the last three years had never happened, for my wife gave me a perfunctory kiss and said only, "Where the hell are your shoes?"

"The Bolsheviks couldn't afford to give me any," I replied. Before she could say anything her mother and sister entered the living room, accompanied by a young man in the uniform of an army political commissar. I glanced from him to the military topcoat hanging on a peg beside me. The insignias were the same. The young man was looking at me with friendly irony, as if to say that as a Communist official he was not in the habit of receiving enemies of the people in his house, but he was after all a tolerant man.

"You are totally insane," I said quietly, trembling with rage, "if you think that I am going to tolerate that uniform in my own house."

Still holding my daughter in my arms, I brushed past them all and went into the bedroom, slamming the door.

"But George," Judith protested through the door, "he's my brother-in-law!"

"Forty-eight hours!" I shouted back. "If your secret policeman and his wife aren't gone by then, I'm leaving and taking my daughter with me."

After this the muffled sounds of animated conversation could be heard from the living room, and in a half hour or so my wife knocked on the door.

"They'll move out tomorrow," she said, her eyes red with weeping and her voice thick with reproach, "and my mother is going too."

"I said nothing about your mother," I replied rather hypocritically, because now that she mentioned it, it seemed an excellent idea. "If she wants to go too, that's fine. When it comes to that, you can go too if you wish."

"Oh, God!" moaned Judith, bursting into tears. "You've been home less than an hour and already you've turned everything upside down!"

"Do you really think I am willing to share my home with one of my jailors?"

"My sister's husband was not one of your jailors!" she replied in sincere amazement.

"He and his kind are the jailors of us all, my dear," I replied, "and if you can't see that, it's you who've learned nothing these three years."

They began moving out the next morning, and for a moment I felt almost guilty—until I remembered that a man wearing that uniform had no problem acquiring a flat, anybody's flat. To avoid their sullen looks, and the ominous smile on the commissar's face, I accompanied Susan to school early, having finally located an old pair of shoes in the back of the closet.

"Why don't they like you, daddy?" asked Susan as I pushed her swing in the schoolyard.

"Well, dear, there are a lot of things we don't agree on," I began fumblingly, wondering how to explain to a six-year-old the sordidness of personal relationships in our dictatorship of the proletariat.

"I know what it is," she announced brightly. "You don't like policemen. Neither do I."

Kissing me good-bye, she ran off to join her schoolmates at the doors, and I imagined her sitting all day beneath the portraits of the Hungarian and Soviet party leaders. The pact I and my friends had made in Recsk to fight in every way possible to bring about change in our country suddenly seemed like hopeless nonsense. I would have given anything to run after Susan, take her in my arms and flee to any country where we would not be forced to breathe this omnipresent atmosphere of political garbage.

I was required to present myself, beginning that morning, at the local police station to ask for a registration form for an identity card from the administrative headquarters of the district. To my surprise everything went easily with the police. The police commissioner of Budapest was now Sandor Kopacsi, who, taking advantage of the comparative liberalism of the Nagy government, was doing everything in his power to make the civil police act humanely.

At the administrative headquarters of the Ninth District, however, it was another story. It appeared that I was the first released prisoner to present himself, and with the highly developed opportunistic instincts of petty bureaucrats everywhere, the staff there, not yet sure which way the wind was blowing, were cautious. Some withdrew in almost physical disgust when my identity was made known to them and passed me on to other offices with open contempt. Others stared in disbelief, as if seeing a ghost, and forgot to be rude to me. And a few, the bravest, greeted me with civility and open sympathy.

Taking stock of the situation, I decided this was no time to change the habits of a lifetime, and when in the third office I entered a clerk addressed me ironically as Comrade Gabori, I leaned across his desk until I was inches from his face. "I am not your comrade and I object to your addressing me as such," I said in a voice loud enough to bring the activity of the whole office to a halt.

"Then stop addressing me as mister," he stuttered.

At this point someone in authority came up behind me. "How did a stinking reactionary like you ever get out of prison?" he asked, and I turned slowly to face the male equivalent of those unattractive women who in former times became reluctant and sour nuns and in our society became party functionaries. He was badly shaved and pasty-faced, overworked, underpaid, frightened and a bully: the very image of the most pathetic class on earth, the socialist white-collar worker.

"I'm not here to listen to the jargon of party hacks," I said slowly. "If I object to being addressed as comrade, it's because I am not your comrade, not even according to your fatuous philosophy. And if I address you as mister, it's for want of a better term—certainly not because I consider you gentlemen!"

A still more senior official, alarmed at this little fraças, came up and smoothed things over, and in a few minutes I was handed identity papers that listed my occupation as quarry worker and, far worse, added that I had been "previously interned for crimes against the state." Knowing it was hopeless, I protested that civil rights had been restored by Imre Nagy and that, moreover, my case had been reopened and I was found to be innocent. This met with shrugs, of course, and I left with a document that condemned me to the lowest category of jobs. With luck I might end up as a street sweeper or a seller of lottery tickets.

On my way home I stopped off at a library and looked up the old edition of *Szabad Nep* that carried the text of Imre Nagy's inauguration speech. It turned out to be as monumentally courageous as I had ever heard. In some detail Nagy listed the crimes of Rakosi and his deputies. He said that the economy of the country had been all but ruined by overconcentration on heavy industry and that farm workers had been forced into the factories, with the result that agricultural production had fallen far below prewar levels. Tens of thousands, he went on—and I could scarcely believe that I was reading a Hungarian newspaper—had been unjustly imprisoned, while many other thousands had been deported to the countryside to live in squalor, even in pigsties. These wounds, announced the new prime minister, would now be healed. The ruthless censorship, which had published political rubbish while forcing our real writers to dry up completely or else hide their work, would be eased. From now on it would no longer be the first duty of an artist to laud the party and the leadership.

Putting the paper down, I stared out the windows of the old library and watched the yellowed leaves drift down along the avenue. It seemed scarcely credible that Moscow would permit this man to be our prime minister. Then, going through other papers, I found the names of those who made up Nagy's cabinet. Most of them were former Rakosi men, which made it clear that Moscow wanted to use Nagy as a liberal front to pacify the population. The real power, evidently, was to be retained by the old guard.

Still, there were grounds for optimism. My treatment by the police had demonstrated that. We had an honest prime minister, Communist though he was. A vast majority of the population would be strongly behind him, and that boded well for change. And finally it appeared that the fermentation had begun: either the wine would be good or else the bottle would explode. The third possibility, vinegar, I would not allow myself to entertain.

My wife went to work every morning and my daughter to school, so I was left alone. For the time being I lay about most of the time, getting back my strength. In general I was feeling fairly fit again but still could not climb the three flights of steps without breathing like a sixty-year-old at the top. Then, with increasing frequency, the telephone began ringing as more and more of my comrades were released from Recsk. These conversations always began with shouts of joy, followed by rather dangerous statements which I did my best to cut short: when I lifted the receiver I still heard the faint click that had been there since 1949. The secret police rarely, for some reason, acted on information gleaned this way, but there was no sense in tempting them. So after the initial greetings we always made a rendezvous, and in this way within a few weeks we formed a circle of friends even more tightly knit, if that were possible, than we had been in Recsk. We were not, as the secret police would no doubt have thought, a conspiracy. Rather we formed a group of totally loyal friends committed to bringing about change in every way at our disposal, an unofficial organization whose one great goal in life now was to wait for the day when we could take an active role in the political life of the country and bring about reforms that would keep scum like Rakosi from ever floating to the top again. If in the past there had been political differences among us, they were forgotten now. And all of us, except for Faludy, who was among the last to be released and who had spent World War II in the US Army, had belonged to that tiny fraction of the population who had actively resisted the Nazis in the underground.

In the meantime, however, there was the problem of surviving from day to day. Now that I had got rid of the commissar, my wife's small wage was our only income and the money my brother had given me was fast running out. So I began making the rounds of personnel offices, where as soon as I produced my documents polite excuses were found for not employing me. At first I openly defended myself, saying that my status as an ex-political prisoner was by far the most honourable in the country. This usually met with a pained smile of sympathy and a shrug of helplessness. Sometimes it merely provided the manager with the excuse he needed to throw me out.

Gradually I began looking, as I had known all along I must, for the lowest paid jobs, and from time to time I was offered one, but never for more than eight hundred forints a month, which would not even replace the old shoes I had worn out tramping the streets. To the offers of salaries of this sort they sometimes slyly and obliquely added that with a little pilfering on the side I might double the salary. After only six years of Marxism that was the level we had sunk to: petty theft was universally recognized as a means of surviving. Everything in my upbringing rebelled against this, but gradually I began to talk myself into it. Jewish law did not forbid a man to steal to save himself and his family from hunger, and neither (if I remembered well something Father John had told me in Dachau about St. Thomas Aquinas) did Christian law.

It rankled, but I decided to do it, and one morning before I went to yet another personnel office I stopped in an espresso bar and was just about to leave when an old friend, Laszlo Frank, came up and gave me a great bear hug.

"My God," I said, looking at him, the very image of prosperity, "how did someone like you manage to keep afloat during the Great Deluge?"

"I'm ashamed," said Laszlo, though with a broad smile that denied any such emotion, "but the day you were arrested I was made general manager of the National Poultry Enterprise. Can you believe it? An old Social Democrat like me?" Then, no longer smiling, he asked, "Where did they send you?"

"To Recsk."

"Oh, Jesus," he said, looking away.

"Do you know about it?" I asked, surprised, for most people did not.

"I didn't, but lately the name's cropped up over and over again."

I was overjoyed by this, because it meant not only that things were loosening up, that people were talking more openly, but also that our Recsk confraternity was spreading the news far and wide.

"Well," I went on, "I'm out, but it seems they mean for me to starve to death now that they've freed me. I don't suppose you happen to know of a personnel manager willing to hire a notorious enemy of the people?"

Laszlo paused and bit his lip a moment, then straightened his shoulders and smiled. "You've found him!" he said. "Come to my office in the Central Market on Monday morning. You can start immediately."

"Splendid, but you know that I can't feed my family on eight hundred forints?"

"My dear George," said Laszlo, offended, "I don't know exactly what sort of job I can come up with for you, but rest assured you'll make far more than that!"

On Monday morning a secretary ushered me into an office that would have looked more at home on Wall Street than in Budapest. Surrounded by leather-upholstered furniture, Laszlo awaited me with a balding, middle-aged man who kept twisting his grenadier-type moustache like a silent-film villain. We were introduced and I discovered that the grenadier, Joe Moldovanyi, was to be my boss. I would be his chief cashier.

"And the salary?" I asked, rather rudely. I still had visions of being reduced to lentils as the pantry in our flat shrank visibly day by day.

Laszlo and Joe Moldovanyi glanced at each other and burst out laughing, and I understood.

"All right," I said. "Who gets robbed? The peasants or the state?"

Both men frowned at me in reproval. "Come on, George!" said Laszlo. "Do you take us for crooks? It's the bloody state that gets robbed, of course, and the more the better!"

A few minutes later I was wandering with Moldovanyi through a crowd of silent, patiently waiting peasants standing beside sacks of fattened geese. The first part of the operation was the only one I had qualms about: national custom far older than the Communists ordained that in return for grading the geese A-1 we, as buyers for the state, were paid off with one of the geese. I was carrying fifty thousand forints to pay the peasants. By the end of the day we had bought all the geese, weighed them, paid off the peasants, then weighed the bribes we had been given and discovered that we had "earned" eighteen hundred forints. Of this Moldovanyi, as chief, kept two-thirds, leaving me with six hundred forints—nearly a month's wages for some categories of workers—for my work.

"This is nothing," said Moldovanyi. "Fridays and Saturdays we really clean up!"

All the way home that evening I struggled with my conscience, but by the time I reached our gate and I thought of the dreary meal the three of us were going to sit down to, my conscience had lost the battle.

"How the hell are we going to live on eight hundred forints a month?" wailed my wife when I told her my official salary.

"With socialism, my dear, all things are possible," I replied, and then, as I saw hysteria cloud her eyes like a squall on Lake Balaton, I told her to get Susan into a coat and come with me; we were going out for a proper dinner.

Within the space of two months I was becoming as rich as a cabinet minister, and if my conscience still troubled me it was also true that I had an impressive argument to pit against it: I was now able to give financial help to some of those from Recsk who had not been so lucky and were living in misery with their families. The state owed us three years of our lives; I was going to exact as much compensation as I could.

Months passed, and more and more people were released from the prisons and camps. Then one day I got a phone call from Esther, who had just been let out of Kalocsa. We met an hour later in an espresso bar—relations between Judith and myself had cooled to the point that the arrival of Esther, old comrade-in-arms that she was, would have brought on one of the hysterical scenes that were now rocking our small flat with tiresome frequency.

"There isn't much change, is there?" asked Esther, and for a painful moment I thought she was referring to herself, who was so thin and pale and haggard that at first I had not recognized her.

"How do you mean?" I asked.

"Under the Nazis we were neck deep in shit. Now we're shoulder deep. Is this what we fought for all that time?"

I begged her to lower her voice. Speech had become comparatively free recently, but there were still informers about and everybody observed the limits. I brought her up to date and listed the things that had improved.

"Nagy may be prime minister," Esther replied bitterly, looking around to challenge any potential informers, "but that bald-headed dung beetle Rakosi is still head of the party. Nagy keeps mouthing about party democracy—which is a contradiction in terms, as we all know by now—and for all his goodwill we're still shoulder deep in shit!"

Quietly I argued with her to be patient, that if improvements continued at the same rate it would not be long before we had a tolerably decent society. Esther gave me a long, quizzical look.

"Do you really believe that, George? We followed Justus, didn't we? Cooperate with the Russians, he said; it's the only way to build social democracy. We believed him, George, and look at us. We both look ten years older than we are. Do you still accept that rubbish?"

"What choice do we have?" I asked her, and she leaned over the little table and gave me the smile Clytemnestra once gave Agamemnon.

"When the time comes," she hissed, "we can choose to rise up and kill them!"

Shaken, I argued with her some more, and in the end she promised to imitate the rest of us for the time being, to agitate for change.

"But don't fool yourself, George. Your Nagy may be an honest man even though he's a Moscow-trained Communist—talk about a contradiction in terms!—but I hope you don't think our agitating can change anything. Nagy will stay in power as long as it pleases Moscow. There is only one way to change that situation, and I've already told you what it is."

In the months that followed it became clear that Esther, not I, was right. By November 1954 the patience of the Kremlin was exhausted. On orders from Moscow Imre Nagy was replaced by Hegedus as prime minister. Returning from Moscow, where he had convinced the Soviet leaders that Nagy was toppling the system, Rakosi began manipulating the strings of his puppet government. Imre Nagy was charged with "rightist deviationism" and expelled from the party.

It appeared that the thaw was over. But when Rakosi tried to restore Stalinist methods, it simply did not work. The power of the secret police had been eroded in too many ways, not least of all in the public mind. There had been no waves of terror under Imre Nagy and few midnight knocks on the door. The attitude of people toward the state and its apparatus was no longer one of abject fear; now there was an element of anger and defiance in it.

Moreover, under Nagy the standard of living had risen. There was more food to buy and people had largely lost the pasty, unhealthy look of recent years. With their bellies filled and their nerves restored, they talked more and more openly. The government tried everything it could think of to stem the flow of free speech, but nothing worked—and it became obvious to everybody that in a totalitarian system such as ours once the government retreated the populace would never again take it altogether seriously.

In 1953 it was still nearly impossible to argue publicly with a party member—exceptions being those of us just out of prison, who, in our fury, disregarded the danger. But by 1955, even with Rakosi back in power, the atmosphere had changed so much that people not only talked back to party members but Communists themselves frequently began ignoring party meetings and directives.

There was still the click as I lifted the receiver of my telephone, but now I began every phone call by telling the secret policemen listening in to go to hell. In this atmosphere the party hacks and ideologists, like Revai, the cultural czar of the country, continued to grind out slogans, prophesies, threats and statistics, but it was hard to find anyone, except of course those who were on the same sort of payroll, who paid the slightest attention to their fatuous nonsense.

Then in 1955 some newspapers, especially *Irodalmi Ujsag* (the *Literary Gazette*), started publishing articles so outspoken that at first I could scarcely believe my eyes. The language was circumspect and no conclusions were drawn; the writers merely described what they saw around the country, the living conditions of workers and peasants. This was a body blow to the government, which had from the beginning proclaimed those two classes as its pets, the darlings of the "workers' and peasants' state." The fact was that in 1955 Hungarian workers were living and working in conditions that had not improved since the era of Admiral Horthy forty years earlier. Rakosi personally read the galley proofs of all newspapers before they went to press, and time and time again he thundered, telephoned and forbade issues to appear;

but more often than not they appeared anyway now and sold out within minutes.

In the theatres something like ninety percent of all plays had in recent years been socialist realist trash from the USSR. The Hungarian national classic *The Tragedy of Man* was now performed again before sold-out houses. It had long been forbidden because the author had a century ago foreseen something of our national future. In his drama he showed Michelangelo in a Communist state, carving chair legs for a living. Shakespeare's *Richard III*, forbidden because of the king's really startling resemblance to Rakosi, now reappeared to crowds so enthusiastic that tickets were going for fabulous amounts on the black market.

The only really depressing note in all this was the absolute uncertainty of our position. It was clear that eight million Hungarians could not keep up this more-or-less open defiance of Moscow endlessly and that the patience of our Russian masters would sooner or later break. In a way, what we were experiencing was simply the latest version of the national fate. For centuries Asia had thrown up wave after wave of mounted horsemen against Europe to rape, plunder and kill: Tartars, Mongols, Turks and now Russians. Each time the wave crested and broke on the shores of Hungary. Vienna was besieged, but it was always Budapest that fell. It was beginning to look as if the West accepted this as Hungary's historical fate and was content that the Russians should occupy us so long as they went no farther.

In this bleak impression, which was the one most of us had formed by now, there was perhaps one intriguing exception. The American secretary of state, John Foster Dulles, made a speech in Fulton, Missouri, that apparently went largely unnoticed in the West. But when the Americans broadcast a translation of it to us it hit like a bombshell. In effect the American secretary of state told us that if ever we rose up against our Russian oppressors, *the Americans were waiting to help us.*

—

In the spring of 1955 I was thrown out of my job, rather to the relief of my conscience, and although I had saved quite a large amount of money, I went out looking for work again anyway. And again, after days of fruitless visits to personnel offices, I dropped into an espresso bar and ran into an old friend. This time it was Rose Biro, who had been a member of the Social

Democratic Party's choir with me during the war. Rose had grown stouter now, downright hefty in fact, and her husband, whom she had in tow, followed beside her like a tugboat helping the Queen Mary into harbour.

"Out of work, eh, George?" asked Rose after we embraced and I shook hands with her husband.

"Not at all!" I replied. "As you see, I'm an inspector for the National Espresso Bar Enterprises."

I looked away as I said this because Rose's huge bosom began to heave with laughter and I was going cross-eyed as I stared in fascination: it did not seem possible that breasts could be that large.

"Don't tease an old friend, George," said Rose, "especially one who's in a position to offer you a job! Zoltan here will hire you, won't you, Zoltan!"

"I'm the chief purchasing agent of the Salgotarjan Machine Works," began Zoltan obediently, "and as it happens I'm looking for someone who understands the wine business. We need a buyer for the canteens of our many factories."

"And the salary?" I asked.

"Twelve hundred a month," he said, "but there is also, well, you know. . . ."

Indeed I did. Only the details were missing, and a week later I became the wine buyer for one of the largest employers in the country. It had been a long time since I had seen my brother, Andrew, so I decided that the Gyongyos district would be a good place to begin wine buying. With ten thousand forints in cash and a vinometre in my briefcase, I arrived in Gyongyos determined to help Andrew recoup some of the losses he had sustained when the Communists confiscated the wine business he had rebuilt with his bare hands after the war. This time my conscience bothered me not at all.

After one night at my brother's house I went around inspecting the local wine, then phoned the Machine Works asking for someone to be sent to take charge of what I bought. Before the company inspector arrived I injected a good deal of pure alcohol into each of the lots I was buying. As a result, when the inspectors measured the alcoholic content the prices went up astronomically. When they drove off with the first of my purchases, the local wine growers flocked around me eagerly. By the time all our deals were concluded, including future arrangements, I had chalked up commissions amounting to some twenty thousand forints. From now on the National Machine Works employees were going to drink wine only from the Gyongyos area.

Somehow in my eventful youth I had failed to have the traditional run-in with a beautiful widow. It was several years overdue, and when one day in the village of Abasar I saw a ravishingly beautiful woman in her mid-thirties, raven-haired and slightly tanned from working outdoors, I said to myself: that, George, is beyond doubt a widow who has been waiting for you.

I approached her with a confident smile and discovered that she was one of the few independent vineyard owners left. Quickly she brought me a sample of her wine, and I recoiled in disgust at the first taste: she had taken a quite good riesling and mixed it with something that tasted like lighter fluid.

"I'm very sorry," I said, spitting it out, "but you ought not to have mixed them."

"My neighbours advised me to do it!" she wailed, sobbing into her apron. "My husband died three years ago and since then I've managed to live only by mixing my wines. How was I to know that someone from Budapest could tell the difference? They never could before!" she added, looking up at me reproachfully.

"I'd buy it, but I'd lose my job," I replied, filled with sympathy for the woman whose qualities were so evidently just those that her wine lacked.

"Well, then perhaps you'd like to rent a room from me? I know you travel back and forth from Gyongyos all the time. Why do that when you can have a room right here in the centre of the wine-growing district?"

She had dried her eyes now and kept casting little sidelong glances at me, which soon reduced me to such a state that, if only she had known it, I would have bought her wine as well as rented her room.

I moved in the next day and discovered that things were not at all what I had expected. Granny slept in the kitchen, the beautiful widow slept in another room with her three children and I was put into a room the size of an AVO cell with nothing but a large bed in it. Even the food was terrible. At the end of the week, utterly frustrated by my failure to add adultery to my growing list of moral irregularities, I asked her what I owed her.

"Oh," said the widow, smiling and waving her hand airily, "we'll just add that to the price of the wine!"

You've been had, George, I told myself, and phoned my employers asking for an inspector and a truck to arrive as soon as possible. It was high time for me to leave Abasar— which, by the way, means Father of Mud. When the inspector arrived I took him to the widow's house and there he was so stuffed with food and the best riesling that by the time he got around to inspecting my purchases he did not bat an eyelash when he tasted the widow's foul brew. You really are an enemy of the people now, I told myself, and made a mental note to dispose of the widow's concoction before the unsuspecting workers of Salgatarjan burned their guts out on it.

I went up to the widow to take my leave, but she and the other peasants of Abasar suddenly insisted on my staying: they had planned a great feast in my honour that night. Reluctantly I agreed, and by midnight, stuffed with goulash and fabulous wine they kept for their own use, I stumbled off through the darkness for my last night at the widow's.

Not bothering to light the oil lamp, I undressed, slipped beneath the huge eiderdown and realized that I was not alone.

"You really did not think, did you," whispered the widow, "that I was going to let you go without payment in full?"

The next morning I sat behind a peasant on his motorbike and left Abasar, bouncing down the dirt road to Gyongyos. The widow stood barefoot, waving good-bye. I think each of us was satisfied with the bargain we had struck.

A few months later the machine-tool workers of Salgatarjan had had enough of the wine I bought for them, and I found myself once more without a job. But this time I had prudently saved nearly everything I earned, so I was able to stay at home for the time being, watching events. For things were happening with unusual speed just then. In Moscow Khrushchev made his startling revelations about Stalin at the famous Twentieth Party Congress; it appeared that the Soviet leadership were going to make peace with their archenemy Tito; and in Hungary there were signs that Rakosi was being forced to loosen his grip still further.

I was sitting home reading one day toward the end of February when the phone rang and I heard Paul Justus's voice at the other end. He had returned home from prison that same morning and asked me to visit him the following afternoon. I remember very little of our conversation just then: I was overcome with confusion, one emotion working against the other. First, I still respected Justus for his learning and for the kindness he had invariably shown me since I was a teen-ager. On the other hand, while it was certainly not his fault that we were under the thumb of the Russians, the fact that some of us had cooperated in our own downfall could be laid at his doorstep.

No sooner had I finished speaking with Justus than the phone rang again. It was George Balazs, the man who had been arrested at the Austrian border with his wife (they were now divorced, I later found out). I told him to come over at once and celebrate his release from prison. What he and his wife must have endured while refusing to denounce my brother Andrew, who had tried to help them escape, was hard to imagine. Hastily I took out the best wine in the pantry, and a few minutes later Balazs arrived, with Esther. He looked quite healthy, so much so in fact that I must have stared.

"Come now, George, I'm not a ghost!" boomed Balazs.

We drank most of the first bottle in silence.

"When they arrested us at the border," said Balazs at last, "they brought me back to Budapest and gave me a life term. After a year or so some of us who knew foreign languages were set to work translating foreign books for the use of the leadership. Our conditions improved a lot then, thanks to the party."

"The party?" I asked, scarcely believing my ears. "What did the party have to do with it?"

"Well, George, for sensitive work of the sort we were doing they selected only those who were deserving, if you follow my meaning."

"Only too well!" I replied, flushing with anger. I was on the verge of rising and throwing Balazs out of my flat, but instead I said, "I understand that we were tortured daily in Recsk for three years and that elsewhere in the prison system there were prisoners who 'deserved well' of the party. Am I right?"

Balazs gave me an odd look, as if he could not understand why such an obvious truth was upsetting me.

"Tell me," I went on, "since you're obviously *persona grata* in party circles, what do you think is going to happen after all these shake-ups are over?"

"Nagy's program has its merits," he said, "and obviously we've got to restore legality. But since you ask me, I don't think anyone has the right to tamper with the achievements of socialism. Nagy has gone too far toward restoring capitalism."

"So, given the choice, you would prefer Rakosi in power?" I asked.

"I didn't say that," replied Balazs expansively. "A middle course, perhaps, between the extremism of both men. But if you insist on my choosing, then I'll take Rakosi. He's the real Communist of the two."

"I find this very interesting," I said, pouring more wine with a hand that trembled with rage. "Actually, I've never seen anything like it. For instance, out of all of us who were in Dachau together I can't remember a single man who was converted to nazism by the experience. The same goes for Recsk. Yet here you are, Balazs, a Communist."

"Well, what of it?" he asked ominously.

"You know that I am grateful to you for what you did for my brother by keeping silent after your arrest. If you had come here today and told me that after years of hunger and mistreatment you had crumbled, had become, say, a police informer, I would have had all the sympathy in the world for you. Nobody knows more about human weakness than I do. But what are the facts? You were unjustly arrested and sentenced to life. You did valuable work for your jailors and, by your own account, proved to them your loyalty to their strange political philosophy. Now you come here not to confess this to me but to boast of it! What shocks me is that someone with the guts to hold out during what I'm sure they did to you at first, that someone like that should have given in so easily later on."

"But I didn't exactly become a Communist!" said Balazs, looking helplessly at Esther, beside him. For her part, she stared at the table. "At least not a Stalinist. It's just that in prison I had opportunity to read a lot of Marxism—especially books printed in the West, and which I helped translate sometimes—and I reached the conclusion that Marxism for all its faults, which the party is even now weeding out, is still by far the best of all possible systems."

"All right," I said, cooling down somewhat. "The last time I saw you, you were a Trotskyite, like me, though I'll be damned if I can tell you now what a Trotskyite actually is! Now here you are, fresh out of jail. All around you former Communists, their eyes suddenly opened, are falling away from Holy Mother Party in droves. But not you! You're just

discovering the truth of the whole thing even while Khrushchev is denouncing it in Moscow. My God, Balazs, it's a pity
you weren't with us in Recsk. We didn't have time to read
trash there, least of all half-assed Western views of Marxism.
We lived communism twenty-four hours a day in Recsk, and
there's not one man of the thousand of us who would not be
ashamed to repeat any of the rubbish you're spouting."

"Be patient with him, George," pleaded Esther suddenly.
"I'm working eighteen hours a day to clean his brains out.
Give him time."

"Tell me, Balazs," I asked, suddenly curious, "who was
with you in your translation bureau in jail?"

"Nobody you know, I think, except Paul Justus." Balazs
paused a second and gave me an ironical look. "I'd like to
know if you're going to play the moralist with him as well
when you see him. He ought to get out any day now."

"I'm glad to hear it," I said, deciding not tell him I had
already heard from Justus.

"You might as well get used to the fact that most of us
being released just now are unwilling to accept right-wing
views like yours."

"Then I'll have to remember, Balazs, not to argue with such
people."

"What sort of people do you mean?"

"People whose political views change according to conditions—and opportunities." Balazs flushed, but I continued.
"I was a democrat and a Socialist when I was arrested and
that's what I am now. I remember how you were horrified,
Balazs, when the Communists first wrecked the Social
Democratic Party and then began the reign of terror that
drove so many to suicide. I remember, in fact, that you had
the quite sensible reaction of wanting nothing so much as to
escape from this lunatic asylum. But now you've changed
your views and you say that I can expect to have trouble as
there are many others like you."

"Yes, that's what I think" he said, trying to remember—as
I had forgotten—that he was my guest.

"Well, there may be a few who have learned to kiss the whip
hands of their masters. But not many, I think. I suspect there
are ten of us for every one of you."

"You're entitled to your views," he replied, standing up
unsteadily—we were through the third bottle of wine now.
"But they're going to cost you a lot of friends."

"They're going to cost me no friends at all, Balazs," I said and handed him his coat.

At this point Esther hustled him to the door, giving me a sad and helpless look over her shoulder. Suddenly I regretted my harshness to Balazs. I ought to have waited awhile and let him come to his senses. In any case, it was the last time I ever saw him. Later I learned from Esther that he had become incurably alcoholic and then had hanged himself.

The next morning my wife announced that she was sleeping in the living room from now on: lately I had begun having nightmares about Turckheim and Recsk and woke up screaming and flailing about. Judith was sick and tired of it and no amount of apology or explanation on my part would calm her down. I left the house with her complaints still ringing in my ears.

A little later I rang Justus's doorbell and then embraced my old teacher, thinner now but fit-looking. His face was lined in a way that only added character to it, and his walnut-coloured hair was streaked with grey. Only his eyes were unchanged, burning and flashing as they reflected the thought going on behind them.

"Balazs visited me yesterday," I began when we reached the drawing room. I was unwilling to put off what was coming.

"George, you and I are no longer master and disciple, but friends. You want an explanation for the translation business in prison, right? Well, you deserve an explanation."

For a few seconds the only noise was the sound of our spoons as we stirred our coffee.

"What particularly infuriated me in my conversation with Balazs," I began, "is not that he gave in to the AVO but that now he's trying to justify the action."

"I think, George," replied Justus, "that what you really want to know is whether or not I became an informer. No, I did not. Nor did I become a Communist. The first two and half years they kept me in solitary confinement in Budapest. Then they offered me a place on the translation staff, and I jumped at it. Wouldn't you have? I added English and Spanish to my list of languages. As for politics, I ignored them. Here, look at these."

He handed me a large manuscript entitled *The Sonnets of Shakespeare* Translated by Paul Justus. Quickly I thumbed through the pages, picking out my favourites, and by the time I had finished I was more than a little impressed.

"Would you be angry with me," I asked hesitantly, "if I told you that I find you a far better translator than political messiah?"

"Not at all," Justus laughed. "As a matter of fact, I decided in prison that I had had enough of politics. From now on I'm going to try to earn my living by doing literary translations."

"Does that mean that you've lost your faith in Marxism?" I asked.

"Of course not! Have you?" he was astonished.

"I'm grateful to you for having taught me Marxism so thoroughly," I said, unable to meet his eyes, "if only because there is no better way of proving that those who lead this country are such thorough traitors to their own cause. Whether or not things would be better if they were *real* Marxists, that I don't know. I suspect not. There comes a time when we have to judge theories for what they turn out to be in practice. Marxism has been tried over and over again and each time it proves to be worse than bankrupt."

"And can you tell me a political philosophy that is not bankrupt at this point?"

"No," I admitted, "but then I no longer think in terms of political philosophies. Obviously we have to have governments, and from what I've seen I'll choose the government that begins and ends with democracy."

"Democracy in itself solves nothing!" said Justus.

"Of course it doesn't," I shot back. "But what you've always forgotten—or never realized—is that nothing can be solved without it! Theorize all you like, the situation is really quite simple. There are two Germanies. One is democratic and filled with problems and injustice. The other is Marxist and filled with problems and injustice. Given the choice of living in either as an ordinary citizen, there aren't ten men in this country who would choose East Germany. That, my friend, is the long and short of it."

"And if you happened to live in West Germany," asked Justus, "where would you stand politically?"

"With the right wing of the Social Democratic Party," I said wearily.

"And why the right wing?"

"Because I worked in the left wing of the party here, with you, for years. And what did we do? We cooperated in the hope that all would be well. And why did we cooperate?

Because we trusted you and your Trotskyite theories. And we were all very, very wrong."

"I am forced to agree with you," said Justus slowly, cleaning his glasses and blinking in the strong light coming through the front windows. "Given the opportunity, there are many things I would do differently. But what can one do now?"

"For my part," I said, "I'm shooting my mouth off all over the country trying to wake up anybody who will listen to me. Apart from that, I've been doing my best to add to the general corruption by stealing money right and left. That came to an end recently, I'm sorry to say."

"Even if we don't agree on everything," said Justus, obviously shocked by my last remarks and wondering if I was serious, "I hope this will not interfere in our future friendship. It's too late for me to stop being a Marxist, George. I can't give up my hope that some day, somehow, someone will put Marxism into practice with good results."

He went on speaking in this vein for a little while, and as I looked at him I saw that Justus was closer to being a broken man than I had at first realized. He was talking to convince himself, not me, and perhaps that had been the way he always talked. Suddenly even the light shining from his eyes seemed that of a lamp burning in a house in broad daylight: utterly pointless.

"Tell me, George," said Justus as I took leave from him in the doorway, "I hope you don't regard our having consented to translate books for the AVO as giving in to them. If they had asked you to do work of that sort, intellectual work of real value, in return for better food, would you have refused? Would Egri and Faludy have refused a simple request like that?"

"While the rest of the prison population starved and died of exhaustion? Yes, of course, we would have refused."

Justus blinked, then smiled sadly and nodded as I turned and made my way down the street.

17

The Revolution

EARLY IN THE SPRING OF 1956 the university students began holding more-or-less public meetings at which the leadership, Hungary's relationship with the Soviet Union and, sometimes, socialism itself were criticized. A group known as the Petofi Circle (named after the great Hungarian nationalist poet) led the way in these activities, and it was at their meetings that many of us who had been in Recsk prison now gathered regularly.

On July 27 there was a public debate in the officers' club of the Hungarian army. Several thousand people were present to hear the writer Tibor Dery attack censorship in the arts. At the end of his speech Dery blamed the central committee of the Communist Party for having thrown out Imre Nagy, "the most decent man in Hungarian political life." There was a moment's silence, then the huge hall burst into spontaneous and prolonged applause—a startling sound to anyone used to the monotonous, rhythmical clapping mandatory at party meetings and rallies. The debate at the officers' club went on most of the night.

Several days later Rakosi called a meeting of the Politburo at which he demanded the immediate dissolution of the Petofi Circle and the arrests of Dery, Nagy and a number of writers and students. As so often in his career, however, Rakosi had timed his move badly. Khrushchev was infuriated by this bit of neo-Stalinism, which belied the much-publicized new humanitarianism and liberalism of the Kremlin. Mikoyan was flown to Budapest to sort things out, with the result that Rakosi was thrown out of his job and another old-time Stalinist, Gero, replaced him. Also reinstated in the leadership was Janos Kadar, just out of prison himself.

By this time a large section of the population, including the workers, was openly bitter against the government. In an attempt to gain some popularity, the Politburo now arrested Mihaly Farkas, a former minister of defense, and his son Vladimir, notorious as the most insanely sadistic torturer in the AVO. The top leaders, however, including Gero himself, generally disregarded popular sentiment in the traditional Soviet way. It was clear to everyone but them, in fact, that the country was reaching the boiling point. On October 20, oblivious to everything going on around him, Gero went off to Belgrade as head of the Hungarian delegation ordered by Moscow to make peace with Tito. We then realized why Moscow had thrown Rakosi out. It was not because of our hatred for him but because Tito had let it be known he would not receive a delegation headed by Rakosi. It was clear that the government was never going to pay the slightest attention to the population unless it was forced to.

Late in the evening on October 21 I received a phone call from Zoltan Benko asking me to come immediately to the Kossuth Club (named after the nineteenth-century nationalist revolutionary leader), where others from Recsk were already assembled with the students. When I arrived I found two strong young men guarding the doorway. Silently I handed them my prison release papers. They glanced at these, smiled and nodded for me to enter.

Inside there was turmoil but finally I found Paul Jonas, who was reading a freshly mimeographed leaflet with fifteen demands made by the university students. Among other things, they asked for the immediate withdrawal of the Soviet army (as stipulated by the peace treaty); the restoration of Imre Nagy; the dismissal of all Stalinists; a new constitutional assembly elected by secret ballot; the right of workers to strike; and the immediate return of all those Hungarians forcibly deported to the USSR since 1945.

"Can you believe it?" asked Benko, and he gave a long, low whistle as he read the leaflet. "There's going to be a mass demonstration the day after tomorrow at the statue of General Bem to show our sympathy with the Poles in their own struggle against Moscow."

"But this is insane!" I said, too loudly, for I was thoroughly alarmed and unable to understand the euphoria all around me.

"What's the matter with you, Gabori?" asked another friend from Recsk. They were all looking at me as if I were ill.

"Gero is coming back from Belgrade tomorrow. Do you imagine he's going to allow this? Do you want a change or a massacre? He'll have the police open fire, you know. And why the fuss about Imre Nagy? He's a Communist, after all. Show him your fifteen points and he'll laugh in your faces."

"Do you think we ought to try to dissuade the students?" asked Zoltan Nyeste. "They wrote this leaflet, Gabori, not us. They've been the pets of the regime, and if *they're* rebelling it's not for the likes of us to stop them!"

Argument raged back and forth, but in the end all of us agreed to take part in the demonstration. I was sure it would be suicidal, but if it were going to happen I was not going to miss it. Finally I grabbed a stack of leaflets and a roll of tape and headed home on foot. It was like old times. With one eye on the lookout for police, I plastered leaflets all over walls and kiosks throughout central Budapest.

I reached home after sunup. Susan was at school and my wife at work. I fell into bed and must have slept immediately, because the next thing I knew the phone was ringing.

"George! Are you there?" I heard the excited voice of Paul Justus at the other end. "What on earth is going on? The city is like an ant hill with everyone running to and fro!"

"What time is it?" I asked him, shaking myself awake.

"Noon."

"The excitement," I explained impatiently, "is over the fifteen points, the things the students are demanding from the government. The leaflets are all over town. The real excitement will occur tomorrow. There's going to be a demonstration." There was a long pause. "Are you there, Paul?" I asked.

"I'm here," he said in a strange voice. "Tell me the fifteen points, please."

I read him the text of the leaflet over the phone and at the end there was an even longer pause, so I said, "I suppose it must be difficult for you to accept the fact that students who have had nothing but a Marxist education can be making these demands on the government and that they hate so passionately a system that has pampered them."

"I consider the contents of the leaflet impossible and irresponsible," he replied. "What astonishes me most of all, however, is not the students, but you—that you of all people should want to reintroduce the old system of opposition parties into our socialist government. I know the system has its faults, but don't you see, George, the fact that you and I are alive and out of prison means that those faults are being rectified. Do you think the government will tolerate open rebellion? Are you willing to share in the responsibility for a massacre?"

"No," I replied, "I'm not. On the other hand, Paul, I'm not willing to repeat what you and I did after the war. I know there was nothing we could have done to stop the Soviet Union from imposing a tyranny on us, but it is not to your credit that you advised us to cooperate while they were doing it, nor is it to my credit that I let you persuade me. Well, the country has now had enough of Soviet tyranny. Are we going to make the same mistake twice? Don't you see? This is your chance to make up for the past. Of course we don't want a bloodbath, but if the students stand up and demand justice, can you and I and people like us sit back and watch silently?"

"It is not a question of demanding justice," said Justus softly. "I find it hard to believe that you, who were my best pupil, should be abandoning socialism at this point, now, after everything we've gone through."

"What we've gone through, Paul, is socialism in its most typical manifestation. For me to remain a Socialist is to kiss the hand of my torturers."

"I can't believe it's you I'm talking to, George," said Justus.

I tried to think of something to reply, but nothing came to mind. I stared at the telephone, knowing suddenly that there was no way to bridge the distance between us, that there was nothing more to discuss. Overcome with weariness, I hung up the phone gently and sat on the edge of the bed with my head down. At last, I thought, you've cut the umbilical cord and now you're on your own. I remembered how when I was about eight or nine my brother and some other boys had thrown me into the local mill pond to teach me how to swim. They shouted encouragement from the shore as I sputtered and thrashed about and finally, to my own surprise, made it to the opposite bank. I felt just the same now.

I reached for the telephone, intending to phone up Faludy, but I let my hand drop again. The poet would happily have helped me, but this was something I had to think out alone. I had learned long before, first from Uncle Eugene and Father John in Dachau and later from Faludy in Recsk, that it is not politics that makes the world go round. But in spite of that, I had still counted on Justus to provide the answers to certain questions. I was not a poet but an ordinary citizen called on to play an ordinary role in affairs; and now I saw clearly for the first time that the man I had always counted on to advise me in that simple role was himself so far removed from reality as to be almost mentally ill.

I took a cold shower, then grabbed my remaining leaflets and went out. All along the Great Boulevard groups of people were reading the leaflets and discussing the demonstration scheduled for the next day. People were talking openly in a way no one had heard for years and the faces of passers-by were alert and alive. I stopped at a corner and watched a man across the way reading out the text of the pamphlet to a crowd that could not reach the kiosk where it was posted. The air was electric with enthusiasm and relief, and I stared at the shining faces of the ordinary people of Budapest, that population about whom I had had such mixed feelings throughout my life. At that moment they looked beautiful, craning their necks to hear the man. Finally I turned away, tears running down my cheeks.

October 23 was a beautiful autumn day. There was not a single cloud in the sky as I made my way toward the centre of Budapest. The workaday crowds jamming the trams looked much as they always did, except for a tricolour in a lapel here and there; only someone long familiar with Budapest would have noticed the changed atmosphere today, a mood of happy expectancy hovering over everyone.

On the Great Boulevard I jumped onto a passing tram and was surprised when passengers on the landing reached out and helped me in, smiling—not at all usual Budapest behaviour. Then at the first stop I watched as passengers waited patiently to board the already overcrowded tram. The sour expressions, the grey atmosphere familiar to anyone who has ever travelled in a Communist country, all this had suddenly been removed from Budapest like a fog blown away by a breeze. Total strangers were wishing each other good morning and all around me people who had never seen one another before were starting conversations.

"Well, colleague," said one of my neighbours to another, "will you be going to work or to this demonstration they're all talking about?"

"Work until noon," replied the blue-overalled labourer, "then to the demonstration."

"My whole shift is going!" a young workman informed me excitedly, as if confiding a secret to an old friend.

As the tram approached the buildings of the university I saw Benko in the street, pacing up and down. Squeezing through the crowd, I joined him.

Benko grabbed me and began leading me in the direction of the statue of Petofi, telling me there was no time to lose.

"Gero's delegation came back from Belgrade this morning," he said, "and he forbade the demonstration—and, the grapevine has it, he's ordered the police to fire on the crowd if his order is disobeyed."

This was more than a little alarming, Hungary being a country in which the wildest rumours frequently have an unpleasant way of turning out to be true. When we reached the rather small square that contained the statue of Petofi it was clear that we would not be able to go farther. There were thousands of people jammed ahead of us and thousands more began to overflow behind us onto side streets. Soon a sharp-featured young man climbed up onto the base of the statue and began reciting the national anthem:

> Arise, Hungarians,
> The fatherland calls on you,
> The time is now or never!

Then Tibor Dery, the novelist, spoke to the crowd, and after that Benko and I joined those who were heading for the bridge to cross to the other side of the Danube to the statue of General Bem, a Polish officer who had come to help the Hungarians against the Austrians and the Russians during the 1848 war of liberation. Banners began to appear now reading Long Live Polish-Hungarian Friendship. And then, for the first time, I saw our own national flag raised by a student—with the Communist insignia ripped off, leaving a hole in the middle.

The ministry of the interior had set up loud-speakers in the street, and from these Radio Budapest could be heard relaying the government's order forbidding public demonstrations. No one was paying the slightest attention. In the meantime streetcars began disgorging large numbers of workers who had headed for the centre as soon as their work shifts ended. It was close to four o'clock now, and the thousands of students and others were joined by shabby workmen. The two classes had seldom had much to do with each other in Hungary, not even under communism. But now they were together, intellectuals and workmen greeting each other like long lost friends, just like the accounts of the Russian revolution all were familiar with from films and textbooks. But the common motive this time was not hatred for the czar but loathing for our Communist masters.

Now the loud-speakers announced that at eight o'clock Comrade Gero, secretary general of the Hungarian Communist Party, would broadcast a speech. This was greeted by derisive laughter, and those marching toward the statue of General Bem took up chants calling for Imre Nagy. Then we passed a military barracks and I grabbed Benko's arm and pointed, open-mouthed with wonder: the windows were lined with soldiers cheering us! And at that moment I think I realized clearly for the first time that what we were doing was a matter of life or death for the country. These soldiers were not going to fire on the crowd. On the contrary, they were at any moment going to join it. Part of my mind rejoiced, and another, more sober part was frightened. We were not going to pressure the government into further reforming itself: we were going to explode.

It was about five o'clock when we reached the Bem statue. Members of the writers' union were speaking, but we could not hear them. There was no public address system and the crowd was so large that it was noisy in spite of itself. Then flags appeared in the windows of the military barracks beside the square. The soldiers of the Hungarian People's Army had followed the example of the students and had torn the Communist insignia out of the centres. Soldiers came down and mingled with the crowd, and when people begged them to take the red stars off their caps they did so. Then the whole crowd began moving toward the parliament building, a great wall of humanity again crossing the Danube bridges. This time they were determined to see Imre Nagy.

Thousands and thousands of people pressed themselves into the large Kossuth Square opposite the buildings. Chants arose calling for Imre Nagy. Others shouted out for the great red star above the parliament to be removed. Darkness began to fall, but the street lights were not turned on, the authorities evidently hoping that total darkness would discourage the crowd. Then people began lighting bits of newspaper and pamphlets, and as darkness descended the great square resembled a cathedral at Easter, with uncounted thousands of little lights burning. The crowd began angrily demanding the appearance of Imre Nagy who, in a way certainly unusual for a Communist, had really become the great hope of the population.

Then Nagy appeared on the great balcony. The street lights came on and he stood silently as the crowd roared its approval. He was waiting for someone to find a megaphone. (As it never occurred to the Communist government to address the population directly, there had not been a public address system on the balcony for several years.)

"Comrades!" began Nagy when a microphone was finally produced.

"No!" the crowd roared back in protest, and people began shouting, "We are not comrades!"

Nagy was visibly shaken by this rejection of a term he had used as a matter of course all his life, obviously unable to grasp that in rejecting it the people of Budapest were rejecting years of terror and hypocrisy, the whole inhuman system that addressed people as comrades while treating them like animals. Nagy was facing a crowd that was begging him to lead them. It was an experience seldom, possibly never before, offered spontaneously by a population to a member of a Marxist government. And Nagy fumbled it tragically. He began again, telling us that he held the youth of Hungary in "great esteem" and that he wanted nothing more than to help lead us to Socialist democracy and that the path to this lovely goal lay in maintaining discipline and order within the party apparatus. Finally he asked the people to return peacefully to their homes. For a moment some two hundred thousand people stood silent.

"We'll stay!" people shouted, and others chanted, "Not us; *you* go home." And then, for the first time, I heard a group

chant the cry that later became famous: "*Russzki haza!
Russians Go Home!*" In desperation Nagy began singing the
national anthem. At this people calmed down and joined him,
until thousands of voices echoed through the square and
across the water of the Danube.

After this many people did begin to head for home, rather
depressed that so little had happened. But very many stayed,
and at eight o'clock loud-speakers broadcast the promised
speech of Gero.

Gero spoke for about fifteen minutes, and during that time
he managed to alienate the entire country with his unpleasant
nasal, high-pitched voice. In a word he condemned the
demonstrators (who were, after all, about a fifth of the entire
population of Budapest; in front of the parliament alone we
were over two hundred thousand!) as a Fascist mob. He
charged us with chauvinism and nationalism. When the
speech ended and the loud-speakers were turned off the
crowd exploded in fury and began shouting threats toward
the now darkened parliament building.

Foldvary had joined Benko and me some time before, and
we stood side by side now, thoroughly dejected.

"Well, is that it then?" asked Foldvary.

"Wait," I said to him. "It's still possible that all this will
force them to put Nagy back in power and that things will
continue to improve."

"And if they don't?" asked Foldvary.

"Then we can begin discussing how to get out of this
country."

Just then one of our friends from Recsk made his way
through the crowd. Sobbing for breath, he told us that he had
just come from Brody Sandor Street, from Radio Budapest. A
crowd of student demonstrators had been there for some
hours already, demanding that the fifteen points be broadcast. The AVO guarding the radio had just opened fire on the
students and a battle was raging. What I had feared most had
happened, and now that I heard it it did not register at all.

"What are you saying?" I asked the man stupidly.

"He's saying that the revolution has begun!" shouted
Foldvary, shaking my shoulders and kissing me on both
cheeks in his glee. "He's saying that we're going to fight the
bastards!"

Then trucks pulled into the square, followed by cars driven
by young people. They offered to take us to the radio
building. Propelled along by Foldvary, I found myself in the

back of a truck, and a few minutes later we could hear gunfire in the distance. At the entrance to Brody Sandor Street students were carrying out the dead and wounded. Then behind us a very large number of soldiers and policemen arrived. For a moment I thought that the students would now be trapped between this new force and the machine guns of the AVO inside the radio building. Far from it: the police and soldiers began distributing arms to the crowd, and just in time. The rumbling sound that had been growing in the distance turned out to be tanks belonging to the AVO. As they arrived, the real battle began. Suddenly a soldier handed me a rifle and a clip of ammunition. Foldvary, joining the students, ran off toward the entrance to the radio building. I ran several steps beside them, then stopped; and still clutching the rifle, I turned and entered a side street.

Very tired now, and with the rifle slung over my shoulder, I headed for home. Several times I turned around to listen as the noise of the battle raged louder and louder and the rattle of machine-gun fire became drowned in the thunder of tanks. It's your duty to join your friends back there, I told myself; but even as I thought it, I knew I would not. Nothing was going to induce me to fire that rifle, not even in self-defence. Nevertheless, as I walked through the dark streets I had an uncomfortable dialogue with myself. Half my mind argued that I had never known anything but violence all my life; now was the time to end it. The other half would reply that this was violence for a good cause: now was no time to become a conscientious objector!

I was still arguing with myself when I arrived at Heroes' Square outside the City Park. Beside it stood the colossal and much-hated statue of Stalin. A mob of people, including women and children, had been hacking at it with hammers and knives and stones. They had tried to pull it over with cables attached to trucks, but it was too strong. Then workers had arrived with blow torches, and just as I came within sight of the monster, they were toppling it. The crowd was hysterical with pent-up rage, helplessly kicking and spitting in the face of the Caucasian Cockroach. Forcing my way through them, I found myself staring into the eyes of the man I hated more than anything else in the world. For a moment I almost joined the others as they kicked at the cold metal in their fury; then I felt my blood run cold, and sickened by this excess of hatred, my own and that around me, I turned away and continued home.

I went through the dark tree-lined avenues following such a meandering path that dawn was breaking when I finally reached home carrying the rifle over my shoulder. I left it propped up against the outside gate of the house for anyone who might want it; then I went upstairs and fell asleep lying in the centre of the living-room floor. Later, awakened by distant gunfire, I turned on the radio and learned that Imre Nagy had just been reappointed prime minister by a panic-stricken government. The incredible fools, I thought, holding my head in despair. If they had had the sense to make him prime minister twenty-four hours before, the bloodbath would probably not have begun. Then Susan woke up from the gunfire, coming closer now, and ran in to hide her head in my lap.

"Are they coming for you again, daddy?" she asked in tears.

"No, of course not!" I forced myself to laugh, and again I regretted that I had not found a way to take my daughter and escape to a country where children never ask such questions or cry because of such fears. On the other hand, the young people of Budapest were bleeding to death at that very moment in the gutters in their attempt to turn Hungary into just such a country—and I could not bring myself to join them.

My wife, who had been with some neighbours, came in a little later and immediately accused me of having spent the night with another woman.

"You probably won't believe me," I said wearily, "but I was at Radio Budapest and then at the Stalin statue."

"I don't know why I bother asking you," she replied and then went on: "If you want to know the truth, I was worried about you. Are you all right? Were you in the battle?"

I told her what had happened and how I had decided not to fight. For once we agreed on something, Judith and I: a compromise with the Russians was the only nonsuicidal course for the country.

For three days I stayed at home, doing nothing but listening to the radio. It was the first time since the age of six or so that something was going on outside without my racing out to join in it. I knew that either I stayed indoors or else I joined the insurgents with a gun in my hand. Most of the population might be watching on the sidelines, but that was not a role I could play.

The radio announced the decision, typically ludicrous, of the central committee of the Communist Party to lift its ban on all public demonstrations. They also asked all workers to return immediately to their jobs. Clearly the party was no more in touch with reality now than ever before. The fact was that most of the workers had joined the revolution, as indeed most of the Hungarian army had. The only people who had not, evidently, were the AVO, the Russian occupiers and a few of their hangers-on.

Late on the afternoon of the twenty-fifth the radio announced that Gero had resigned as first secretary and Janos Kadar had replaced him. Then Imre Nagy himself came on the air and delivered a speech promising extensive reforms and immediate negotiations with the Russians concerning their withdrawal from our borders.

That same evening a neighbour arrived to say that the AVO had opened fire on an unarmed crowd before the parliament building and that hundreds were lying dead in Kossuth Square. It was hard to believe that even the AVO goons could be that stupid; but it turned out to be true.

The next morning the radio was still referring to the "unfortunate events" before the parliament, adding that the insurgents were, however, entirely responsible. So on the third day of the revolution the government, new leadership and all, were still insisting that the overwhelmingly popular rebellion was in fact some sort of Fascist plot.

Early in the morning of October 27 I awoke to the sound of banging on the door. Once again my wife and daughter huddled behind me as I opened it, certain this time that it was the NKVD, the Soviet police themselves, who had come for me—it seemed likely, according to the Marxist logic we lived under, since this time I really had done absolutely nothing!

Two young men stood in the doorway. They looked like pirates or highwaymen, loaded down with weapons and belts of ammunition. One was short, stocky and menacing-looking; the other, a tall, blond youth, smiled and asked if I was Gabori. He lifted a grimy hand to push back the bandana wrapped around his brow as he spoke. Whatever they were, they weren't Russians. I invited them in but asked them to leave their tommy guns in the entrance hall. Blushing at their own incivility, the two youths hastily put down their weapons and added hand grenades and ammunition belts as well to the stack.

My wife served coffee with trembling hands and Susan,

delighted, kept trying to make off with the arsenal in the hallway. Then the young men came to the point.

"We're part of Joe Dudas's group," said the taller youth.

"We're taking you to him," said the short one.

"We've been sent to *ask* you," said the blond with a furious glance at his colleague, "if you would be willing to come and act as a political adviser to our leader. We've occupied the offices of the *Szabad Nep* newspaper. All the commies are gone, of course, and our group has direct lines to every government ministry, and even abroad!"

I remembered Joe Dudas the last time I had seen him, in the punishment cells in Recsk. Even beaten half to death, as he had been then, he had spirit enough to lead ten revolutions, and for all my determination to keep apart from this uprising I knew I could not resist helping Dudas.

"The presses are working again," added the blond, still trying to entice me to come. "We're printing our own paper, *Hungarian Independence*."

"And what is this paper politically?" I asked.

"It's hard to say," replied the boy with a genuinely puzzled look—anything not dictated from Moscow was bound to be puzzling to his generation until they had time to learn. "But our first headline is 'We Do Not Recognize the Present Government.'"

"That won't make you popular with those who consider Nagy our only hope," I said, "but from what I've heard of our new government on the radio it's only marginally better than the old one."

"Then you'll come?" asked the blond.

"Yes."

They had an armoured car at the curb, manned by still more youths bristling with hand grenades and ammunition belts. The first thing that was evident was their discipline and loyalty to Dudas. He had summoned me as an adviser, and because of that they treated me with a respect that just bordered on the comic. There was little traffic, at least little that cared to risk an encounter with our armoured car, so we sped at breakneck speed through the city and soon arrived at the former Communist newspaper offices.

Dudas and I embraced, laughing with pleasure to see one another in such changed circumstances, and at this even the short young tough beside the blond boy stopped narrowing his eyes at me.

"I hereby appoint you my chief political adviser, George," said Dudas in his rather theatrical way. It would never have occurred to him to ask me if I consented. He stood in the centre of the wildly disordered teletype room with a leather coat flung over his shoulders like a cape. Like his troops, he gave the impression of being not altogether serious, a Hollywood idea of a revolutionary. But after a few minutes' talk I realized just how serious Joe Dudas was. He was absolute leader of one of the three major revolutionary groups, the other two being led by a man named Szabo and by Colonel Maleter. The other groups were cooperating up to a point with the Nagy government even as they fought to drive the Russians out; as for Dudas, he was unwilling to compromise with either the Russians or with Nagy himself, who, for all his liberalism, was still a Communist.

"As far as I can see, you're doing quite well without an adviser," I suggested at one point in our talk.

"True, but all this is just the beginning. From now on, whether I like it or not, I'm going to have to deal with Nagy and Maleter and the others. You know me, George. I'm no politician. I had them bring you here because you know how to talk to those idiots better than I do. But for the time being, the teletype machines are working, we control the switchboard, we're in communication with the whole world. I want you to sit in here and read everything that comes in. Get a complete picture of everything, including foreign reaction to what's going on here, and brief me regularly."

"I haven't lifted my little finger in this revolution so far," I said, "and before I do I have to ask you certain things and give you my conditions."

Dudas gave me a hard look. Obviously he was not used to conditions from his subordinates, but he nodded.

"First of all, I refuse to handle a weapon. I'll help you in any way I can, but I won't kill anyone, not even a Russian, not even in self-defence. All right?"

He looked surprised, but nodded again.

"Secondly, I don't know who your men are or where they come from. A lot of the Communist leadership have been Jews, though, and there's a lot of bad feeling about that—understandably. When I look at a picture of Rakosi it's enough to make an anti-Semite out of me! But if anything like that is going on in your group I'm not staying around for a minute. If you're interested in justice, I'm with you."

"You know me better than that," replied Dudas, looking hurt. "On the other hand, in a situation like this one doesn't have time to screen recruits. Some of these bandits may very well turn out to be raving anti-Semites. I hadn't even thought about it. First case I see, though, I assure you I'll blow the bastard's brains out. You see? I do need advice, and you've already given me some."

I spent the rest of that day piecing together the situation inside the country and the reaction from abroad. The more I learned, the more horrified I was. Suslov and Mikoyan had arrived from Moscow two days previously. It was they who had ordered Gero to resign in favour of Kadar. As for the rest of the government, it was in complete disarray. Some sided openly with the revolutionaries; others were in hiding, loyal to Moscow and afraid of being captured—though the revolutionary groups were behaving scrupulously for the most part. Their targets were Russians and the AVO. The latter especially were hated, and a few of them were lynched by the public before they could be brought to justice—or shot by the insurgents. Some thought this a black mark on the revolution. Those of us who had been tortured by the AVO could not see it that way. They had put themselves beyond the pale of humanity; it could be argued that the judicial process was inappropriate in their case—as it would be if during an uprising in Auschwitz one got one's hands on an SS man.

Reports indicated that the revolution had spread all over the country and that losses were terrible on both sides. There was a general strike in effect, communications were breaking down and the capital would have begun to starve if peasants had not voluntarily brought large amounts of food into Budapest in horse carts! As it turned out, Budapest was being better fed than it had been in years.

I managed to contact George Egri later that day, and when he arrived he gave me the news that Foldvary had been killed just after I left him in front of the Radio Budapest building on October 23. Overcome with horror and guilt, I slumped over my desk and wept, bitter beyond words that I had left Foldvary alone. Those whom the gods love best. . . . Of all of us, Foldvary had been not only the youngest but the one most loved by the gods in every way.

A little later Dudas arrived and told me that he had arranged a conference with Imre Nagy and Colonel Maleter

for the following morning at eleven o'clock. It would be in the
parliament building and I would accompany him as his
adviser.

"What's the rush?" I asked.

"You're falling down on the job, Gabori; you haven't been
listening to the radio. There's going to be a truce. Nagy has
got the Russians to agree to a complete withdrawal! He
actually finished his speech by saying, 'Long.live our free and
independent Hungary!' Did you ever hear a Communist say
anything like that? By God, we've won!"

"You've asked me to advise you, so I will. I advise you to
remember that we have not won at all. This has been the first
round. As for the Russians leaving the country, I'll believe it
when I see it. Think, man! When have the Russians ever made
a humiliating concession like that before? Do you think they
haven't figured out yet that they can do what they like and
the Americans will say 'naughty! naughty!' and look the other
way? We've caught them unprepared. As for the Americans,
when aren't they unprepared? Moscow is playing for time. In
the meantime Imre Nagy will ask us to surrender our arms to
his government, you can be sure of that."

"And?" asked Dudas, raising his eyebrows.

"It's your decision," I replied, "but I can assure you that if
you do surrender your arms it may well be the last decision of
that sort you will have the power to make."

"And what about our line concerning some of the men
around Nagy? There are some old-time Bolsheviks there, not
to mention the writers and journalists, the fellows who are all
good democrats now although a week ago they were still
kissing Gero's ass."

"I suggest we look straight through any old-time Bolsheviks we find across from us at the conference table. We have
nothing to say to people like that. As for the writers, they're a
special problem. As far as I know, Faludy is the only writer in
the country who refused to knuckle under to the leadership
during the past ten years. And he's the only one who went to
prison. If you want anyone else to write for your paper, you're
going to have to pick someone from that crowd at the Writers'
Association. They're all beating their breasts now and crying
'mea culpa'; the fact is, however, that there's not one of them
who would not have cleaned Rakosi's shoes with his tongue in
order to stay out of prison."

"In the report you gave me last night," said Dudas, "you

said that the Anglo-French attack on the Suez Canal would have serious consequences for us. How?"

"First of all, you've been sending direct appeals to the United Nations asking for armed intervention in Hungary. Realize that they are going to do nothing and that the British and the French have taken the pressure off them even to discuss the matter. From now on they're going to howl about Suez at our expense. The Soviets can be counted on to take advantage of this—if Anglo-French imperialism is raising its ugly head in the Middle East, why should not the Russians recapture their colony in Eastern Europe?"

"And in what way," asked Dudas, "does all this affect our discussions with Nagy tomorrow?"

"I think the Russians are going to invade in force to keep their colony and their prestige. Nagy is going to ask you to surrender your forces and your arms to the government. Maleter and Szabo will, no doubt, obey. But I can tell you this: when the Russians come back in force the only way you are going to be able to fight them is if you hold onto your weapons now."

"What?" asked Dudas, standing up like Napoleon dismissing Marshal Kellerman; he raised one eyebrow and slung his leather coat over his shoulders to depart. "Is this you I hear? Is our humanist suddenly giving the battle cry?"

"Far from it," I replied. "I have no intention of fighting. I'm just telling you what any five-year-old could advise: if you want to keep fighting, don't give away your guns."

The following morning Dudas and I stepped into an armoured car at the curb. It had recently been captured from the Russians and still bore Soviet licence plates, although a Hungarian flag with the centre ripped out flew above it. I had not been outside the headquarters in several days, working and sleeping beside the teletype machines and subsisting largely on black coffee. I was dazzled by the sunlight and intoxicated by the mild October breeze as we raced through the battle-scarred streets toward the parliament. People were everywhere in the streets and, in spite of the suffering they had just undergone in the battles which had left so many dead, their faces were radiant with happiness.

As the guards admitted us into the parliament building, one of Dudas's deputies stepped up and whispered to him that he had just been talking with the leaders of the new

Catholic People's Party. Their slogan was "With Christ for the People, and with the People for Christ."

"It appears Cardinal Mindszenty is trying to sound like a democrat," said Dudas. "What else are they up to around here?" He really looked like Captain Kidd as he strolled ahead of us through the corridors of parliament, cigarette dangling, leather coat trailing.

"One last thing," said Dudas as we approached the council chambers. "What do you think about a vote on leaving the Warsaw Pact? I understand some of the others are going to propose it."

"Don't vote for leaving the pact!" I begged him. "If we get away with everything else, we won't get away with that. The Russians won't tolerate it."

"I disagree," said Dudas. "How can we build a democracy if we're linked to that pack of Russian toadies?"

"I'm telling you, Joe, don't do it! To the Russians it will mean not only that we've turned our backs on them but that we're allying ourselves with the West. Our only hope now is to let them save face. But before we go in there, there's something else I'm afraid of. And I'm afraid certain parties in there are going to bring it up."

"What's that?" asked Dudas, stopping in surprise.

"In the past thirty-six hours various people have been telling me things about you. For instance, that you are an anti-Semite and a murderer, the head of a gang of thieves, not revolutionaries. One man told me that in the battle in Republic Square there was not only Jew-baiting but there was the public hanging of several Jews."

"Yes," Dudas replied evenly, "there was. But they were hanged because they were AVOs, not because they were Jews. As for the things my men said, I've warned them, but I can go only so far. Do you believe me?"

"Yes, but that doesn't mean that everyone else is going to."

"Is Maleter responsible for the 'excesses' of his troops? I regret these things, but we're in the middle of a revolution, you know. When it comes to atrocities, if half of what I've heard about Maleter's men is true they've lost their self-control far more often than we have. Yet when all this is over he'll be the hero of the revolution and Joe Dudas will be the head of a gang of thieves."

He was right. Maleter, the ex-Communist, and Nagy, the liberal Communist, understood one another completely.

Dudas, on the other hand, had held aloof from both parties and now they were going to make him pay for it.

As we entered the second-floor conference room we found some twenty-five or thirty people already seated at a long oak table. Nagy had not yet arrived. I had expected a cold or even hostile reception, but several of those present had been prisoners in Recsk.

A moment later Nagy entered the room and we stood and applauded. He exuded self-confidence and warmth; his tubby little body, far from being ridiculous, bespoke well-being and friendliness. He paused in the doorway a moment and looked at us, eyes twinkling behind his pince-nez. The man invited instant confidence in himself in a way I have never seen with anyone else. Quickly the atmosphere of the room became charged with optimism, as if it were radiating from his eyes. It was all a great game, he seemed to be saying; he was the gamesmaster and we were his chief players.

He began by telling us that he was aware of the basic demands of all our groups and that he not only agreed in principle with them, he wanted rather more. He was at the moment having a series of meetings with the Russian military commander and with Mikoyan. As I had foreseen, however, he went on to say that for the time being the Russians refused to hear anything about our withdrawing from the Warsaw Pact.

"That," continued Nagy, "is an extravagant demand even from my own point of view. You must realize, gentlemen, that our economic and political ties with the Socialist bloc are so close at this point in our history that to try to cut or even loosen them would be to invite catastrophe."

At this point someone interrupted to point out that the West had already offered us emergency assistance, twenty million dollars to begin with, and no doubt more would be offered later. Nagy looked for a moment as if he were going to laugh at this piece of naïveté; then in a rather gruff voice he said, "No country can live off the charity of others. We have been exploited. In a sense it would be better to continue that way than to return to what we used to be: a nation of beggars." Then he went on to tell us that we would of course form a new government as soon as possible, one based on free elections and proportional representation. As for the press, there was no need to revise the laws. The existing ones were admirable, and the revolution had finally implemented them.

He called on us to do our best to persuade the workers to return to their factories and end the general strike.

Then Nagy touched on the one issue where Dudas was likely to balk, the formation of a national guard and the question of each revolutionary group surrendering its arms to it. I cast a glance at Dudas, but for once his face betrayed nothing but contentment. He too seemed to be under Nagy's spell. As Nagy finished speaking, discussion broke out all around the table. Dudas rose and took me aside and was just about to say something when Nagy himself came up.

"Mr. Dudas," he said, "Colonel Maleter and Sandor Kopacsi, the police-president of Budapest, are waiting to speak with you in the next room."

Dudas looked startled but nodded and headed for the doorway, stopping halfway there to beckon me to follow. As we entered, Pal Maleter stood up and approached. He was a tall, good-looking man who would have looked no less a soldier even in mufti. Except possibly for Nagy, he was the most popular man in the country at the moment, the leader of the largest armed force and the hero of the battle of the Killian Barracks. We all shook hands in silence and then faced Sandor Kopacsi, head of the civil police, in civilian clothes and somewhat warmer in his manner than Maleter.

We sat around a table in silence. At last Maleter spoke.

"You know that we are forming a national guard," he began, "and naturally I have turned over all my arms to it. Now the prime minister has asked me to confer with you, Mr. Dudas, on the same matter. First let me offer you my congratulations on the splendid work you and your group have done for the revolution. Now that that work is completed, we hope you will follow us in putting yourselves under the authority of the new national guard."

I expected Dudas to reply immediately and forcefully, but instead he cleared his throat and said rather gruffly that I, as his political adviser, would state our position. Caught off guard, I mouthed a few platitudes about how of course we all had to work together. Then, realizing that there was no help for it, I faced the most powerful man in Hungary and told him what I conceived to be the truth.

"We are democrats," I began, "and will do everything we can to help you restore democracy to our country. As for surrendering our arms, our point of view, bluntly, is this: Russian forces are still in the country. It is not at all certain that they intend really to withdraw from our borders. The men who lead this government, starting with the prime minister, are liberal in their views but they do not have a record of standing up and resisting Moscow. We, not the government, have fought the Russians. What grounds have we for believing that if we have to fight them again the present government will have the courage to do so?"

"But even now the Russians are agreeing to leave," said Maleter uneasily.

"When they have left, and when it is clear that they mean not to come back, then we will hand over our weapons to the national guard," I replied.

At this point Maleter's patience broke and he turned to Dudas, who, to my intense relief, began speaking as leader of the group. They argued a long time and at the end neither side had budged an inch. Nevertheless, when we parted the atmosphere was somehow more friendly than when we had entered.

"I suppose you'll leave my group once the Social Democrats get back on their feet," said Dudas as the guards opened the great wrought-iron gates and we descended the steps of the building into the square where only a few days before the AVO had machine-gunned a crowd of peaceful demonstrators.

"Well, of course, I'll have to work for the Social Democrats," I said, "but that doesn't mean I can't keep on working for you too, though I'll be damned if I have any real idea where you stand politically, Joe Dudas!"

"Stand politically?" Dudas sounded rather vague, as if the question had never occurred to him before. "I've been everything politically, a Communist, a Smallholder, you name it. I guess I can't think in those terms any more. So I'm shooting the bastards and trying to defend the decent people. We're likelier to get somewhere that way, don't you think?"

I glanced at him and saw that he was completely serious, so I smiled and nodded as Dudas's young men came to attention and opened the door of the armoured car.

As Budapest caught its breath and began reorganizing itself along the lines of a free society, I no longer spent all my time with Dudas but, increasingly, ran all over town trying to do ten things at once. First I tried to get some of my friends from Recsk to volunteer for Kopacsi's police. He had promised officer's rank to the best of them, and there seemed no better way for former prisoners to prevent a recurrence of anything like their own past experience. I spent part of every day helping put out our newspaper, *Hungarian Independence*, and was relieved to see that Dudas did not try to prevent other newspapers, even some fairly right-wing ones, from using the presses we controlled.

The Social Democratic Party regrouped now in its old headquarters. Unfortunately the obvious leader of the revived party, Anna Kethly, had left for Vienna to attend an international conference, and a lot of the best choices were either dead or in exile. I tried to keep up all these activities, as well as others, on four or five hours' sleep a night and a diet of bread, rolls and black coffee; and as Budapest was restored to life I began to crumble.

Finally I went home for a few days and slept. Budapest was functioning beautifully without any help from me. Factories and shops were reopening; even the telephone worked again from time to time. The revolution had not only freed us, it seemed even to have purged the country of a lot of bad blood. Open boxes were left at street corners where the population tossed in money for the widows and children of the dead—for as the count went on, it became apparent that many thousands had died fighting the Russians and the AVO. These boxes quickly filled up with money and no one ever touched a penny of it. It was hard to believe one was in Budapest.

Early on the morning of November 1 I awoke to find Joe Dudas hammering on my door. He came in and slumped down in an armchair next to the door.

"I've just come from parliament," he said. "Soviet troops have reentered Hungary at three points."

I jumped into my clothes and we drove to his headquarters.

"If this is really true," I said, still hoping against hope that it would prove to be false, "then there's not going to be any more hesitation on Moscow's part. They mean to crush us and they don't give a damn what the world thinks about it. Perhaps they've made one of their famous under-the-table deals with the Americans—they order the British and the French out of Egypt and let the Russians stay in Hungary!"

"What are we going to do?" said Dudas, staring at the empty surface of his desk. I had seen him at a loss before, but never so close to despair.

"The West is going to leave us in the lurch, of course. We have more communications equipment here than anybody else. Why don't you ask the UN to send an army?"

I was half joking, but Dudas's eyes lit up and he proceeded to do just that. Nothing came of it, as the whole world knows, but it served to stir Dudas into action again and, through him, his men.

Then we sat beside the radio, sent messengers out constantly to get more information and gradually became frantic as we learned the seriousness of the situation. The Russians were moving in with massive amounts of men and equipment this time. And there were two armed groups to resist them in Budapest: the national guard under Maleter, and the much smaller force of Joe Dudas.

To our astonishment, in the afternoon the government of Imre Nagy declared that we were withdrawing from the Warsaw Pact. Nagy for his part was behaving magnificently. He had decided for the first time in his life to fight Moscow and he meant to do it. Through various foreign legations he also requested that the United Nations guarantee the independence and neutrality of Hungary.

By early evening the whole population knew about the invasion and a huge mob of enraged citizens had collected before the Soviet embassy. The ambassador, the much hated and despised Andropov, gave Nagy an ultimatum: either the national guard dispersed the crowd or the Russians inside would open fire. I was just going to suggest that we ourselves go and fire on Andropov, when suddenly one of Dudas's troops, as it happened the blond boy who had come for me the third day of the revolution, burst in out of breath. He stood panting in the centre of the office, rain dripping from his hair and jacket. Then he told us.

"Budapest is surrounded by Soviet tanks. There are hundreds and hundreds of them!"

The following evening Dudas summoned all his fighters and briefed them on the situation. The UN was not going to help. The Russians were meeting armed resistance all over the country. Imre Nagy and Pal Maleter were calling out all the troops of the national guard, and now it was our turn.

"In a few hours they'll be here," shouted Dudas to the crowd of fighters spilling out of the hall into the passageways. "Those of you who want to fight them, here are the weapons and ammunition before me. If any of you does not want to fight, no one will think the worse of you."

At this a roar came from the throats of the young men and all ran forward and began grabbing rifles, tommy guns and hand grenades. Within a few minutes I was the only man present not armed to the teeth.

I went home that night. For the first time it was really cold, and I awoke about three in the morning and put an extra blanket on Susan. I was just about to return to bed when I heard the first distant rumbling of artillery. The Russians were entering Budapest.

About two hours later the radio finally came on and Imre Nagy announced the invasion, adding: "They have the intention of overthrowing the legal and democratic government of our country. The government is at its post and we are fighting back." Then the radio played the national anthem, and instead of being stirred by it, I sank my head into my hands and despaired. A little later I learned from the radio that Pal Maleter had the previous evening gone to the Soviet high command to negotiate with them: he had been arrested!

By seven in the morning the real battle of Budapest had begun. I got halfway to Dudas's headquarters and realized I would never make it. Russian tanks were everywhere and battles were raging at five points. I returned home and learned that Imre Nagy, his family, and a number of other government ministers and officials and their families had taken refuge in the Yugoslav embassy.

The strongest military power in the world was being met head on by bands of enraged citizens, some armed with nothing but rocks, and by children throwing Molotov cocktails. And to the astonishment of the whole world, for a moment they managed to hold the Russians at bay. But it could not last. For every tank the teen-agers of Budapest put out of action others quickly arrived, and in retaliation the Russians began destroying whole residential blocks, firing at ground floors until buildings collapsed in on themselves, floor by floor.

Then the Russians began rounding up people indiscriminately, especially young people, and deporting trainloads to the Soviet Union. Just as they had done after their first "liberation" of Hungary in 1945, again they sent tens of thousands off to Siberia.

Because of Kopacsi a lifeline was left open between Budapest and Austria, and it was along this that the uncounted thousands of refugees began making their way westward with nothing but the clothes on their backs. It took the Russians twenty-two days to take complete possession of the country, and even then there were sporadic outbursts of resistance in the hill country of the north and west. Imre Nagy, still given asylum by the Yugoslav embassy, would soon be turned over to the new puppet government, the one that had "begged the Soviet Union to come and help put down the Fascist counterrevolution." Kadar, the new prime minister, would have him tortured and hanged.

On November 26 I had had enough. My family were hiding, and I had moved from flat to flat, hiding out with friends in anticipation of a raid by the Russian secret police. With great difficulty I met with Dudas and begged him to come to Austria with us while there was still time. He refused, even though he knew he would be among the first they hanged. I told him that all of us from Recsk had decided to leave— Faludy, Nyeste, Garamvolgyi, all of us.

"I know I'll be one of the first to hang, and that's as it should be," said Dudas. Then we shook hands and, seeing there was nothing more I could say or do, I took leave of him.

At two the next afternoon I met my wife and daughter. Judith had made a last foray into our flat to get some warm clothes for Susan but had been stopped by the concierge: the Russian secret police were inside turning the place inside out! Several of us had managed to get a truck and were just about to leave when the blond youth who always acted as Dudas's messenger came running up and handed me a slip of paper. It read, "Good-bye and good luck to all of you. Forgive me; I've got to stay and fight for what I believe in."

Armed only with the documents issued by the Budapest police, we headed westward toward the Austrian border and the unknown. The army, the police and the government had surrendered to the overwhelming might of the Soviet Union but they could not bring themselves to turn back those of their fellow citizens who had had enough and were leaving. Weary, defeated soldiers waved us on as we approached the border, and the next morning at dawn we crossed on foot into Austria and I turned to look, for the last time, on the only country I had ever had—a country that had never really had a place for me or my kind but that, in spite of everything, I shall always continue to love.

Epilogue

"WHAT IS THAT DREADFUL NOISE?" asked my grandfather, exhaling smoke from his long-stemmed pipe and frowning.

"It's the Arabs, grandfather," I replied. "Ramadan is over and people are celebrating."

"Ramadan?" he said with disgust. "Next you'll be taking us to live with *Turkischers!*"

I was about to defend myself but could not, for grandfather faded away in a flood of blinding light as I opened my eyes. Jumping out of bed, I threw open the window of the hotel bedroom reverberating with the noise of traffic, shouts, drums, brays—all the raucous sound any Arab city produces between the first and last calls to prayer every day. The odour that in Algiers and Tangier I had thought to be camel dung was just as strong and exotically pleasant here in Tunis, with no camels in sight. In the distance rose the building-block jumble of the casbah, floating in a blue mist even the Mediterranean sun could not burn off.

I lay back on the bed and, not for the first time in the past two months, was overcome by a wave of homesickness, and with disgust for myself at feeling it. The dream of my grandfather had, with variations, become a recurring one. Disconcertingly, it had come to be a comfort: some nights I repeated the Ma-nish-tana with him, sometimes he reprimanded me, other times comforted me. And each morning I awoke knowing that, whatever happened or wherever I went, he was with me permanently, my most important possession.

It was January 30, 1957. Two months earlier I had left my wife and daughter in good hands in Vienna and found myself invited by an American organization of rather mysterious origin, function and purpose to go on a lecture tour of North Africa with George Egri. The American organization had gradually revealed itself as something closely resembling a secret policeman's idea of the CIA—which is what it was.

"Well, old man," I addressed the haggard stranger in the hotel shaving mirror, "you're rising in the world. At two this afternoon you're being received by the president of Tunisia. For years you've got into trouble for shooting off your mouth, telling the truth about the Bolshies, and now they're paying you to do it? Smile! What more do you want?"

It was true. By my usual standards I had every reason to smile. The Austrian Social Democratic Party had welcomed me with open arms, the French Socialist Party had offered me a job and a home in France, then the CIA had got me to agree to the lecture tour, where, day after day, I could harangue through an interpreter audience after audience about the nightmare world from which over two hundred thousand Hungarians had just fled. So why wasn't I smiling? That was a rather complicated matter.

First of all, I had grown up effectively cut off from what, except for the Nazis and then the Communists, I might have considered my birthright, namely a Western education culminating in a German or Austrian university. Arrival in the West had meant for me, as for many of my generation, first the euphoria of being free, delight in the face of so much prosperity, then, gradually, the realization that much of the glitter was on the surface only. Liberty and respect for human rights was one thing—one very important thing—but slowly one began to realize that the West was, in its way, almost as soulless as the East. The Europe of Bach and Voltaire had changed from a community of nation-states into an economy obsessed with prosperity. Crawling through the barbed wire, one suddenly found oneself in the glittering corridors of Europe, Inc.

Secondly, one was embarrassed by all the fuss. Hungary had exploded and all but bled to death trying to free itself from the grip of its Russian overlords. Now a sizable part of its population had fled and were being treated as heroes by a world with a guilty conscience. Many were heroes but, like any other heroes, they would soon be forgotten. Human nature being what it is, people love to read about disasters and other great events at the breakfast table. But Hungary had been a bit much for the West. Very thrilling and moving, no doubt, but we had rocked the boat, had caused a grave inconvenience by arriving in such large numbers and, worst of all, had for a moment threatened the stability of the Western world. No, in a month or two we would be forgotten, and it would be business as usual. Including, of course, business with the USSR.

And finally there was self-disgust. A few days before I had been in the studios of the Voice of America—the same station that had criminally encouraged the Hungarians to revolt and promised them American aid!—listening to myself make a broadcast against the new puppet regime, which I had just learned, to my sorrow, had already deported thousands of young-Hungarians to Siberia and was hanging many others, including Joe Dudas. Worse than the feeling of having left Joe in the lurch was the deeper, sickening feeling of relief at having myself escaped his fate.

I was still standing before the mirror, the soap dry on my face, when Egri and our French interpreter strode into the room without knocking.

"While you were sleeping," Egri began in a tone of moral superiority, "I was up all night preparing our next lecture."

"Dear George," I replied wearily, "there's no need for a new text. Nothing new has happened."

Egri was taken aback by my cynicism. The fact was he had stood up better than I had to the endless one-night stands for the Americans, telling the political facts of East European life to Arabs and Frenchmen who inevitably greeted our speeches with thunderous applause and total incomprehension. By now I had the feeling that I could not take very much more. I was out of Europe but by no means far enough away from it.

"What do you know about Canada?" I asked Egri.

"In three hours," he wailed, "we're seeing President Bourguiba, and you want to chat about Canada! Why Canada?"

"I see. You don't know anything about it."

"It's large and pink on the map," ventured the interpreter lamely.

"And except for Australia it's about as far away as you can get, isn't it?" I went on.

"Away from what?" he asked, even more bewildered.

"From all this shit," I replied, watching his eyebrows shoot up, as I knew they would. "All these countries where in twenty-five centuries people still haven't learned enough to stop treating each other like animals."

Egri's reply was forestalled by the telephone. The car from the president's palace had arrived for us. I hacked away with my razor, threw on my only suit and dashed after the others, who were sitting in the back of a limousine accompanied by a tall, muscular and decidedly sinister Arab, an aide to the president. After a long drive we pulled up to a jetty extending out into the sea and were conducted aboard a motor launch. The president, it seemed, lived on an island. We bounced across a choppy sea at full throttle and the aide shouted at me through the wind, "His Excellency is suffering from a cold and will receive you in bed." This sentence, accompanied by unmistakable gestures, produced an effect of incredulous horror in me until finally my mind, unused to hearing French for thirteen years, at last realized what the man was saying.

Soon we were being led through gardens and then into halls of gilt and marble with masses of Persian rugs everywhere. Marble tables were weighed down by huge golden bowls piled high with fruit and other delicacies I could not identify, the sort of food the majority of Hungarians had not seen since the war.

Tunisian trade union officials and their wives were brought in to meet us, and elaborate and linguistically confused greetings gradually gave way to indifference and finally to frank boredom on all sides. Attempting to relieve this, I approached a veiled lady and, murmuring an introduction, attempted to kiss her hand. The result was a shriek, and the matron ran in panic from the reception hall. What the upshot would have been I was deprived of learning, for just then we were summoned by still more aides and taken to see the president.

The bedroom was pure Hollywood, but the figure lying in bed, buried under satin and brocade, was not Mae West but the Father of His Country, President Bourguiba. He sat up and beamed at us.

"I am proud of you," said the president in more than usually nasal French. "I know what you have suffered in the Communist grip, and I know how you had the courage to rise up against it and, if only for a moment, force a tyranny to its knees."

We lined up to shake hands and Egri, smiling all the while, fairly hissed at me, "Stop looking like that!"

Perhaps I was unjust. Tunisia was and is the closest thing to a democracy that Africa has ever seen. I smiled, shook hands, and then we were led away.

Several days later, completely exhausted by now, we were in the far south of the country, delivering our last lecture to the natives of a desert town before returning to Europe. We droned away automatically that night and the translator chattered in French without so much as listening to us. Afterward, at the inevitable reception, we shook the hands of long queues of people and, having nothing else to say, mumbled something in Hungarian to each dark face. Gradually, I am ashamed to admit, exhaustion, despair or, for all I know, innate wickedness had prompted me to begin smiling and murmuring a Hungarian obscenity over each handshake. This night the last man in the queue of trade union officials and other dignitaries did not let go of my hand when we exchanged greetings. I looked up sharply and saw a European face smiling into mine.

"And up yours, too, my boy," he replied cheerfully. He was from eastern Hungary, and after many years in Tunisia he was now a representative of the Ministry of Labour.

Two days later we stumbled off the plane in Paris and were met by a little Hungarian sent by the CIA from Washington. He identified himself cloak-and-dagger-style only as Frigyes.

"Mr. Griffith wants to see you," said Frigyes mysteriously, then hustled us into a car. Frigyes was obviously annoyed at the idea of more Hungarians being involved with the CIA—if indeed that was the case; we had no idea why the CIA were interested in us—and all the way into Paris kept making remarks about "third-rate people" and about not knowing "why Griffith is bothering with you," until finally out of the blue Egri turned to him and said: "Shut up."

"What did you say?" asked Frigyes.

"He said shut up," I interrupted.

Frigyes blinked several times, and one's heart went out to him as he tried hard to think of a reply impressive enough for a representative of the Central Intelligence Agency, but he had done no more than stammer when the driver stopped before a posh-looking building. A few moments later I was ushered by a furious Frigyes into the office of the mysterious Mr. Griffith (whose name I remember because I have never met a Hungarian who could pronounce it quite correctly).

"Your US visa has come through," he said with a smile that was devalued by Frigyes's surly translation. Then he handed me a cheque, my fee for two months' lecturing. "Your friend Egri's visa has been turned down, I'm afraid," he went on.

"It's all right," I said. "We're going to Canada anyway."

"Canada?" Griffith sounded as if he were trying to place the name. Behind him a gilt eagle atop a flagstaff glowered at me in open hostility.

"Canada," I repeated, smiled, and turned toward the door.

There was a mumbled consultation and, as I left, Frigyes, looking quite eager and friendly now, called after me, "You can still change your mind, you know! We can always use a man of your experience."

"I'm sure he can find all the flunkies he needs," I said softly and left.

A few minutes later Egri returned from his interview with a cheque in his hand and a scowl on his face.

"Canada isn't much colder than this, is it?" he asked as we stepped out into the biting wind of a Paris February.

April 1957 was not an ideal time for sailing the Atlantic. Weak-kneed and wretched after ten days of seasickness, some hundreds of Hungarians, including my family and myself, stumbled out on deck and stared at the rooftops of St. John huddling together beneath a leaden sky. It might be expected that penniless, homeless, largely friendless and altogether frightened refugees would take heart at the first sight of a land they knew to be welcoming them, a land, moreover, they knew to be free and prosperous. But that was not the case.

After a twenty-five-year love affair with Canada I think I can risk the revelation that it was not love at first sight. No one who knows me will accuse me of being an aesthete; but like many others brought up in the midst of ancient, patinaed symmetry, I took it for granted that cities—at least at a distance—were beautiful. The haphazard, mining-camp look of most built-up areas in North America had a strange and profoundly depressing effect on me at first. I could not figure out why well-fed, well-dressed people would put up buildings no one would want to look at. It was some years later, having at last saved the money and secured the time, that I returned to Europe and realized that what I had thought a North American phenomenon was in fact a twentieth-century one. Frankfurt, risen from the ashes, was the same jumble of sterile and forbidding concrete and glass as Toronto or Dallas.

Montreal, however, looked more like home. And if the Canada of 1957 was not quite the welfare state it has since become, that suited me just fine. All the world loved a Hungarian for the moment, but that did not bring down the rent of apartments, and it was with some difficulty that I finally found one we might be able to afford. We settled into two bare rooms, slept on mattresses on the floor and arose before dawn each morning to tramp the mysterious streets of Montreal in search of work.

For most of that first year I worked as a bricklayer eight hours a day, then dashed off to do a six-hour dishwashing stint in the underground kitchens of a large hotel. Putting raw hands into steaming water, there were times when I felt almost as wretched physically as I had in Recsk. But it did not matter: I was free, I was paid a just wage, and I was building a life, not watching one disappear. Not even in my childhood had I been happier, and when my grandfather appeared in my dreams it was usually to congratulate me for having brought "us" to a good place.

Slowly I saved a bit of money and bought a knitting machine and taught myself to use it. My wife was a skilled dressmaker, and by dint of working day in and day out—never less than fourteen hours—we put ourselves in business, working away at knitted-wear beneath a bare bulb until late at night. Often I awoke at dawn lying on the cutting table.

We prospered, as one is apt to do in a free society by hard work, and by 1961 I had three employees and we were thinking of buying a house. But then something happened that caused me to sit back and, for a moment, wonder if I had not been living in a fantasy. A mailbox was blown up in

Montreal; then another. The FLQ were out to rescue their long-suffering French Canadian compatriots from the grip of English domination, as they saw it, and a Jew from Putnok, who knew a thing or two about explosives and when to use them sat back in horror and disbelief.

As upset as most English Canadians were in the early sixties and, more recently, in the late seventies by events in French Canada, I think most of them did not understand the near panic among the immigrant population of Quebec, especially the Jewish population. The explanation is simple. The new Canadian of Central European and Jewish origins is a man who grew up in streets that were, often quite literally, soaked with the blood of his kin. For centuries his ancestors, deprived of the right to own land or to enter most professions, had known only one means of security: the amassing of money, money with which to buy protection and hence a bit more life. It takes at least a generation in a country like Canada for the children of such a man to take security, justice and liberty for granted. There is a look to certain uniforms, a sound to certain political manifestos that is all too familiar to him, and when he confronts these, or the beginnings of them, in a place like Canada, his blood freezes. Here too? he asks himself, and looks around for somewhere he will be left in peace.

I turned to my three French Canadian employees, hoping to learn. Two of them shrugged, but the youngest taught me the phrase "Nous sommes les nègres chez nous"—We are the negroes here. Shocked, I asked him if he was unhappy with his job or with his wages. "No," he replied, "but it's always you people who own the business; always us who work for you."

"What people?" I asked.

"The English—or the Jews."

Slowly I walked down St. Catherine's Street, depressed and perplexed. I wondered if Justus had not been right after all. Was it impossible to prosper, even in the minimal way I was prospering, without stepping on someone? Was I oppressing my employees by giving them employment? Everything in me rebelled at the simplistic stupidity of the idea, but I could not argue with the look in the eyes of Gilbert, the cutter. Far from being the look of a Nazi, it was the look I myself had in all probability worn during those years in Budapest when life consisted largely of survival, making one's humble way through a society thoroughly owned and controlled by others.

By Central European standards, however, there was something a bit silly in that look on Gilbert's face. If he did not like his situation he was free to change it. If he did not like being an employee he could turn his mind toward becoming an employer. Angrily I compared Gilbert's life with my own at the same age. But it was no good: pain was pain, and his was real. As the weeks went by there was more violence, more people were killed or maimed. Next on the agenda, I thought, will be the finding of a scapegoat; and I knew, or thought I knew, who that would be. I sold the business at a loss and we packed our bags.

Happiness, I write to my friends in Hungary, is driving a taxi in Toronto. And after driving a taxi for twelve hours a day, six days a week, for fifteen years, one is made even a little happier by owning the taxi one drives. The man who drives it at night, being a Hungarian Jew, does not feel that I am oppressing him by giving him the job.

Over the years a large number of Recsk graduates have settled in Toronto and all of us, I think, harbour a fierce sense of gratitude and attachment to the country and the city that has let us build happy lives. Of course many educated Europeans living in Canada are apt to grumble privately about a lack of history and culture. But in their lucid moments they know, on occasion even admit, that the history they profess to miss is what drove them here in the first place.

As for culture, Canada does not need to be defended. It took me a long time to realize that the Canadian preoccupation with the matter, including periodic outbursts of printed despair, is in fact a kind of national pastime. Canada has not produced a Bach or a Michelangelo; but neither, since the year of Canadian Confederation, has Europe. And farther down the scale of Europe's cultural decline, a taste for Wagner or Flaubert can be cultivated as easily in Vancouver as in Paris, not to speak of Budapest.

As for history, it is true that few of the greatest names in Western civilization have ever strolled down Spadina Road or put pen to paper in the shadow of the Rockies. But there is more to history than that, and Canadian history is distinguished by the fact, almost unheard of in our civilization, that never has one section of the population burned and whipped another section out of their homes and driven them off to the slaughter house. In the eyes of some, perhaps, this means that Canada is a bit short in the history department. As for me, I regret the load of "history" I had to bring with me. Canada does not need it.

One morning a few years ago my cab dispatcher sent me to an address in Forest Hill where, before an impressively solid-looking Victorian mansion I picked up a middle-aged gentleman whose tweed-and-leather look was as redolent of privilege as the house he stepped out of. Halfway to the airport he said that he surmised from my accent that I was Hungarian. His tone was oddly hostile, so I replied with a curt yes. "Then," he continued, "I assume you are one of those Fascist counterrevolutionaries."

I took a deep breath. Not even in Canada is one permitted to bloody a man's nose because of what he says.

"No," I replied evenly. "I'm a Dachau- and Gulag-type Jewish Fascist." Then, as if talking to a child, I began a lecture that lasted until the airport, at which point, to my surprise, the man shook my hand and asked me for my phone number.

Thomas Mann once remarked that Americans are the best Europeans. I think he was speaking out of politeness and ignorance, for he did not know Canada. There are a lot of types in Canada like my Forest Hill customer: rich, secure, drawing-room Marxist revolutionaries. Sometimes it is a little depressing to watch them get their suntans in Cuba, taste the wine in Bulgaria and hotly deny the extermination of half of Cambodia (or worse, dismiss three million lives with the phrase "you can't make an omlette without breaking eggs"). They are enacting a fantasy I cannot begin to understand, having spent so much of my life attempting to escape from the bliss they wish for their fellow citizens, and presumably for themselves. Perhaps it is the "Swedish disease" that has infected them, that strange boredom that overcomes people when they have too much security, too much to eat and nothing to strive for—the lust for a change, any change, to make them feel alive. Or perhaps they feel themselves such failures in their personal lives that they could welcome a Castro or a Pol Pot to come and roughly rearrange their lives for them, even at the price of a little blood in the streets.

Whatever it is, most Canadians happily are not infected by it. To my vast astonishment, my Forest Hill Marxist turned out to be a sensible man. Curious, he phoned me for another tirade, which he got, and then, in coming months, something more like conversation. We became friends, and he became one of many Canadians I was happy to present to George Faludy, who, finding sixty years of European history more than enough for one lifetime, settled in Toronto about that time.

I recognized the look of panic in the eyes of the aged poet as we drove him through miles of concrete into Toronto, and in the coming weeks and months George Egri, my new wife, Ibi, and I took great pleasure in introducing him to our Canadian friends and watching that look of panic give way to a smile. And so we had the pleasure of cheering the poet whose verses, memorized, have cheered two generations of Hungarians around the world and whose first lines written in Canada were perhaps too pessimistic:

> In this country I speak freely, without fear;
> But who, in this lethargy, will ever hear?
> Back there, all listen to what I have to say—
> Especially the secret police, as they lead me away.

For many Canadians have now listened to Faludy and others who have told them the truth, and it is because of those Canadians especially and the country they represent that those of us with the scars of history on our backs are apt to sing *O Canada* a little more loudly than necessary. No one knows better than we do what will happen if we fail to stand on guard for her.

SEAL BOOKS

Offers you a list of outstanding fiction, non-fiction and classics of Canadian literature in paperback by Canadian authors, available at all good bookstores throughout Canada.

The Canadian Establishment	Peter C. Newman
A Jest of God	Margaret Laurence
Lady Oracle	Margaret Atwood
The Fire-Dwellers	Margaret Laurence
The Snow Walker	Farley Mowat
The Dionne Years	Pierre Berton
St. Urbain's Horseman	Mordecai Richler
Act of God	Charles Templeton
The Stone Angel	Margaret Laurence
Love Affair With a Cougar	Lyn Hancock
Judith	Aritha van Herk
My Country	Pierre Berton
When Lovers Are Friends	Merle Shain
The Diviners	Margaret Laurence
Lunar Attractions	Clark Blaise
Bronfman Dynasty	Peter C. Newman
The Edible Woman	Margaret Atwood
Men for the Mountains	Sid Marty
Needles	William Deverell
A Bird in the House	Margaret Laurence
Never Cry Wolf	Farley Mowat
Children of My Heart	Gabrielle Roy
People of the Deer	Farley Mowat
Life Before Man	Margaret Atwood

The Mark of Canadian Bestsellers

THE CANADIANS

by
Robert E. Wall

A MAGNIFICENT FIVE-VOLUME HISTORICAL SAGA OF THE SPECIAL BREED OF PROUD MEN AND PASSIONATE WOMEN WHO DARED TO CONQUER A CONTINENT.

THIS IS THEIR STORY

With primary emphasis on the Canadian setting, **THE CANADIANS** vividly paints tales of romance and adventure, loyalties and vengeance against the vast canvas of 18th and 19th century America, before these groups of European colonies were transformed into the nations of Canada and the U.S.

"Wall's five-book saga, THE CANADIANS, is a publishing sensation. BLACKROBE (volume 1) is a fascinating and exciting book...keeps the reader happily enthralled from the first page to the last. One is left with something to look forward to: namely, book two of THE CANADIANS."

The Gazette, Montreal

BLACKROBE, vol. 1 (1720-1745)
BLOODBROTHERS, vol. 2 (1745-1759)
Volumes 3, 4 and 5 will be published in
1982 and 1983

Available in paperback at all good bookstores throughout Canada

C1RW

MARGARET ATWOOD

ONE OF CANADA'S BESTSELLING AUTHORS

Margaret Atwood ranks among the most important of today's writers. She injects honesty, introspection and humor into characters who become vivid reflections of each one of us. The *Toronto Star* hails her for the "knack of getting right inside the souls of her characters and creating people who are literally unforgettable."

☐ 01588-1	**EDIBLE WOMAN**	$2.50
☐ 01629-2	**LIFE BEFORE MAN**	$2.95
☐ 01681-0	**DANCING GIRLS AND OTHER STORIES**	$2.95
☐ 01704-3	**LADY ORACLE**	$2.95